DESIGNING FICTIONS

Designing Fictions

Literature Confronts Advertising

MICHAEL L. ROSS

McGill-Queen's University Press
Montreal & Kingston • London • Ithaca

© McGill-Queen's University Press 2015

ISBN 978-0-7735-4535-9 (cloth)
ISBN 978-0-7735-4536-6 (paper)
ISBN 978-0-7735-8397-9 (ePDF)
ISBN 978-0-7735-8398-6 (ePUB)

Legal deposit second quarter 2015
Bibliothèque nationale du Québec

Printed in Canada on acid-free paper that is 100% ancient forest free
(100% post-consumer recycled), processed chlorine free

This book has been published with the help of a grant from the Canadian
Federation for the Humanities and Social Sciences, through the Awards to
Scholarly Publications Program, using funds provided by the Social Sciences
and Humanities Research Council of Canada.

McGill-Queen's University Press acknowledges the support of the Canada
Council for the Arts for our publishing program. We also acknowledge the
financial support of the Government of Canada through the Canada Book
Fund for our publishing activities.

Library and Archives Canada Cataloguing in Publication

Ross, Michael L., 1936–, author
    Designing fictions: literature confronts advertising/Michael L. Ross.

    Includes bibliographical references and index.
    Issued in print and electronic formats.
    ISBN 978-0-7735-4535-9 (bound). – ISBN 978-0-7735-4536-6 (pbk.). –
    ISBN 978-0-7735-8397-9 (ePDF). – ISBN 978-0-7735-8398-6 (ePUB)

    1. Advertising in literature. 2. Advertising in popular culture. I. Title.

PN56.A284R67 2015   820.9'355   C2015-901341-0
                                              C2015-901342-9

This book was typeset by Interscript in 10.5/13 Sabon.

To Lorraine

Contents

Figures

Acknowledgments

Any work of literary analysis grows out of a broad context of conversation and exchange. Here, that context has been enhanced by friends and colleagues who have offered valuable suggestions and who have in some instances read versions of chapters: Sarah Brophy, Ron Granofsky, Rob Hemmings, Paul Huebener, Linda Hutcheon, and Lynn Shakinofsky. Bill Schwarz provided needed encouragement at a time of some duress. Blake Morrison graciously read and commented on my discussion of his novel *South of the River*; he saved me from embarrassment by pointing out my foolish error concerning a plot detail. Lorraine York has read all the chapters of this study, some of them – masochistically – more than once. I owe her, as always, a great debt of gratitude.

At McGill-Queen's University Press Jonathan Crago has been a constant source of support, sympathy, and wise advice. The readers for the press made, from their different vantage points, criticisms that have contributed substantially to strengthening the shape and substance of the book. I would like to thank Elena Goranescu and David Drummond for producing the handsome cover design, and Ryan Van Huijstee for overseeing the later phases of the book's production. Shelagh Plunkett's scrupulous copyediting has made her an indispensable and much appreciated collaborator. It goes without saying that none of the people on the foregoing list can be held responsible for shortcomings in the work I have produced.

I wish to thank Margaret Atwood for permission to quote from her archive at the Thomas Fisher Rare Book Library, University of Toronto.

I have energetically endeavoured to ascertain the holders of rights to the six illustrations contained in this volume: three from H.G. Wells's *Tono-Bungay*, two from Diana and Geoffrey Hindley's book *Victorian Advertising* (ads for Cadbury's cocoa and Beecham's Pills), and one by the artist Constantin Alajaloff from the 1956 illustrated edition of Herman Wouk's *Aurora Dawn*. After a number of inquiries over an extended period of time, I was unable to obtain the information I had solicited from the publishers and agents concerned. Since these visual materials are closely relevant to the argument of this study, I have reproduced them here notwithstanding.

From Marner to Gatsby:
Literature, Advertising, Commodity Culture

Come To Sunny Prestatyn
Laughed the girl on the poster,
Kneeling up on the sand
In tautened white satin.
Behind her, a hunk of coast, a
Hotel with palms
Seemed to expand from her thighs and
Spread breast-lifting arms.

She was slapped up one day in March.
A couple of weeks, and her face
Was snaggle-toothed and boss-eyed;
Huge tits and a fissured crotch
Were scored well in, and the space
Between her legs held scrawls
That set her fairly astride
A tuberous cock and balls

Autographed *Titch Thomas*, while
Someone had used a knife
Or something to stab right through
The moustached lips of her smile.
She was too good for this life.
Very soon, a great transverse tear
Left only a hand and some blue.
Now *Fight Cancer* is there.

Philip Larkin's "Sunny Prestatyn" (CP 149) is a fable of mass advertising and the resistance it inspires, an opposition that sounds the
keynote of this study. The poem, composed in 1962, comments sardonically on a defining fact of modern life: the nexus between promotional promptings and the enveloping surround of commodity
culture. It anticipates an insight by the French filmmaker and theorist Guy Debord: "The spectacle ... is both the result and the project
of the existing mode of production. It is not a supplement to the real
world, an additional decoration. It is the heart of the unrealism
of the real society" (section 6). Larkin's voluptuously posed beauty
personifies such socially produced unrealism. That is why she triggers in reaction an orgy of corrective indecency, until the image of
delusory *dolce vita* is finally supplanted by an all too circumstantial
memento mori.

Larkin's Prestatyn poster can stand for the myriad appeals with
calculated designs on the observer (and potential consumer) that
we all, nowadays, regularly encounter. This study's title, *Designing
Fictions*, refers to that feature of modern life, and the study's aim is
to shed light on the consequent social and literary implications. At
the same time, Larkin's poem, too, can be read as a designing fiction
– a project of carefully contrived persuasion. What the poem invites
us to do, of course, is nothing so straightforward as actually coming
to Prestatyn, let alone fighting cancer (a battle Larkin, sadly, was
himself to lose). Instead, the aim of persuasion here is scrutiny:
an alert recognition of the commercial fantasies comprising what
Debord calls "the society of the spectacle." That design aligns
Larkin's poem with my own broader investigation.

And yet there is more going on in "Sunny Prestatyn" than simple
exposé; the poem's emotional import is divided. Plainly, the Prestatyn
belle can be censured as a mildly pornographic image doing duty as
a commercial shill; but Larkin's feelings about pornography itself
were far from dourly judgmental. A propos of the earlier poem
"Lines on a Young Lady's Photograph Album," Andrew Motion
remarks: "By covertly admitting to the pleasure it takes in fantasy,
the poem connects with the other pictures Larkin liked to gaze at:
the photographs in pornographic magazines" (234). Phrases like
"My swivel eye hungers from pose to pose" (CP 71) support Motion's
insight. In "Sunny Prestatyn," the terse epitaph for the poster girl,
"She was too good for this life," is of course to be taken ironically;
the sentimental cliché clashes wryly with a promotional image that

is itself clichéd. Still, looked at more indulgently, that flaunting icon does embody something "good," an ideal, if meretricious, object of desire opposed to the meagre rations "this life" doles out.

Such collisions between bald factuality and wistful fantasy will emerge repeatedly in this study, generating a comparable ambivalence. The works I examine tend to manifest an endemic split: a tension between critique of advertising as a mode of misrepresentation – a devious confidence game – and a sympathy, overt or subtextual, with the scheme of seduction. This peculiar dividedness is deftly captured in "Connections," a story by the Canadian writer Alice Munro from her 1982 collection *The Moons of Jupiter*, where the narrator confides:

> I used to love to look at magazine advertisements showing ladies with chiffon dresses with capes and floating panels, resting their elbows on a ship's rail, or drinking tea beside a potted palm. I used to apprehend a life of elegance and sensibility, through them. They were a window I had on the world … Well, now that I think of it, what were those ladies talking about, in the balloons over their heads? They were discussing underarm odor, or thanking their lucky stars they were no longer chafed, because they used Kotex. (17, ellipsis in original)

In the chapters to follow, I will examine a group of fictions in which the designs of advertising offer such alluring windows on the world, even if the prospects disclosed embarrassingly fade into vistas of drab banality. Time and again, the thrill of billboard fantasy yields to the cheerless but imperative task of fighting cancer – of facing up to the discomfort of unenhanced reality. The tensions are seldom resolved; but, I will argue, these conflicted narratives offer valuable insights into contradictions that have become intractably embedded in the culture we all must navigate.

While the disharmony between ideal promise and sobering factuality is an ancient literary topos, the specific pattern in question here is a relatively recent development, one that hinges on the evolution of a culture engrossed with commodity values. From the middle of the nineteenth century to the early decades of the twentieth, relations between fictional characters and the objects surrounding them

underwent a momentous shift. Consider first a familiar passage from
George Eliot's *Silas Marner* (1861). Wrenched from his native habitat, Silas the weaver has retreated into a psychological shell.

> Yet even in this stage of withering a little incident happened,
> which showed that the sap of affection was not all gone. It was
> one of his daily tasks to fetch his water from a well a couple of
> fields off, and for this purpose, ever since he came to Raveloe,
> he had had a brown earthenware pot, which he held as his most
> precious utensil among the very few conveniences he had granted
> himself. It had been his companion for twelve years, always
> standing on the same spot, always lending its handle to him in
> the early morning, so that its form had an expression for him
> of willing helpfulness, and the impress of its handle on his palm
> gave a satisfaction mingled with that of having the fresh clear
> water. One day as he was returning from the well, he stumbled
> against the step of the stile, and his brown pot, falling with force
> against the stones that overarched the ditch below him, was bro-
> ken in three pieces. Silas picked up the pieces and carried them
> home with grief in his heart. The brown pot could never be of
> use to him any more, but he stuck the bits together and propped
> the ruin in its old place for a memorial. (69)

The object featured here has doubtless been purchased at some
point, but it could hardly be called a "commodity." We are told nothing about its manufacture, its sale – its price. Instead, what counts is
its unique significance for the subject, Silas. The pot is clearly a fetish,
but it is not one whose worth stems from its capacity to be exchanged
for money. Instead, it could more aptly be described as a *talisman*.
It begins its life as merely a "utensil," albeit a precious one, but over
years it acquires the affective weight of a comrade; indeed, the only
one Silas can boast. It becomes a companionable agent in the organic
processes of Silas's life, bringing water to a parched sensibility,
releasing "the sap of human affection." The pot assumes a quasi-
human personality, meeting Silas's fondness half way; it "lends its
handle" to him and has "an expression ... of willing helpfulness." Its
shattering mimics the fracturing of Silas's pre-Raveloe life, which
has left him stranded in alien terrain, severed from nurturing past
associations. Its mending proleptically foretells the eventual healing
of Silas's psyche through his fostering of the child Eppie and his

integration into the rural community. Its use-value is annulled, but it assumes larger importance as a memento of the continuity and tending that Silas's existence has sadly lacked.

The tale, set back decades before the novel's date of composition, unfolds in a half-mythologized rural England innocent of mass marketing, untroubled by advertisement. Silas gains his lonely livelihood by weaving cloth and selling what he produces, but it is the reliability of his workmanship that promotes his "business," abetted by local word of mouth. When he at last revisits his old urban haunts he finds shops and factories – a world of getting and spending – but nothing he can recognize and no one who recognizes him. The shards of his early life cannot be reassembled. The entire narrative frames a nostalgic recreation of a social order that, by Eliot's time, was passing or already past, where the community was knitted together by values largely independent of commercial exchange, a personal network emblematized by Marner's pursuit of weaving, but menaced by the scything onrush of industrial society. Eliot's vision looks ahead to the insights of the twentieth-century French social philosopher Jean Baudrillard, as summarized by George Ritzer: "Baudrillard paints a picture of a world that has fallen from the glories of primitive society and the symbolic exchange that characterizes it. During the industrial era, symbolic exchange was replaced by exchange dominated by use-values and exchange-values" (20–1).

To grasp the consequences of that replacement, we can flash forward (and across an ocean) to F. Scott Fitzgerald's *The Great Gatsby* (1925). Jay Gatsby, grown immensely wealthy, is displaying his mansion to his erstwhile, and now married, sweetheart, Daisy Buchanan. Gatsby's neighbour, Nick Carraway, narrates:

Recovering himself in a minute he opened for us two hulking patent cabinets which held his massed suits and dressing-gowns and ties, and his shirts, piled like bricks in stacks a dozen high.

"I've got a man in England who buys me clothes. He sends over a selection of things at the beginning of each season, spring and fall."

He took out a pile of shirts and began throwing them, one by one, before us, shirts of sheer linen and thick silk and fine flannel, which lost their folds as they fell and covered the table in many-colored disarray. While we admired he brought more and the soft rich heap mounted higher – shirts with stripes and scrolls and

plaids in coral and apple-green and lavender and faint orange,
with monograms of Indian blue. Suddenly, with a strained sound,
Daisy bent her head into the shirts and began to cry stormily.

"They're such beautiful shirts," she sobbed, her voice muffled
in the thick folds. "It makes me sad because I've never seen such
– such beautiful shirts before." (93–4)

Judged literally, Daisy's storm of emotion over Gatsby's mountain of
shirts makes no sense. It is explained only by a fundamental change
in the social meaning of produced goods. Here, for both the con-
vulsed woman and the infatuated man, impersonal objects become
carriers of symbolic value (though symbolic in a different sense from
the one Baudrillard intends). Now those objects, the "soft, rich heap"
of shirts, function unmistakably as commodities; that is their point.
As Bill Brown observes, "[A]fter the [twentieth] century turned ...
Americans lived in an 'age of things,'" characterized by "the effort to
sell things, to purchase things, and to accumulate things" (5).
Gatsby's shirts are colourful banners blazoning the new spirit of
accumulation. They originate in a fashionably foreign place (as the
social theorist Thorstein Veblen had observed, in the United States
"leisure-class tastes are to some extent shaped on usages and habits
which prevail ... among the leisure class of Great Britain" (144)).
They have been culled by someone with no doubt impeccable taste,
and they have presumably cost a fortune to purchase and transport.
They are, to apply Veblen's famous term, tokens of conspicuous consumption – as is, for that matter, the glamorous Daisy herself.

In the first, feverish weeks of their courtship, Daisy had made
a stunning impression on the young Gatsby through her aura as a
prized, sumptuously packaged female commodity:

There was a ripe mystery about [her house], a hint of bedrooms
upstairs more beautiful and cool than other bedrooms, of gay
and radiant activities taking place through its corridors, and of
romances that were not musty and laid away already in lavender,
but fresh and breathing and redolent of this year's shining motorcars and of dances whose flowers were scarcely withered. It
excited him, too, that many men had already loved Daisy – it
increased her value in his eyes. (148)

The images come straight out of fashion magazine ads of the time.
What so moves Daisy now is her recognition that Gatsby has amassed

his plethora of shirts, and is marshalling them for her, as a tribute to the fairy-tale world of consumerist opulence from which she springs. Gatsby's wealth, despite its mysterious and probably scandalous origins, has at last qualified him to inhabit that Veblenesque fantasyland of ostentatious acquisition. As Veblen had shrewdly observed, "Property is ... of the nature of trophy" (28), and the grandiose spectacle of Gatsby's trophy wardrobe could be called Veblen eroticized. It dramatizes another of that thinker's pronouncements: "The consumption of expensive goods is meritorious, and the goods which contain an appreciable element of cost in excess of what gives them serviceability for their ostensible mechanical purpose are honorific" (154–5).

For this set, poor Silas's cherished jug could not be honorific unless it had been gold-encrusted by certified adepts in Byzantium. And yet what is at stake here is of course not simply the gross monetary value of Gatsby's possessions nor even the size of his bank account. Instead it is the pair's *shared reverence* for the wealth-engorged style of life that exalts them far above the workaday drudgery of the world's Marners. Gatsby's shirt-mountains are harbingers of the still more rampant commodity culture that would emerge in the decades to follow. Another comment of Baudrillard's is precisely to the point: "Profusion, piling high are clearly the most striking descriptive features" of the consumer society (26). The metaphor of *glut* is one that will recur in texts to be considered in later chapters of this book, most notably Joshua Ferris's *Then We Came to the End*.

True, Silas too "piles high" his hoard of gold coins, but in an utterly opposed spirit; the coins are meant to delight his own eyes, not to dazzle the eyes of society moguls. His obsession, indeed, causes him to *abstain* from consumption. It gains him notoriety as a miser but does not otherwise control his perceptions of his world. Ironically, the gold hoard that draws him away from human exchange preserves in him (like his unfortunate jug) the latent "sap of affection." He is thus enabled to form an emotional bond with the golden-haired child, Eppie, whom he suddenly discovers in a scene of magical transformation that reverses the familiar, tragic "golden touch" of King Midas.[1] By contrast, people of Gatsby and Daisy's ilk are gripped by an altogether different kind of magic. They are, to quote Baudrillard once more, "condemned to a magical economy, to the valorization of objects as such, and of all other things as objects (ideas, leisure, knowledge, culture): this *fetishistic logic is, strictly, the ideology of consumption*" (59, emphasis in original). "The world of objects and needs," Baudrillard concludes, "might thus be seen as a world of *generalized hysteria*" (77, emphasis in original) – a spot-on description of the affective habitus Gatsby and his tribe occupy.

The decisive difference between that world and Silas Marner's is the advent, on a gargantuan scale, of what the sociologist Andrew Wernick calls promotional culture. That culture is absent from the social arena of Eliot's novel but suffuses that of Fitzgerald's. Not that George Eliot was blind to promotional ploys, as witness the amusingly deft sales pitch of the packman, Bob Jakin, in *The Mill on the Floss* (Book V Chapter 2). Eliot had grasped the fact that advertising was a growing force in the England of her time; the absence of that force from *Silas* is a deliberate exclusion. But it is safe to say that no object in all of Eliot's oeuvre takes on the kind of commoditized *aura* that the shirts have for Gatsby and Daisy. And while the shirts themselves may or may not have been advertised, in a vital sense they *are* advertisements – for Gatsby's fortune, his taste, and above all his abiding romantic passion. In a later scene Daisy, just after signalling in public her love for Gatsby, acknowledges that he occupies for her the exalted realm of high fashion publicity: "'You resemble the advertisement of the man,' she went on innocently. 'You know the advertisement of the man – '" (119). She is cut short, but "the man" in question is probably the dapper swell shown full-face adjusting his cravat in a celebrated ad for "Par, the Aristocrat of Arrow Collars": "Cluett Peabody's 'Arrow Man' depicted by Joseph Leyendecker became the symbol of fashionable American manhood in the '20s – a dignified, educated man of taste, manners, and money" (Miller 350).[2] But ultimately the exact identity of "the man" hardly matters; his distinction derives from his presence in a glossy ad, just as Gatsby's distinction derives from the imputed resemblance. As Ronald Berman points out (64), Myrtle Wilson's infatuation with Tom Buchanan follows a parallel logic: Tom, Myrtle says, "had on a dress suit and patent leather shoes, and I couldn't keep my eyes off him, but every time he looked at me I had to pretend to be looking at the advertisement over his head" (*Gatsby* 36). Again, the decoy advertisement and the nattily accoutred man merge into a single object of adulation. Later, with gruesome irony, Myrtle herself is conspicuously "consumed" by Gatsby's top-of-the-line motorcar, Daisy at the wheel.

Fitzgerald had worked, briefly and not happily, at the Manhattan advertising agency Barron Collier, and it stands to reason that the genius of advertisement should preside over his most famous novel.

Its earthly avatar is the stark, dilapidated signboard vaunting the merits of the oculist T.J. Eckleburg. After his wife Myrtle's fatal mishap, the distraught George Wilson stares at "the eyes of Doctor T.J. Eckleburg, which had just emerged, pale and enormous, from the dissolving night," and pronounces "God sees everything" (160). His friend Michaelis gently corrects him, "That's an advertisement," but Wilson's conflation of divinity with publicity has its own irresistible logic. The one true god governing the world of Gatsby and Daisy is the god of almighty promotion.

The shift in values and perceptions in question here reflects a deep transformation in the social history encompassing Eliot and Fitzgerald. Underlying those changes, partly cause and partly symptom, is the novel importance of advertising as a major force. Berman cites a "pioneer study of advertising," *Packages That Sell* by Richard Franken and Carroll Larabee (1928), which "identified 1925 as the crucial period for marketing in America; it was then that advertising really learned, through packaging and picturing, 'to create a desire in the consumer's mind'" (68). As it happens, 1925 is the publication date of *The Great Gatsby*, with its copious array of artfully cultivated desires. But that portentous year did not see the gods of advertising suddenly spring, fully formed, from the brains of myriad ecstatic ad men; those deities had been romping in their infancy and adolescence since before the turn of the century. The present study will bear witness to the spectacular growth of the promotional gods to their robust maturity, and will examine some of the attempts by makers of literary fictions to confront and even possibly to tame them. Again, such confrontations are apt to betray the authors' own covertly divided allegiances; even the censorious Nick Carraway – with, one senses, the indulgent backing of Fitzgerald himself - finds in Gatsby, the "man in the advertisement," "something gorgeous ... some heightened sensitivity to the promises of life" (2). The chapters to follow will trace a series of precarious contests between promise and disappointment.

DESIGNING FICTIONS

Introduction:
Baudrillard's Dream

The premise of this book is that, for the past century, advertising has exerted a controlling force on industrial society and has provoked in response an important body of work by a varied roster of imaginative writers. The study shows how a number of fictional texts have engaged with advertising as a social praxis and/or a means of professional livelihood. It observes how such narratives pit promotional business against "artistic" pursuits, often, though not always, to the detriment of promotion. One common motive for the disparagement of advertising is its imputed utilitarian or "venal" nature. I argue, however, that these critiques tend inevitably to be conditioned by their own participation in modern commodity culture. (On the most practical level, books must be publicized and sold; television shows must be funded.) Thus, the works to be considered here manifest, again and again, a tension between an oppositional view of advertising as an enterprise and identification with those engaged in it.

According to George Ritzer's introduction to Jean Baudrillard's *The Consumer Society*, the French theorist "holds to the dream of an art that, instead of being in the thrall of the consumer society, would be able to decipher it" (16). The literary works I examine, though diverse, all share in Baudrillard's dream. Whether they manage to escape society's thrall will be a difficult, perhaps imponderable, question. Anyone embarking on such an inquiry is confronted with an *embarras de richesses*; the number of arguably relevant fictional texts is too vast to be contained within a single critical envelope. One's principles of selection, therefore, risk looking arbitrary.

I would, nevertheless, claim that some method underlies the madness of my choices. In part, the rationale has been defined by principles of exclusion. To begin with, my specimen texts are almost all prose works. A consideration of the treatment of advertising by poets like E.E. Cummings, Robert Frost, Sylvia Plath, or indeed Philip Larkin, though tempting, would raise somewhat different issues from those I highlight here. Among novelists, the most glaring omission is no doubt James Joyce, whose canvasser Leopold Bloom ranks as the nonpareil fictional practitioner of the advertising business. But while Joyce cannot be called either dismissive or uncritical of advertising, *Ulysses* is not a book that attends consistently to promotion as a practice. In any case, Joyce's relation with that activity has been amply treated by Jennifer Wicke in her 1988 book *Advertising Fictions* and by others since then. Theodore Dreiser's sprawling 1915 novel *The "Genius"* might have been tempting to consider, especially because its protagonist, Eugene Whitla, abandons his artistic ambitions in favour of a more lucrative career in advertising, prefiguring the trajectory of George Orwell's Gordon Comstock. However, advertising cannot be considered a thematic centrepiece of Dreiser's book, and space does not permit the inclusion of all such "might have beens." A bestseller like Sloan Wilson's *The Man in the Gray Flannel Suit* (1955), along with the 1956 screen adaptation, could have made an interesting companion piece to the popular 1940s novels by Wouk and Wakeman I consider in chapter 4, but Tom Rath, Wilson's hero, works not in advertising but in the allied field of public relations, and little in either the book or the film would significantly extend the arguments relating to the texts on which I focus. Again, other television shows besides the current AMC series *Mad Men* have featured characters involved in advertising, most notably the popular 1970s series *Bewitched*, which fancifully juxtaposed the "magic" of advertising affairs with magic of the bona fide, old-fashioned kind. However, neither *Bewitched* nor any comparable production has probed the social import of promotion in *Mad Men*'s compelling fashion. While, as I will argue, *Mad Men*'s take on advertising is acutely self-divided, that very fact makes the series an illuminating complement to the literary works discussed earlier on.

What sorts of texts, then, have managed to escape the cutting-room floor and why? By and large, they are – predictably – works that, over the past century, have made promotional culture and its proliferation a central concern. Henry James's 1903 *The Ambassadors* (chapter 2), where the subject is not treated *in extenso*, may appear to be an exception. Despite its seemingly peripheral status, however, advertising turns out to have a crucial bearing on the protagonist, Lambert Strether's, understanding of the *jeune premier*, Chad Newsome and of his own poignant predicament. James has in common with his friendly enemy H.G. Wells, whose *Tono-Bungay* takes up the lion's share of the chapter, a fascination with the way promotional matters can impinge on or warp personal relations. Writing in the opening years of the twentieth century, both James and Wells evince a prescient awareness of the portentous significance of advertising for the age to follow.

The thread of the discussion next leads to books by two writers who, working in Wells's large shadow and in the grimmer shadow of a world war, both registered the growing influence of promotional culture: the American Christopher Morley and the Englishman George Orwell. As with James and Wells, this is again a transatlantic coupling. It should be said, however, that nationality will occupy at most a secondary place in the chapters that follow. This is not to deny that the advertising industry developed in distinctive ways in the America of James and Morley as opposed to the Britain of Wells and Orwell or, for that matter, the Canada of Munro and Atwood. Earlier twentieth-century writers like James and Wells and Orwell were inclined to regard innovations in mass marketing as a peculiarly American phenomenon. Yet in its further phases the industry proved, as everyone knows, to be emphatically global. What I think matters above all for the literary works I discuss are facts of chronology rather than geography. Thus, while it is right to remember that Morley and Orwell were writing on different sides of the Atlantic, a still more salient fact is that they were writing on opposite sides of a temporal watershed, a period that saw a dramatic expansion of the advertising industry and concurrently a drastic shrinkage of financial means for many would-be consumers.

The bestsellers by Wakeman and Wouk, discussed in chapter 4, drew momentum from the new modishness of mass advertising as a topic for debate in the years following the Second World War. The burgeoning of commercial radio (and later television) as a channel for publicity lent the subject a palpable urgency, which the two authors exploited effectively for a popular audience. Both novels chronicle the pitfalls of working in the dangerously worldly purlieus of advertising. Wakeman's book (and even more the cinematic spin-off) takes the form of a moralized melodrama, while Wouk's strikes

an archly facetious note of satire. Both novels were successfully marketed as Book of the Month Club selections; not surprisingly, neither
manages to elude the "thrall" of consumer society.

The works (by male authors) mentioned thus far pay on the whole
little attention to the impact of consumerist pressures on women –
typically the front-line targets of promotion. The discussion of
Margaret Atwood's 1969 *The Edible Woman* (chapter 5) aims at
redressing this imbalance. The tribulations of Atwood's protagonist,
Marian MacAlpin, wittily dramatize how promotional culture can
configure a woman's subjectivity, especially as manifested in her intimate personal relations. The novel's stress on the deforming impact
of advertising on perception itself is a groundbreaking insight, looking ahead to the enhanced emphasis on interiority that characterizes
more recent fictional treatments of promotional affairs. That emphasis distinguishes two novels of 2007 dealing with advertising as an
occupation: Blake Morrison's *South of the River* and Joshua Ferris's
Then We Came to the End (chapter 6). Actors in both books deal
with the awkward question of whether their professional lives can
be deemed artistically "creative," an issue glanced at a century earlier by Wells and pursued further by Morley and Orwell. Finally,
with a nod to the growing dominance of the visual dimension in
contemporary promotional culture, chapter 7 turns to the televisual
series *Mad Men*, in which themes prominent in the print texts – the
conflict between literature and promotion, the motif of prostitution,
the troubling prevalence of dishonesty and infidelity – get replayed
with hectic immediacy.[1]

All these texts can be called outgrowths of the seismic shift separating the world of *The Great Gatsby* from that of *Silas Marner*.
Each comments on what might be called the manufacturing of preference: the hold commodity culture and its confederate, advertising,
have come to exert on the public. The marketed items featured range
from the trivial to the preposterous to the deadly, from soaps and
patent medicines to prunes and ginger cubes to cigarettes and even
(*pace* Larkin) cancer. The narratives generally purport to be exposés
of the distorting grip promotion exerts upon individual human consciousness and society as a whole; yet the exposés have a way of
paradoxically exposing themselves to question. As Simone Weil
Davis has said of Fitzgerald and his contemporaries:

> These authors were not only "treating" the phenomenon of sub-
> jectivity and commodity culture, they were living in it, constructed

by it, illustrative of it – as is the modern-day critic hoping to comment on them. Essentially, they were marketing themselves and their work to a predominantly middle-class consumer culture, addressing and simultaneously participating in it. (14)

The more one attempts to pin the works of such writers down to consistent stances on their main preoccupations, the more anomalies and contradictions emerge. Both the writers and those who read and attempt to understand them are, as Davis points out, preconditioned by a common immersion in consumer society. It is best therefore to be both circumspect and resolute when entering this sometimes hazardous literary terrain.

Advertising is an inescapable presence in our society, yet it is seldom given sustained or even serious attention. According to the authors of the article "Toward a Critical Theory of Advertising," "[A]dvertising appears on the surface to be insignificant and is easily dismissed as something irrelevant or tangential to production, social life, and personality development" (Harms and Kellner 16). We register advertising as peripheral, as a sideshow cluttering the margins or interstices of "main events," as fleeting images and "messages" undeserving of more than a bemused shrug, but this is a response that overlooks promotional culture's real and growing centrality. To quote Davis, since the 1920s "advertising has become an ever more influential part of a hegemonic matrix of social and economic institutions" (1).

My main concern here will be with literary representations of advertising's steadily encroaching social influence. To quote Harms and Kellner again, "[A]dvertising plays a key role in the transition to a new image culture, and thus in the transition from a discursive book/print culture to a figurative media culture" (5). If that is true, then the two modes – the promotional and the literary – would seem to be, by their very natures, at odds. In its earlier phases, of course, promotion itself depended largely on print for its diffusion, but in an age of ubiquitous electronic feeds, above all television, it has increasingly turned to visual images for its persuasive impact. Decades ago the economist Joseph Schumpeter voiced a sceptical view of the potency of such means: "The picture of the prettiest girl that ever lived will in the long run prove powerless to maintain the sales of a bad cigarette" (263). While nobody would nowadays talk about "bad" cigarettes as if good ones existed, Schumpeter's doubt regarding the capacity of pictures to control consumer preference remains a live issue. If anything, in a twenty-first-century milieu saturated with persuasive images to a degree the economist could not have imagined, the question has become even more urgent.

True, debunking stances like Schumpeter's now look passé. Advertisers themselves are the first to complain when visual modes of persuasion are deployed against them. A revealing instance is reported in Stanley Fish's *New York Times* piece, "The Tobacco Horror Show" (14 November 2011), in which Fish comments on tobacco companies' attempts to thwart "the FDA's plan to augment the textual warnings on cigarette packages with graphic color images, including diseased lungs, a cadaver on an autopsy table and a man blowing smoke from a hole in his throat." The firms sought a court injunction on the grounds that "the purpose and effect of the warnings is [sic] to drown out Plaintiff's own constitutionally protected speech and replace it with the Government's emotionally charged anti-smoking message." The nub of the complaint is the Federal Drug Administration's move to upgrade its antismoking efforts by gearing them to the transition from an older print culture (textual warnings) to the new visual culture.

Fish takes issue with the companies' distinction between objective fact and emotional impact, contending that "in the case of the tobacco warnings ... the emotions intentionally produced by the graphic images bring a cognitive message home." In Fish's view, "What alarms [the companies] is not that the proposed images distort the truth, but that they tell it." Nevertheless, the presiding judge issued the requested injunction and "gave as a reason the illegitimacy of images as conveyors of information." Fish asks rhetorically, "Is the factual and uncontroversial assertion that 'smoking can kill you' ... without persuasive intent or effect?" He concludes that neither words nor images, singly or in combination, can yield "a 'neutral observation language,' a super-literal language uninflected and uninfected by the distortions of any human, or ... 'subjective' perspective."

Fish's case for questioning strict boundaries between verbal and visual persuasion is intellectually sound. Still, by employing inflammatory graphic design to counteract the purchasing of cigarettes, the FDA is arguably fighting fire with fire – or, if you like, smoke with smoke. That is, it is participating in a runaway culture of emotionally loaded appeals that, more and more, act as surrogates for rational discourse. Cutting-edge advertising techniques can cut both ways; they have infiltrated areas remote from the marketing of baked beans or bananas.

A number of recent, more formal philosophical and sociological texts have maintained that advertising lies behind many of the ills in modern or postmodern society. Among the most influential commentators has been the Polish sociologist Zygmunt Bauman. In his 2007 *Liquid Times* Bauman claims that we have moved from an older, more established "solid" phase to a "liquid" phase of modernity in which social forms tend to mutate persistently from one configuration to another. According to Bauman, we are now living "in a world ... in which each individual is left on his or her own while most individuals are tools of each other's promotion" (24). This "new individualism" based on mutual promotional exploitation resembles the post-Emersonian free-for-all evoked by Ferris's novel *Then We Came to the End*, or the no-holds-barred 1960s commercial arena of *Mad Men*. It conduces to "the fading of human bonds and the wilting of solidarity" (24). It is a "deregulated, individualized society of consumers" (104) where "'progress' seems to have moved from the discourse of *shared improvement* to that of *individual survival*" (103, emphasis in original).

Bauman argues that "[i]n postmodern society, it is the advertisers who set standards of taste and create consensus within the population, not the general intellectuals – heirs to the *philosophes*" (Smith 118). For Bauman, the intellectuals might as well be labeled the ineffectuals; their power "has been expropriated by the advertiser, the marketing manager, the public relations expert, the television producer, the game show host and other agents of mass seduction" (Smith 117). The consequence of dwelling in this Vanity Fair of promotion, surrounded by enticing images, is that instead of "being" what you do for a living, "in a postmodern habitat you *are* what you buy" (Smith 157, emphasis in original).

Two recent reports on the advertising industry in the United Kingdom by and large corroborate Bauman's theses: *Think of Me as Evil?* (2011), published by the Public Interest Research Centre and *The Advertising Effect* (2010), published by Compass – Direction for the Democratic Left. Both surveys call attention to important technological advances in persuasive methodologies; both stress the need for vigorous resistance through concerted public action. (The whole debate about advertising tends to divide opinion along

political fault lines; opponents of promotion often identify as pro-
gressives who favour government intervention, while proponents are
frequently conservatives devoted to free-market principles.)

Among a garland of tributes prefacing *Think of Me as Evil?:
Opening the Ethical Debate in Advertising, Guardian* columnist
George Monbiot asserts that "nothing quite like it has been written
before" (7). Such a claim is certainly exaggerated; it becomes more
understandable, however, if one grants that issues connected with
advertising have been less widely canvassed in Monbiot's Britain
than in North America and continental Europe. The authors of the
report focus on ecological concerns, contending that "modern advertising's impact on British culture is likely to be detrimental to our
wellbeing, and may well exacerbate the social and environmental
problems that we collectively confront" (14). They note that "economic growth can usually be maintained through *the artificial creation of needs through advertising* (18, emphasis in original), and
argue that "[t]he goods that are produced and sold in this way are
often unneeded, and therefore are essentially waste" (18). "Such
trends," they add, "threaten to exacerbate global poverty and pose
grave challenges for just and equitable development" (18). To the
familiar defence that advertising merely echoes the values of society,
they counter that far from being value-neutral, advertising naturalizes and reinforces unexamined attitudes and behaviours: "Advertising
... will tend inevitably to establish social norms which condition us
to accept certain values, and which will suppress expressions of alternative values" (26).

The authors draw a key distinction between "extrinsic" values,
"contingent upon the perceptions of others – they relate to envy of
'higher' social strata, admiration of material wealth, or power" (27)
– and "intrinsic" ones, based on "a sense of community, affiliation to
friends and family, and self-development" (27). Advertising, they
maintain, speaks principally to extrinsic values (30) and thus favours
pursuits that leave "a higher ecological footprint" (28). They cite
Anat Bardi's diagnosis of the intensifying effects of advertising: "As
... values are primed repeatedly, they are likely to be strengthened"
(31), The dichotomy they posit between "intrinsic" and "extrinsic"
objects of affiliation runs the risk of looking arbitrary when
applied to the intricacies of concrete cases. (Can one claim with
confidence that Gatsby's shirts are "extrinsic" and Marner's cracked

jug "intrinsic"?) Still, the dualism at least provides a rule of thumb for making helpful discriminations.

Like some other recent commentators, the authors are concerned with "how brain science can contribute to marketing" (40) by equipping advertisers with insidious means of playing on consumers' "intuition" (40). Such innovative techniques can, they claim, "extend advertising's pervasiveness" (45) and work to limit the consumer's real freedom of choice. They may overstate the actual power of these novelties, such as product placement, to control consumer choice among competing brands. However, they argue plausibly for the need "to reduce the negative impact that advertising has on cultural values" along with "the pervasiveness of advertising, reversing the trend to communicate with us as consumers in every facet of our lives" (49). Above all, "the choice to avoid advertising must be made open to us" (51). The authors' blueprints for accomplishing such laudable goals, for example the prohibiting of advertisements in public spaces, tend toward the utopian, but they are motivated by a palpable sense of urgency.[2]

The authors of *The Advertising Effect* pursue a broadly similar agenda. Their report, too, warns that advertising "encourages us to run ever faster on the treadmill of modern consumer life" (5) and that the world "is becoming a vast advertising hoarding to sell us more stuff" (7). They find it all the more imperative that we "take back our streets, towns, and cities as places to be citizens rather than just consumers" (5). They believe that "the crucial role of advertising" is "creating wants and turning them into needs" (8); the goal of advertising is thus "the creation of a mood of restless dissatisfaction with what we have got and who we are so that we go out and buy more" (8). The demoralizing result is that "[d]riven on by the seductive images of success and aspiration we compete with each other for status, but simply make ourselves feel like failures as we out bid each other for the latest car, gadget or holiday" (9). In short, "We are buying more but are increasingly less fulfilled and a multi-billion-pound industry is working flat out to make sure we stay that way" (13).

What these studies say about the controlling grip of advertising on British society holds good at least equally for countries like the United States and Canada. One long-established avenue for contesting this promotional hegemony – one the reports neglect to mention – is imaginative literature. Admittedly, we are unlikely to encounter in novels or short stories the sort of unsparing remonstrance that characterizes the British reports I have been summarizing. To begin with, we would do well to ask whether such works are even distinguishable in their essence from commercial publicity. Are we dealing here with apples and oranges, or rather with two variants of genetically the same fruit? D.H. Lawrence, an imaginative writer who was not normally an admirer of business, points out the shared ground between the two genres.

> And when a word comes to us in its individual character, and starts in us the individual responses, it is a great pleasure to us. The American advertisers have discovered this, and some of the cunningest American literature is to be found in advertisements of soap-suds, for example. These advertisements are *almost* prose-poems. They give the word soap-suds a bubbly, shiny individual meaning which is very skilfully poetic, would, perhaps, be quite poetic to the mind which could forget that the poetry was bait on a hook. (*Late Essays and Articles* 237–8, emphasis in original)

Lawrence wittily identifies a genuine affinity here, the common affective charge that advertising and literature alike deliver. Still, his damningly italicized "almost" punctures the poetic soap bubble. A baited hook is not to be mistaken for a Shakespeare sonnet, and even the "cunningest" American literature, by implication, fails to qualify as literature in the full sense.

Some more recent commentators, while not flatly equating advertising with literature, grant promotional discourse at least equal cultural standing. One ground for this move could be termed quantitative: the sheer magnitude of advertising's clutch on collective consciousness. As Rob Walker claims, "[T]he grammar and syntax of commercial persuasion [constitute a language] that everyone has, for better or worse, learned to speak" (207). Jackson Lears, an eminent chronicler of promotional culture, considers advertising and its "fables of abundance" "perhaps the most dynamic and sensuous representations of cultural values in the world" (2). James Twitchell goes farther, calling such fables "the dominant meaning-making system of modern life" (253). Unfazed by baited hooks or literary canons, Twitchell extols advertisement on a national scale as a prime agent of social cohesiveness: "[I]t is precisely the recognition of jingles and brand names, precisely what high culturists abhor, that links us as a culture" (7). (Baudrillard, though with scant enthusiasm, similarly asserts that consumer society hinges on an "*exchange of differences which clinches group integration*" (93, emphasis in original).) Twitchell declares grandly that "[n]ot only are we willing to consume, and not only does consuming make us happy, 'getting and spending' is what gives our lives order and purpose" (110).

According to this euphoric view, advertising has rightfully shouldered aside literature as the dominant mode of discourse in our print-weary consumer culture. Other observers see the two modes not as grappling rivals but rather as comrades-in-arms. Even here, though, advertising tends to be cast as the senior partner. Jennifer Wicke, author of the pioneering 1988 study *Advertising Fictions*, speaks of "the centrality of advertisement to modern culture, and its radical reshaping of both literature and ideological production in general" (2), a claim that merits some extended scrutiny. Wicke wishes to see advertising "as a language and a literature in its own right – as a pre-eminent discourse of modern culture" (1). Although she acknowledges the residual tensions between advertisement and formal literature, Wicke stresses the cross-fertilizing capacity of the two. She argues that "the dialectic between advertising and the novel reveals both how advertising was able to take on the status of a mass literature, enforcing its own codes of social reading, and how the novel relies on the conditions of advertising to permit it to become the major literary form" (1). She rejects the positions of well-known critics of mass promotion – Raymond Williams, both Leavises, Horkheimer and Adorno – who, she says, construct advertising as literature's "demonized twentieth-century rival" (7). Rather than antagonism, Wicke foregrounds symbiosis as the hallmark of the dialectic. She summons ample historical evidence to document how published works of fiction, from the nineteenth century on, regularly contained advertising matter and how the texts of advertising made profuse use of literary allusion. One might logically object that the kindred origins of advertising and literary fiction do not establish their ongoing affinity; genesis does not strictly determine essence. Still, Wicke's analysis documents the extensive indebtedness to advertisement observable in novels by Dickens and Henry James, and in Joyce's *Ulysses*.

While gesturing toward some negative social repercussions of mass promotion, Wicke avoids dwelling on them in the fashion of the British reports I have discussed. Instead, her major stress falls on the power of promotional discourse to inform and energize literary works, a signal instance being Joyce's modernist classic. But because it is formulated categorically, as an axiom with little elaboration, her pivotal claim that advertisement constitutes a "literature" in its own right becomes difficult to verify. In a summative passage, Wicke states that

> [a]dvertising performs enormous cultural work ... on the order of a social literature with its genres, traditions, self-references, and material transformations. It is unlike literature in that it gains this power only across the range of its artifacts, only in its constellation as a floating cultural corpus – the individual instances of advertisement are too embedded in the discursive matrix of advertising for them to be anything other than slight when taken in isolation. (175)

Although advertising's "work" is proclaimed with assurance here, precisely how a "floating cultural corpus" bears comparison with the voluminous body of texts that comprise world literature is left to the reader to ascertain – no simple task in the absence of individual instances, slight though these may be.

Wicke is not alone in viewing promotional discourse as composing, in aggregate, a "corpus" of signification. Baudrillard's theory of consumption, and by extension advertising, in some ways aligns itself with hers. Baudrillard defines commodity culture "as a system of communication and exchange, as a code of signs continually being sent, received and reinvented – as *language*" (93). However, his estimate of the social benefits of the code is less sanguine than Wicke's:

> [I]t is the function of advertising in all its forms to set in place a *social fabric* ideologically unified under the auspices of a collective super-patronage, a kindly super-feudality, which provides all those "extras" [gifts, special offers and the like] the way aristocrats laid on feasts for their people ... No matter that this munificence, like that of potentates, is only ever a functional redistribution of a part of the profits. (165, emphasis in original)

The "cultural work" Wicke extols as democratically available to all amounts, for Baudrillard, to a strategy of feudal conscription meant to bolster and extend a profit-thirsty hierarchical order. Stuart Ewen would concur: "Modern advertising must be seen as a direct response to the needs of mass industrial capitalism" (*Captains* 31).

Wicke's exaltation of advertisement to the status of literature is weakened by vagueness on a crucial point: how exposure to myriad advertisements might replicate the kinds of *experience* delivered by more orthodox literary texts. Granted, it would be misleading to posit a reified edifice called "Literature" with impermeable boundaries and identical attributes in all its component units. And, indeed, as Lawrence suggests, there is appreciable overlap between literary works in the usual sense and promotional texts. For example, the majority of ads, whether television commercials or graphic displays, rely for their persuasive payload on narrative, overt or implied; this holds good even for the crude sketches meant to publicize the Tono-Bungay elixir in Wells's novel (see chapter 2). But the *expectations* one normally brings to works of fiction are not homologous with those one brings to a television commercial. Few would expect even the most clever or imaginative promotional vignette to supply the kind of emotional sustenance or intellectual stimulus one looks for from *The Great Gatsby*. The famous skywriting scene in Virginia Woolf's *Mrs Dalloway* (Part One, Section Two), where the words traced by the airplane are variously decoded by strollers in the city below, features a recently developed promotional technology, but makes no attempt to nudge readers into a preference for Glaxo dried milk or Kreemo toffee. Instead, it memorably dramatizes the way in which the subjective responses of individual observers to an arresting event come together to compose a variegated tapestry of perception.[3] Such probing of subjectivities is antithetical to the persuasive strategies of most advertising, which, *contra* Lawrence, usually aims not so much at an individual as at a preprogrammed, stereotyped response.

Promotional work can, to be sure, manifest genuine creativity: inventiveness, flair, verbal or visual wit. The run of "Think Small" ads for Volkswagen automobiles produced by the Doyle Dane Bernbach agency in the 1950s represents one vintage example of such persuasive brilliance, but numerous others come readily to mind. An annual event, the Cannes Lions International Festival of Creativity (formerly, and more drably, the International Advertising Festival) honours ads that excel in originality and impact, and there seems no good reason why artistic merit in this field should go unrecognized. Certainly, audiences with no personal stake in the products promoted find compilations of such work entertaining to watch.

An impressive gallery of imaginative writers have found in promotional culture a brio they can admire and even emulate. John Updike declares, "I have no doubt that the aesthetic marvels of our age, for intensity and lavishness of effort and subtlety of both overt and subliminal effect, are television commercials" (Twitchell vii). Aldous Huxley discovered in American print ads a new world he could deem truly brave: "The advertisement is one of the most interesting and difficult of modern literary forms. Its potentialities are not yet half explored. Already the most interesting and, in some cases, the only readable part of most American periodicals is the advertisement section" (Twitchell 14).

On a practical level, promotional employment has furnished a lifeline for writers who might otherwise have languished in penury. As Lears observes, "Since the late nineteenth century, advertising has given people who like to write, draw or shoot film the opportunity to get paid regularly (maybe even well) for it. The industry has attracted many extraordinarily talented people" (261). He concludes: "The story of the artist in advertising is part of the larger story of the artist in American society" (262). Ewen characterizes the promotional industry as a Maecenas for moderns: "Artistic patronage, a province of the wealthy since ancient times, now was doled out through the economic avenues provided by advertising and its related industries" (*Captains* 62). He deplores, however, "the psychological attrition" visited on artists and writers by such work: "Artists, often gifted in their sensitivities and sympathies to human frailties, were called upon to use those sensitivities for manipulation" (65–6). This will be, essentially, the grievance of Orwell's struggling poet, Gilbert Comstock, in *Keep the Aspidistra Flying*.

Like the fictional Gordon, a good many flesh-and-blood writers have found the *instrumental* nature of promotion inimical to their imaginative freedom. Wicke, doubtless with opposed theorists like Baudrillard and Ewen in mind, cautions that "[t]he intentionalist [sic] fallacy can rear its head in studies of advertising language, under the guise of seeing in it a monolithic totalization of capitalist control" (147), but Wimsatt and Beardsley's hoary "fallacy" has only a tenuous relevance to promotional language. Granted, ads, despite their predominantly homogenizing intent, may be received differently by diverse subjects; the skywriting episode from Woolf offers an instructive paradigm. Nevertheless, as Lears concedes, the *underlying intention* remains transparent: the copywriter's "art, like the realistic novelist's, required a mix of imagination and accurate observation. But the aim of ad copy was strictly instrumental; it was meant to sell goods. If it failed to accomplish that task, its beauty was irrelevant" (284–5).

How reliably advertising does in fact accomplish its aim has long been a matter of dispute. Baudrillard makes his doubts plain; for him, the product's brand name is "the only real message" of an ad (148), and he repeatedly voices scepticism as to the effectiveness even of that rudimentary message. By contrast, according to William Meyers's 1984 book *The Image Makers*, marketers "are now able virtually to dictate the foods we eat, the soda or beer we drink, the cigarettes we smoke, the clothes we wear, the cars we drive, even the Presidents we elect" (4). Perhaps so, but a lengthy and bedraggled roster of failed promotional campaigns (not to mention the travails of the industry that produces "the cigarettes we smoke") challenges the force of a word like Meyers's "dictate." Walker cites the much-heralded launch of "New Coke" in 1985 (a year after the date of Meyers's book) as "one of the most spectacular marketing flops of all time" (80). He concludes that, "it's not quite right to say that everybody used to be perfectly passive couch-potato 'androids' who did whatever advertising told them to do" (80).

Even the power of branding must itself contend with the counter-force of public wariness. A popular truism holds that brand names merely attempt to inscribe chimerical distinctions between virtually identical products. According to Evan Evans, the despotic soap magnate in Wakeman's *The Hucksters*, the "secret" about the business that has enriched him is that "[t]here's no damn difference between soaps" (23). The function of advertising is, in this view, to manufacture spurious grounds for preference where substantive ones are lacking. Along these lines, Meyers asserts: "Apart from a small price gap ... the only major differences between vehicles made in Tokyo and those made in Detroit are the ones Madison Avenue has created" (86–7). Such blanket application of the "no damn difference" dictum invites, however, intuitive objections, which even a hasty

glance at a buyer's guide to auto makes will reinforce. Despite
Meyers's assurance, advertisement does not exert a Svengali grip
over consumer choice; *caveat emptor*, though a maxim in a "dead"
language, lives on in the minds of nervous buyers.

Still, one does not run afoul of an intentional fallacy by calling
manipulation, barefaced or covert, an intrinsic strategy of promotion, as many commentators have long insisted. Baudrillard loftily
debunks the notion of advertising's hortatory potency – "[T]o
denounce advertising for its manipulation of the emotions is to pay
it too great a compliment" (148) – but his is distinctly a minority
opinion. While literary works too sometimes fall back on time-tested
triggers for emotion, ads tend to rely far more heavily on such psychological props. To quote Marshall McLuhan, advertising agencies
are "constantly striving to enter and control the unconscious minds
of a vast public, not in order to understand or to present these minds,
as the serious novelist does, but in order to exploit them for profit"
(*Bride* 97). In her McLuhan-inflected novel *The Edible Woman*, the
serious (yet funny) novelist Margaret Atwood weaves this motif of
psychic manipulation deftly into the perplexities of her protagonist.

The method of control McLuhan pinpoints works not by reasoned
argument but by endowing commodities with a magical, seductive
aura. As Judith Williamson explains: "That is why advertising is so
uncontrollable, because whatever restrictions are made in terms of
their verbal content or 'false claims', there is no way of getting at
their use of images and symbols. And it is precisely these which do
the work of the ad anyway" (*Decoding* 175). Soapsuds, to reprise
Lawrence, are given "a bubbly, shiny, individual meaning." It is
no accident that the metaphor of "magic" crops up recurrently in
accounts of promotional strategies. To quote McLuhan once again,
"[A]ds can be seen as a kind of social ritual or magic that flatter[s]
and enhance[s] us in our own eyes" (113). Raymond Williams's
chapter on advertising in *Problems in Materialism and Culture* is
entitled "Advertising: The Magic System" (170). Even for Baudrillard,
consumption itself "is governed by a form of *magical thinking*" (31,
emphasis in original). It seems fitting that the American apparel
industry's twice-yearly trade show, occupying "two million square
feet of exhibition space at the Las Vegas Convention Center," should
be entitled "Magic" (Walker 3). Wells presents Edward Ponderevo's
sudden rise to fame and fortune through advertising as, at bottom, a
magic stunt, done with promotional smoke and mirrors.

Magic, of course, is a quality also commonly attributed to the stirring impact achieved by literary works, here too an outcome of the crafty manipulation of language and imagery. In advertisement, however, such rhetorical sorcery normally takes the form of solicitation to purchase commercially produced goods, whether useful, useless, or downright noxious. Even the marketing of reputable products generally depends on calculated suggestiveness. Discussing an ad for Chanel No. 5 in which a glamorous image of a film star is posed behind a suite of the product line, Williamson notes the naturalizing effect of the montage: "After a while, we just start to connect Catherine Deneuve with Chanel and this takes on a sort of inevitability that seems to give the link status in some 'real' or 'natural' order" (29). While Williamson plainly does not mean to deny the merits of Chanel fragrances, she finds that this "linking" effect has troubling social consequences: "The form of advertisements, and their process of meaning through our acceptance of implications in that form, constitute an important part of ideology" (29). One negative result is the screening off of more urgent connections: "Advertisements obscure and avoid the real issues of society, those relating to work: to jobs and wages and who works for whom. They create systems of social differentiation which are a veneer on the basic class structure of our society" (47). It follows that "[i]mages of nature ... and of magic, do not 'represent' nature and magic but *use* these systems of reference to *mis*-represent *our* relation to the world around us and the society we live in" (144, emphasis in original). The clash between advertising and "the real issues of society" will get staged and restaged in the literary works considered in this study. Recent writers like Blake Morrison and Joshua Ferris foreground issues concerning "jobs and wages and who works for whom" by focusing on advertising agencies themselves as conflict-prone and precarious workplaces.

Like Williamson, Andrew Wernick spotlights the associative process that lends "magic" to consumer brands: "[T]he brand-imaging of mass produced consumer goods links them symbolically to the whole world of social values. ... By representing such values as just part of the visual furniture the ad naturalizes them, and to that extent reinforces their hold" (22–3). The use of subrational persuasion inducts consumers into a culture heavily configured by preset stereotypes. Not all of these items are as innocuous as French perfume. Dissecting an advertisement for Eve cigarettes, a brand targeted at female smokers, Wernick comments:

[I]n order to summon the relevant audience and persuade them
to try the product, the Eve ad sets out to construct a personal
and social identity for its potential users. And it simultaneously
grafts this identity – "Today's Eve" – on to the daintily decorated
cigarettes which bear that name. It should be added that the
glamorization of a gender identity which equates femininity with
self-love and moral weakness rests on giving it social as well as
sex appeal. (30)

Such advertisements construct a narrative of interpellation, invei-
gling the user to occupy a subject position predesigned to fit a generic
(and gendered) personality model. Wernick concedes that "commodity imaging can, to a degree, be ideologically creative" (43), but he
maintains that creativity of this sort comes only at an exorbitant
psychic cost. Like the authors of the report *Think of Me as Evil?*, he
rejects the notion that advertising simply mirrors the values of its
parent society:

In projecting commodities as the road to happiness, ads redefine
as soluble through consumption any negativity which clings to
the process of capitalist production as such. ... In short, imagistic
advertising may build on the values, desires and symbologies that
are already out there, but by no means does it simply reflect
them. It typifies what is diverse, filters out what is antagonistic or
depressing, and naturalizes the role and standpoint of consumption as such. (42)

Ewen makes a kindred point about the anodyne effect of the propa-
gation of desire through advertisement: "The nature of this desire,
and not incidentally the nature of capitalism, required an unques-
tioning attitude toward the uses of production. The use of psychological methods, therefore, attempted to turn the consumer's critical
functions away from the product and toward himself" (*Captains*
370).

In his early work *Mythologies* (1957) the French theorist and
critic Roland Barthes displays a prescient understanding of such
"psychological methods" that deflect scrutiny away from the product, and the suasive ends, both commercial and political, to which
those methods could be turned. In several of the essays, Barthes

argues that promotional campaigns for seemingly disparate items in fact run along parallel grooves. In "Operation Margarine," for example, he observes that "[t]o instill into the Established Order the complacent portrayal of its drawbacks has nowadays become a paradoxical but incontrovertible means of exalting it" (41). For Barthes, the Hollywood blockbuster *From Here to Eternity* (1953) epitomizes the stealthy use of this rhetorical subterfuge:

> Take the Army; show without disguise its chiefs as martinets, its discipline as narrow-minded and unfair, and into this stupid tyranny immerse an average human being, fallible but likeable, the archetype of the spectator. And then, at the last moment, turn over the magical hat, and pull out of it the image of an army, flags flying, triumphant, bewitching, to which ... one cannot but be faithful although beaten. (41)

An equivalent flip of the magical hat governs a commercial for margarine:

> The episode always begins with a cry of indignation against margarine ... And then one's eyes are opened, one's conscience becomes more pliable, and margarine is a delicious food, tasty, digestible, economical, useful in all circumstances. The moral at the end is well known: "Here you are, rid of a prejudice which cost you dearly!" It is in the same way that the Established Order relieves you of your progressive prejudices. (42)

According to Barthes, the marketing of both authoritarian regimentation and insipid food products conforms to a single, specious narrative paradigm: "What does it matter, *after all*, if margarine is just fat, when it goes further than butter, and costs less? What does it matter, *after all*, if Order is a little brutal or a little blind, when it allows us to live cheaply?" (42, emphasis in original).[4]

Barthes's objections reach beyond the manipulative agendas of individual ads; what concerns him, along with McLuhan, Wernick, and Williamson, is the way such local instances of deception feed into more general patterns of control in society at large. It is above all the *cumulative effect* of the avalanche of promotion that troubles such commentators and that is repeatedly pondered in the novels by

Wells, Orwell, Atwood, and Ferris to be discussed later. Daniel Pope comments incisively on the promotional industry's growing collective hold over society:

> [E]ven if consumers could consider themselves still sovereign, the advertisers were far more than mere courtiers seeking customers' favor. National advertisers were big businesses, themselves largely sovereign in the world of work and powerful (though not omnipotent) in the political arena. Many of these advertisers found themselves at the core of an economy they had fundamentally transformed. Their advertisements did more than entreat and inform the consumer. Singly, ads tried to persuade Americans to buy manufacturers' brands. *Collectively, they presented an invitation and an injunction to partake in a consumer society.* (111, emphasis added)

In short, as Simone Davis argues, "Ads do 'Work,' but their primary function is not to lead a consumer to choose between brands. Rather, through inundation, ads serve to produce an all-around ambiance that encourages consumerism in toto, making it seem desirable and natural as air" (1). The stress on the naturalizing impact of promotion *en masse* is crucial. What national advertising, in the form of a blizzard of messages in manifold media, was ultimately selling was the belief in getting and spending as a master key to personal self-definition, the faith that (to paraphrase Zygmunt Bauman) we are what we buy. Baudrillard provides a vigorously argued account of how the "code" of advertising is universalized:

> [A]dvertising is perhaps the most remarkable mass medium of our age. Just as, when it speaks of a particular object, it potentially glorifies all of them, and in referring to a particular object and brand it speaks in fact of the totality of objects and brands, so, in targeting each consumer, it is targeting them all, and in addressing each individual, it is addressing them all, thus simulating a *consumer totality.* ... Every image, every advertisement imposes a consensus – that between all the individuals potentially called upon to decipher it, that is to say, called on, by decoding the message, to subscribe automatically to the code in which it has been couched. (125, emphasis in original)

The universalizing impetus of which Baudrillard writes has been a driving force behind the momentum of modern capitalism. For the authors of the vintage textbook *Advertising Theory and Practice* (first published 1936, repeatedly revised and reissued thereafter[5]), carefully calibrated persuasion is needed "to stimulate consumption to a point where it would balance production" (Sandage and Fryburger 31); advertising thus becomes identified as "the spark plug of the total industrial machine" (31). Sandage and Fryburger contend that the spark plug is an integral component of the capitalist engine it activates and cannot sensibly be viewed in isolation from it: "A good deal of what has been said and written about advertising should be applied to our economic system rather than to one phase of it" (34). While their argument is reasonable in itself, such advocacy tends conveniently to elide the social impact of the relentless stimulus it applauds, not bothering to reflect that the spark plugs may ignite other things besides the overall vigour of the economy. It has been left to creative writers like Fitzgerald, Wells, Orwell, and Atwood to trace where the sparks may fly and to what effect.

As I have noted, social analysts have issued repeated warnings about the aggregate cost of unremitting advertisement. Thus Wernick: "From top to bottom ... promotional culture is radically deficient in good faith. ... [T]he total impression it makes (against which, of course, we screen ourselves through wise inattention) is not merely vacuous, but emetic in its perpetual untruth" (194). Such vehement charges of misrepresentation have elicited spirited rebuttals. Wicke stages a counterattack against claims that the "untruth" of advertising is stifling the "truth" of literature: "It is politically a bit hysterical to look on this scene [of advertisement's predominance] as if a vampirish reified Advertisement were caught turning away in bloody glee from the ebbing body of innocent Literature – an allegory that wends its way into the most unlikely of critiques" (173). The picture Wicke paints here seems itself a caricature; though it may be harshly criticized, advertising is not commonly vilified as Dracula come back to ghoulish undeath. What is demonstrably true is that there has been a long history of friction between champions of literature on the one hand and advertising on the other, a sense of radical incongruity based partly on the differing orientations of the two modes.

As Wicke documents, James Joyce displayed a warm receptivity to advertisement; his curiosity bordered on enthusiasm. But while it is good to know that at least one major literary figure harboured kindly feelings toward promotion, it must also be said that Joyce was in this respect (as in many others) exceptional. Certainly, most of the authors treated in this book, from James and Wells on down, have approached the fact of advertising with attitudes ranging from suspicion to aversion. One might, of course, dismiss such authorial negativity as merely a reflex action, a knee-jerk defensiveness in the face of the onrushing triumphal chariot of promotion. Twitchell offers a sarcastic diagnosis of the uncomplimentary accounts of advertising in modern fiction: "Naturally, we would expect hostility from highcult because advertising was besmirching print" (235). He provides a list of celebrated authors, including Sinclair Lewis and Fitzgerald, as exemplars of such hostility.

There may be some basis for Twitchell's surmise that this literary disdain stems from elitism, from a conviction that the marketing of goods is "shoppy" and that it therefore "besmirches print." In a time when conventional vertical hierarchies, high as opposed to low, have become increasingly challenged by deconstructive doubt, the ramparts guarding the inner sanctum of the literary may get doggedly shored up against the mob clamour of consumerist propaganda. The actual case, however, is more complicated. Writers like Lewis, Fitzgerald, and those I discuss in later chapters cannot all be summarily dismissed as so many squeamish snobs shunning contamination by the scurf of commerce, or as so many tremulous divas dreading the loss of their celebrity status. Indeed, Twitchell's smirking contempt for "highcult" suggests the presence of a reverse snobbery, a shrugging off of effete intellectuals who cower before the red-blooded buyer-in-the-marketplace.

———————

It is, ultimately, the instrumental nature of advertising that explains a striking by-product of literary animus: the frequency of the motif of prostitution in fictional treatments of the business. Sherwood Anderson, who worked for five years in a Chicago agency, habitually described advertising as a "universal whoredom" (Lears 359). The painter Thomas Hart Benton was moved to declare, "I'm not a prostitute and I'm sick of advertising" (Lears 360). In William Gaddis's novel *The Recognitions*, two admen ring changes on the pet metaphor: "This [business] is the whoring of the arts and we're the pimps, see?" (Lears 371). Behind the metaphor lies a notion, or possibly a myth, of artistic work as ipso facto endowed with integrity and of marketing as inherently corrupt. According to Guy Debord, the modern promotional industry depends on the replacement of "economic necessity ... by the necessity for boundless economic development, the satisfaction of primary human needs ... by an uninterrupted fabrication of pseudo-needs, which are reduced to the single pseudo-need of maintaining the reign of the autonomous economy" (section 51). Applying one's creative talent to such dubious ends for the sake of lucre might naturally present itself as "selling out." To advertising's practitioners, as Lears puts it, "[a]rt and commerce" can come to seem "hopelessly entangled in a common net of duplicity" (371).

Such entanglements abound in the texts featured in this study. From Philip Larkin's flaunting poster girl to the television series *Mad Men*, whose main character, as a boy years and miles removed from Madison Avenue, proclaims himself a "whore child," the fact of advertising persistently casts over fictional identities a lurid bordello tinge. The commoditizing of the personal comes to figure as an inevitable offshoot of the marketing of impersonal goods. Those characters engaged in advertising typically face a choice between either fleeing the promotional brothel, like Wells's George Ponderevo, or, like George's Uncle Teddy, asserting ownership of it and leading hollow lives of moral confusion. For some, like Orwell's Gordon Comstock, there is no satisfactory avenue of escape from money-driven promotional drudgery into an artistically fulfilling alternative. For others, like Atwood's Marian MacAlpin, an exit from the meretricious snares of consumerism becomes the key to emotional and perceptual sanity.

And yet, after all, the choice between disinterestedness and venality is seldom clear-cut. One reason for this has been advanced by both Wicke and Davis: works of literature are, *inter alia*, themselves commodities and have long depended on promotional enhancement for their diffusion. Some authors – Wells, Morley, Atwood – have vigorously involved themselves with the task of promoting their own work. Writers may aspire to live in an ivory tower, but they still tend to keep an alert eye on the price of ivory. The result of this contradiction is that a certain duplicity often attaches itself to literary treatments of advertising, a looking askance that may verge on bad faith. The debunkers of promotion are seldom loath to benefit from its magical fruits. Such division of allegiances repeatedly fosters an undercurrent of tension in fictional texts, a tension whose effects can be destabilizing but also energizing. Even Orwell, whose abhorrence of advertisement seems thoroughgoing, clothes its recollected glitter with an aura of nostalgia in *Nineteen Eighty-Four*. By the time of the television series *Mad Men*, a production utterly immersed in the promotional element, nostalgia for the glamour of a bygone golden age of advertising clashes disconcertingly with a scathing critique of the industry and its mores.

Beyond the marketable status of literature itself, there are other reasons why literary treatments of advertising are seldom single-minded. While I would grant that there are vital distinctions between advertisement and literary work, between "instrumental" and "non-instrumental" modes of persuasion, even in pursuing its instrumentality promotion can exhibit real imaginative flair. It is the spectacular display of such creativity that endows *Mad Men*'s Don Draper with his magnetic appeal, and in Blake Morrison's novel *South of the River* it is such a gift that distinguishes the advertising-adept Libby Raven from her uninspired "literary" husband, Nat. One can marvel at the brilliancy of the means while decrying the meanness of the ends. This ambivalence, which comes with the promotional territory, has been amusingly acknowledged by yet another notable refugee from advertising, Salman Rushdie. In his memoir *Joseph Anton*, Rushdie, summing up in the third person his early experiences in British advertising agencies, gives an account of his divided feelings. "Advertising itself, in spite of its reputation as the great enemy of promise, was good to him, on the whole," he reminisces (51). Still, "[I]n the summer of 1981, he became a full-time writer, and the feeling of liberation as he left the agency for the last time was heady and exhilarating. He shed advertising like an unwanted skin, though he continued to take a sneaky pride in his best-known slogan, 'Naughty but nice' (created for the Fresh Cream Cake client)" (58). One can understand Rushdie's pride in his catchy marketing coinage, but one presumes that he takes a more heartfelt pride in *Midnight's Children*.

One might say that the tag "naughty but nice" sums up the attitude toward advertising of a good many writers besides Rushdie; "naughty" because it is an enticing distraction from serious literary production, "nice" because it can guarantee a decent income and sometimes provide a glimmer of artistic satisfaction. It may be an unwanted skin that seems extraneous to the core aims of imaginative writing, but it can also be a source of comfort and warmth. Such ambivalence links figures as far removed in time and outlook as H.G. Wells and Jonathan Franzen, or Christopher Morley and Joshua Ferris. And yet chronology matters. The technical advances in the diffusion of publicity have willy-nilly conditioned the form and perspectives of literary works that deal with it.

Since the turn of the twentieth century, the vast proliferation of promotional activity has had social consequences which writers like James and Wells could not have foreseen but which have excited and alarmed their literary successors. Although much has remained constant, the image of advertisement transmitted by literature has been an irregularly evolving one, and my aim is to trace a few of the twists and turns that image has executed. My guiding belief is that the task of coming to terms with promotional culture, whatever confusions and contradictions it involves, is an urgent one for works of literature to undertake.

Henry James and H.G. Wells:
The Seductions of Advertising

"America!" the aspiring pharmacist Edward Ponderevo bursts out to his young nephew in H.G. Wells's *Tono-Bungay*. "I wish to Heaven, George, I'd been born American – where things hum" (57). The "things" Teddy has in mind comprise business ventures in general but more especially the newly humming industry of advertising. Wells was an English writer, his older contemporary Henry James an American transplanted to Britain, but to both men the United States was the scene of a buoyant new wave of promotion, a phenomenon both found at once fascinating and alarming, though for different reasons. At bottom, James's objections to advertising were aesthetic, while Wells's were social and economic; their contrasting positions thus obliquely foreshadow their famous literary quarrel of 1914–15 about the relative importance of form and content in the writing of fiction. And yet, up to that terminal breach the two had felt a warm admiration for each other, a fact suggesting that they had had more common ground to stand on than might at first seem plausible.

James's novel *The Ambassadors* (1903–09) is prima facie concerned not with advertising but with the clash between European and American sensibilities and values. However, the "American" prompt-ings of promotion come to serve as a focus for that broader subject. The standard-bearer of European tradition in the novel is Madame de Vionnet, the lover of the American industrial scion, Chad Newsome. At the behest of Chad's mother, the protagonist, Lambert Strether, has made a reverse voyage of discovery, travelling to Paris to "rescue" the young man from foreign female clutches. Strether is disconcerted to find himself captivated by the French woman's charm, a quality expressed as vividly by the rooms she occupies as by her own elegance of person and bearing. She is defined, in Strether's eyes, by the objects framing her:

> He had never before, to his knowledge, had present to him relics, of any special dignity, of a private order – little old miniatures, medallions, pictures, books; books in leather bindings, pinkish and greenish, with gilt garlands on the back, ranged, together with other promiscuous properties, under the glass of brass-mounted cabinets. His attention took them all tenderly into account. They were among the matters that marked Madame de Vionnet's apartment as something quite different from Miss Gostrey's little museum of bargains and from Chad's lovely home; he recognised it as founded much more on old accumulations that had possibly from time to time shrunken than on any contemporary method of acquisition or form of curiosity. Chad and Miss Gostrey had rummaged and purchased and picked up and exchanged, sifting, selecting, comparing; whereas the mistress of the scene before him, beautifully passive under the spell of transmission ... had only received, accepted and been quiet. ... There had been objects she or her predecessors might even conceivably have parted with under need, but Strether couldn't suspect them of having sold old pieces to get "better" ones. (145–6)

Silas Marner's fractured pot and Madame de Vioneet's heirlooms sit at opposite ends of almost any spectrum one could name – economic, aesthetic, social – but they have essential attributes in common. They stand for continuity over time and are precious because of their intimate meanings to their possessor; they are cherished for their accumulated associations, not for their mercantile cachet as items of accumulation. James places the word "better" in quotation marks to intimate that de Vionnet's relics rebuff the appraising eye of an auctioneer. They have never occupied space in a shop display case. They are talismans pointing to a world untainted by profiteering cupidity. (Even when Strether later learns that de Vionnet herself could be called a "promiscuous property," that jarring revelation does not cancel the impression made by her living space.) That is why, when Chad suddenly swerves toward advertising as a calling, he has already, in spirit, jilted his Parisian paramour. His investment in the realm of commodity exchange spells a disinvestment from the realm of storied European culture.

Not until the end of the novel does Chad confide to Strether that, as James reports, "he had been getting some news of the art of advertisement" (339). "Advertising scientifically worked presented itself as the great new force," the passage goes on, with Chad concluding, "It really does the thing, you know." "Affects, you mean, the sale of the object advertised?" Strether asks ingenuously, drawing from the younger man a lyrical flight:

"Yes – but affects it extraordinarily; really beyond what one had supposed. I mean of course when it's done as one makes out that, in our roaring age, it can be done. I've been finding out a little; though it doubtless doesn't amount to much more than what you originally, so awfully vividly – and all, very nearly, that first night – put before me. It's an art like another, and infinite like all the arts." He went on as if for the joke of it – almost as if his friend's face amused him. "In the hands, naturally, of a master. The right man must take hold. With the right man to work it *c'est un monde*." (339)

One can easily imagine poor Strether's "face." What the stern directives of Chad's mother have failed to encompass, the vision of promotion as a dazzling new avenue of ambition has brought about. Chad now pictures himself as something more thrilling than a mere captain of industry: an "artist" of commerce – a maestro of marketing. He has found a vocation suited to "our roaring age," the "our" plainly referring to "us" Americans, leagues removed in spirit from the "beautifully passive" quietude of his Parisian mistress and mentor and from the indifference to brute acquisition signalled by the heirlooms (most tellingly, the old books) in her rooms. It is this dispassionate regard that sets her apart from American "collectors" like Chad and Maria Gostrey. As Edwin Fussell notes, "No acquisitor *she*, de Vionnet, unlike Chad and especially Maria, who 'rummaged and purchased and picked up and exchanged,' just like upstart Americans" (105, emphasis in original).

The culminating note in Chad's rhapsody is his offhand use of French vernacular – *c'est un monde* – to mark his embrace of a crass, "roaring" new world of publicity and his rejection of the gracious old *monde* his Gallic lover has bestowed upon him. It is the unkindest cut – or *coupe* – of all. As Alwyn Berland comments, "For Chad to be lured back for the advertising side of the family business is a final confirmation, if any be needed, of his fatal acquisitiveness. Europe has become his apprenticeship for Madison Avenue, and James gives us a prophetic first portrait of the huckster in American literature" (208).

Other commentators have proposed alternate readings of this pivotal scene. Jennifer Wicke sees Strether's rejection of Chad's new venture as a symptom of his bondage to sterile anachronism: "Strether, in his eighteenth-century guise, must suffer the shock of encountering an unknowable or at least unpredictable style of art," i.e. advertising (110). For Wicke, advertising is psychologically tied to vibrant erotic longings that Strether wilfully censors from his psyche. In his 1997 study *Henry James and the Culture of Publicity* Richard Salmon, whose reading of James's novel is broadly consonant with Wicke's, comments on what he calls the "remarkable and puzzling" (151) late scene between Chad and Strether, again highlighting the motif of repression: "The significance of the theme of advertising is disclosed in an act of naming which then permits the retroactive inscription of this content into earlier textual lacunae, from which, we begin to realize, it has been carefully evacuated" (152). Both Salmon and Wicke's readings invite the objection that they ignore period conventions, because they assume a deliberate linkage in the text between promotion and libido. Such a connection would be more likely to colour a twenty-first-century television series like *Mad Men* than an Edwardian narrative like James's. To credit James with, in effect, a lusty embrace of advertising would mean attributing to him a fondness for "our roaring age" hardly detectable either here or elsewhere in his oeuvre. One might compare his comments in *The American Scene* (1907) concerning "the unredeemed commercialism" (52) that flourishes in "our [American] vast crude democracy of trade" (53), and the "drummers" he encountered in the American South: "the brawny peddler more or less gorged with the fruits of misrepresentation and blatant and brazen in the key of his 'special line of goods' and the measure of his need" (313).

By choosing the path of advertising, Chad shows his eagerness to feast on the fruits of misrepresentation, a term that will be central to Wells's *Tono-Bungay*. This choice entails his betraying the European

cultural and historical heritage, implicitly gendered female, in favour
of the aggressively male, "brawny" commercialism of the United
States. In his own life, James had long since irrevocably opted for
the contrary path. And yet it could be that, on a subliminal rather
than overt level, Wicke and Salmon are justified in seeing a link in
James's text between the "art" of promotion and libidinal energy.
The Ambassadors may well project a sense, however oblique, of the
potentially damaging contrast between the stasis of the Continental
milieu, as personified by de Vionnet, and the headlong momentum
embodied by Chad, with his newfound commercial zeal. That subtextual tension in James's novel finds an unexpected echo in Wells's,
which, as shall be seen, features a comparable tension between iner-
tia (represented by the ancient estate of Bladesover) and dynamism,
exemplified by the promotion of the fabulous, fraudulent elixir to
which the book owes its title.

If, in *The Ambassadors*, advertising acts as an important guide to the
shifting allegiances of the principals, it remains a subordinate strand
in the narrative. In *Tono-Bungay* (1909) advertising occupies an
altogether different position; Wells's book stands as the first major
English novel to place promotion at centre stage. Although the
book's narrator, George Ponderevo, is the nominal protagonist, the
most compelling focus of interest is George's uncle Edward, producer and promoter of the titular elixir. Uncle Teddy, whose career
describes a tragicomic arc of meteoric rise and vertiginous fall, sees
himself as above all a man of imagination. "'Magination. See?" he
counsels George. "You must look at these things in a broad light.
Look at the wood – and forget the trees!" (111). As befits an apostle
of imagination, Edward has a knack of reciting poetry from memory, invoking Milton, Shelley, Whitman, and others on what he
deems apt occasions. Even on his deathbed he deliriously mutters
scraps of Wordsworth's Immortality Ode: "He fell into a broken
monologue, regardless of me [George]. 'Trailing clouds of glory,' he
said, and 'first-rate poet, first-rate'" (297). But whatever his claims to
poetic status, the clouds Edward trails have been composed not of
glory but of money and of mendacity. They are, in James's phrase,
the fruits of misrepresentation.

Wells's treatment systematically scuttles all of Teddy's pretensions.
George's friend Ewart, an artist and the book's acerbic *raisonneur*,
puts his finger on what is "revolutionary" in Teddy's approach to

trade: "The old merchant used to tote about commodities; the new one creates values" (130), a judgment Patrick Parrinder rightly calls "an acute and prophetic comment on modern advertising" (Huntington 42). In his native vein of sarcasm, Ewart professes to find the Tono-Bungay project an apt theme for eulogy: "What I like about it all, Ponderevo, is its poetry ... And it's not your poetry only. It's the poetry of the customer too. Poet answering to poet – soul to soul. Health, Strength, and Beauty – in a bottle! – the magic philter! Like a fairy tale" (128–9). As Ewart's satire implies, the presumed homology between huckster and bard, "'magination" and imagination, is a sham. The commercial transaction amounts, he shrewdly implies, to no more than an exchange of puerile fantasies between producer and consumer. While Ewart is not the book's main centre of interest, his pronouncements repeatedly bring its key issues into sharp focus. The "creation" of values, he intimates, is an altogether different affair from genuine artistic production.

While Ewart professes to believe that Edward's promotional tactics are revolutionary, when viewed within its historical context that approach to advertising loses much of its novelty. And, although Teddy locates the wellspring of dynamic salesmanship in the New World, Wells's account of the great Tono-Bungay scam draws heavily on British promotional culture of the time. As Diana and Geoffrey Hindley note, "By the end of Victoria's reign, advertising was firmly launched in England" (55), and in making a patent medicine the cornerstone of Teddy's fortune Wells displayed an alert responsiveness to commercial trends. According to T.R. Nevett, "[P]atent medicine vendors ... appear to have been the heaviest advertisers of the period [the early years of the twentieth century]" (71). Jackson Lears claims that "[t]he golden age of patent medicines, from 1880 to 1906 ... was also a golden age of commercial rhetoric, iconography, and performance" (141). Lears is referring expressly to the United States, but events in Britain trailed close behind, and the years specified span precisely the trajectory of Edward's ascent and fall.

As Nevett shows, the patent medicine fad had a decisive impact on the more general evolution of British advertising techniques. He observes that branding was "a logical development" for the marketing of such nostrums:

A product available in its own separate and distinctive packaging was an obvious candidate for advertising, particularly since the

medicine area was extremely competitive, with so many products, most of which offered to cure an incredibly wide variety
of complaints, as well as performing other socially useful tasks
such as sharpening knives. Sordid though this form of enterprise
unquestionably was, the medicine vendors may well be regarded
as the pioneers of modern marketing, branding their products,
advertising them widely, and distributing them over large areas
of the country. (24)

Wells's Teddy, whose Tono-Bungay campaign conforms closely to
Nevett's account, is marching in the vanguard of the innovators. He
is Wells's study of the modern marketer as adventurer, a feat of fictional exploration that was itself venturesome.

Other pioneering ventures of the time were advertising agencies,
which were just coming into their own. "According to … early
advertising executives, patent medicines represented the most profitable investment opportunity among all consumer goods: costs of
production were low and an efficient distribution system in place; all
that was needed was a lavish expenditure on advertising – and
therein, of course, lay the agencies' opportunity" (Lears 98). The
agencies were a powerful force driving the development of modern
marketing. As the Hindleys comment, the American firms took the
lead, but the British were close on their heels:

> The [British] agency men eagerly studied events in America, and
> they could see an ocean of unlimited possibilities opening out
> before them; but before they could launch a business, there had
> to be advertisers to earn them their ten percent. At a time when
> the whole operation was much simpler, even the man who did
> advertise regularly might well do it himself, bypassing the agency,
> and asking the printer to set up his copy. … The idea that an
> advertisement required design or laying out was still new in the
> 1880s. (31–2)

It was in the 1880s, as Daniel Pope notes, that agencies began using
professional artists to design advertisements (139–40). This innova-
tion coincided with a dawning awareness that, to do their job, ads
needed to be eye-catching – that they could act as a mechanism not
just to satisfy but (as Ewart insists) to *create* consumer demand
(Pope 234).

In one respect Teddy Ponderevo may seem behind his times: he is the man who "does it himself, bypassing the agency," making his own copy. George recalls that his uncle "wrote every advertisement; some of them even he sketched" (*Tono-Bungay* 120). In fact, how-ever, such a mode of proceeding conforms to the advice of the flag-ship advertising trade journal: "At the end of the [nineteenth] century *Printer's Ink* was urging that the merchant should supervise or write his own advertisements so that they would show his personality and not that of some expert such as [agents] Gillam or Powers" (Hindley 97). Edward could serve as a poster boy for the *Printer's Ink* edito-rialist; it is his peculiar gift – George considers it his "genius" – to infuse the ads he devises with his own singular personality. Nevett records that "[a]round 1900 freer format for advertising copy (more display space, the picture block etc.) became possible" (80). As George testifies, Uncle Teddy anticipates such advances by more than a decade.

While advertising's new dynamism had attracted attention in trade journals like *Printer's Ink*, Wells's decision to make advertising inte-gral to a fictional narrative was an unprecedented move. What is especially arresting is his inclusion of Edward's sketches for ads to be used in Tono-Bungay publicity: the "Beach scene poster" (121), the "Fog poster" (122), and the "Phagocyte poster" (123). The mock-ups display an intuitive awareness of the ploys likeliest to touch consumer nerves; they thus stand as remarkably prescient pre-dictors of trends in the century to follow.

The graphic content consists of stick figures accompanied by scribbled directives to the compositor. The one headed "Beach scene – sea life" (figure 1) foregrounds an athletic male, labeled "Discobolus" to recall the classic Greek statue, in the act of hurling a projectile. Stylized radiation emanates from the figure's midsec-tion, with the notation: "Lightning flashes from his liver and lungs." To one side stand several smaller female observers – "Beautiful girls admiring him" – with the notes "good figures," "graceful, refined," and (discreetly) "bit of leg, not too much." Beneath the tableau runs the legend wickedly mocked by Ewart: "Health, Beauty, Strength: Tono-Bungay." The sketch displays a savvy awareness of the impor-tance of layout; it features instructions such as "same size all letters" and "nice *clean* colours" (emphasis in original). While the over-all effect is parodic, and would draw laughter from present-day con-sumers, for its time Edward's ad evinces real canniness in the use of

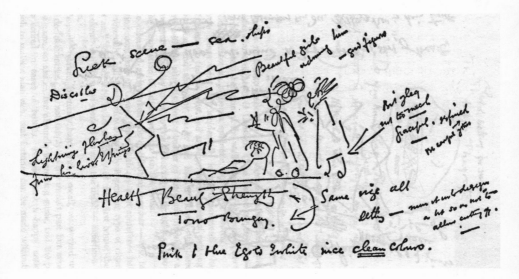

Figure 1

demand-creating suggestion. The primary appeal, of course, is to male fantasies: the yen for physical vigour and for the allied magnetic power to attract desirable females, boons to be secured through the regular ingestion of the vaunted elixir. To the working of that product is attributed a magical efficacy, as witness the lightning bolts emanating from the heroically virile Discobolus.

The sketch for the "Fog poster" (figure 2) also features a central male figure, but the approach here is different. Instead of preening before girls on a beach, this man – again, a confirmed Tono-Bungay user – is making his way through a dense fog (the scene is presumably London-specific), but he is comparably favoured by fortune. As Teddy's notations indicate, he is the "picture of health"; he has "curly hair" and (like the beach girls) a "good figure." "Young and strong," taking "big strides," he blithely strolls past others – not bathing beauties but stooped and coughing "miserable figures seen through fog." The moral is again driven home by the caption: "He does not mind a fog – or any sort of weather" because Tono-Bungay "holds <u>him</u> tight." The primary appeal here is not to muscular triumphalism but rather to valetudinarian self-concern. (Such commercial scare tactics would become standard; Ewen notes that "Listerine was offered as an agent to militate against 'The Hidden Wells of

Figure 2

Poison' that lurk and conspire against the 'program[s] of pleasure' of even the most beautiful women" (*Captains* 38).)

A similar appeal to infection-based anxiety underlies Edward's (ultimately rejected) "Happy phagocyte" sketch (figure 3). The ad references a topical scientific development: the 1882 discovery by the Ukrainian scientist I.I. Mechnikov of "phagocytes," white blood cells that play a vital role in the immune system by "devouring" and thus neutralizing toxic agents. Teddy's graphic design depicts an amoeba-like phagocyte with a gaping mouth ingesting a scattering of rod-like objects, presumably bacteria. Up to this point, however crude the personification of a physiological process, the ad has some basis in scientific fact. That basis is left far behind, however, by the conclusion Teddy appends: "So that what Tono Bungay [*sic*] itself is is a sort of Worster Sauce [*sic*] for the phagocyte. It gives it an appetite. It makes it a perfect wolf for the Influenza Bacillus." Here the world of clinical research yields to the world of fairy tale, in which the miracle elixir magically transfigures the torpid phagocyte, not into a big bad wolf but into a little good one. Teddy certainly "shows

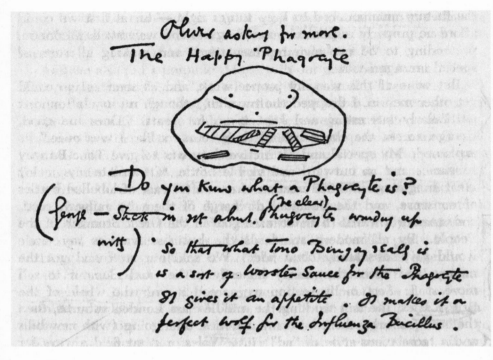

Figure 3

his personality" in this sketch, and once again the effect of the exposure is comic. Still, the exploitation of "Science" as a mystique for hoodwinking the gullible has implications that are by no means amusing.[1]

Although they are at once absurd and dishonest, within the emotional economy of Wells's novel Edward's posters embody a force that is, paradoxically, liberating. Their bumptious dynamism contrasts with the stasis of Bladesover, the ancient, aristocratic estate where George has grown up, whose immunity to change is epitomized by a female friend of George's mother whose repartee consists entirely of musings on seasonal recurrence: "The evenings are drawing out nicely" or "How the evenings draw in!" (20). George's mother herself, when in company, sits "with an eye upon me, resolute to suppress the slightest manifestation of vitality" (19). Vitality is precisely what Edward has found lacking in Wimblehurst, the scene of his abortive debut in business, a place he sums up as "Cold

Mutton Fat! – dead and stiff!" (57). Tono-Bungay may offer only mendacious promises of renewal to its duped users, but to its producers and promoters it brings a momentum missing from the dead and stiff milieus, the "cold mutton fat," of their earlier years. As George says, "My uncle was the first real breach I found in the great front of Bladesovery the world had presented me" (56); and the image of smashing through a restraining wall gestures toward the future careers of both men.

If the ads Edward devises mirror his own febrile restlessness, they also harmonize with the strident publicity of his age. Consider a pair of widely circulated contemporaneous ads displaying the same predilection for up-to-the-minute modernity. The first, for Cadbury's cocoa (Hindley figure 3.5, present text's figure 4) shows a firefighter in full regalia posed next to his resplendent equipment; as the Hindleys note, "The fire engine was in the forefront of technological development in the 1890's." The motto at the top, "Cadbury's Cocoa Makes strong men Stronger," proclaims a theme recalling Edward's Discobolus: masculine potency and control. The likely intent is to counter cocoa's possibly effete image by giving it muscular, macho associations and thus to broaden the consumer base by minimizing gender deterrents. The phallic boilers, one of which is spitting steam, are cleverly accented by the vapours rising both from the cup the fireman is holding in one hand and the saucer he blows upon to cool the smouldering liquid. Cadbury's cocoa, one infers, is not a beverage for the tepid of heart.

The other advertisement, for Beecham's Pills (Hindley figure 5.4, present text's figure 5), interestingly reverses the masculine thrust of the Cadbury example. It shows a woman boldly cross-dressed in the fashion of a male "swell," sporting a broad-brimmed black hat, a smart cravat and waistcoat, bulky shoulder-pads and pantaloons – and casually smoking a cigarette. The ad is pointedly headed "A Startling Effect," and the dialogue-scroll next to the woman testifies to her satisfaction: "Since taking Beecham's Pills I have been a New Woman." The concluding phrase, of course, plays upon the women's movement of the *fin-de-siècle*; as the Hindleys comment, "The new woman paraded her emancipation in the face of shock and then derision from conservatives of both sexes. Beecham's cashed in with the kind of joke that Victorians found highly entertaining." Derision,

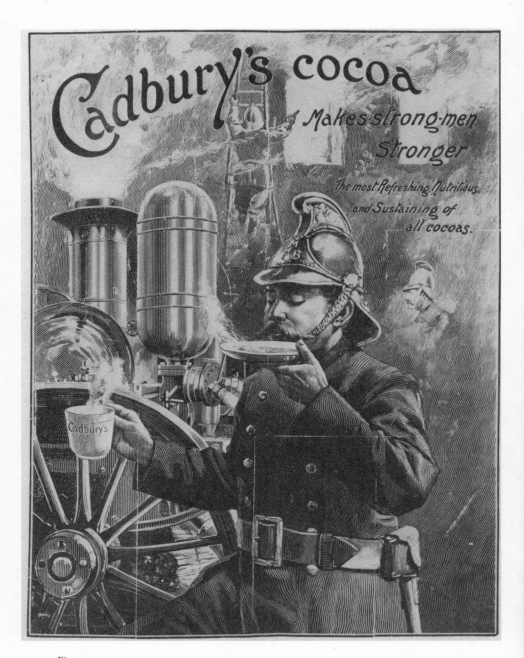

Figure 4

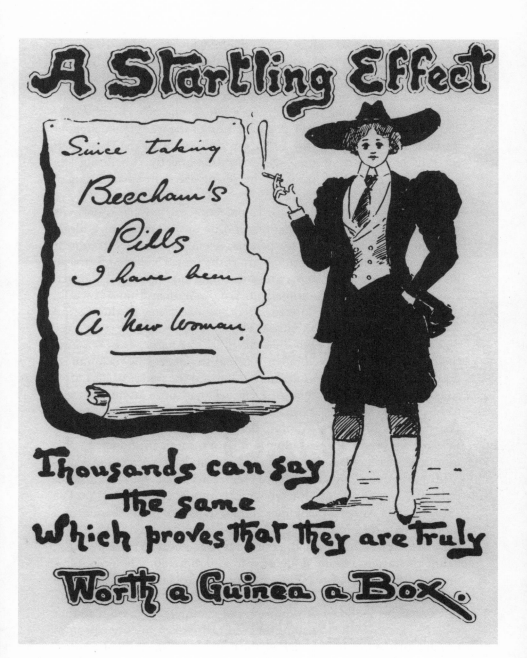

Figure 5

indeed, is by no means absent here; the rakishly cross-dressed female is plainly a figure of fun. Supercilious males, after all, were also consumers to be wooed. However, owing to the nature of the pills – they were a laxative, which (for once) did accomplish the promised "startling effect" – the task of addressing a female clientele risked indelicacy. By offering a magical transformation of the staid female reader into a brazen iconoclast, the ad bids to titillate rather than offend. If the pills have (in a punning sense) so dramatically "liberating" an action, then they must truly, as the oft-repeated Beecham's slogan insists, be "Worth a Guinea a Box."

Thus, the hallmarks of Edward's posters – the emphases on male vigour, on magical transformation, and on *au fait* modernity, along with the use of deft nuance for persuasive ends – occur in prominent specimens of British promotional art of the time. Uncle Teddy, for all his quirks, is moving in step with some of the most widely recognized commercial forces of his homeland. True, as Edward himself would grant, the boldest practitioners of mass marketing in this period were not British but American. The Hindleys concede that "the really alert advertising men did tend to be in America" (82), noting the relatively "slow development of English advertising techniques" (110). Edward's horizons extend well beyond the shores of his native island; William Kupinse plausibly argues that more attention needs to be paid "to the role of America in the larger social and economic system [*Tono-Bungay*] attempts to describe" (52). As Kupinse observes, Edward harbours a keen admiration for American go-getters; his fondness for the eupeptic poetry of Whitman is no accident.

Into the advertisements Edward creates he infuses his private compulsions, above all his urge to "make things hum" with Yankee energy. Linda Anderson comments that "Edward, in his search for a more intense and fulfilling way of life, invents a supposed cure for [the] disease of unsatisfied longing from which he also suffers" (144). While the insight is valid, longing is not all that Teddy pours into his inventions; there is also a good measure of sheer credulity, which he shares with prospective buyers. Attempting to explain Tono-Bungay to George, he confides, "It's the secret of vigour. Didn't you read that label?" (107). With disarming bravado, he takes his own promotional blurb as firmly *establishing* the truth about the item promoted. And yet vigour is a quality that Teddy does undeniably possess. It is also a quality, as he senses, yearned for by legions of British consumers: tired businessmen, tired housewives, tired idlers, and the like.

For Anderson, "the central irony of Edward's career" stems from his failure to transcend his society: "[I]n his urge to prove his unique individuality he demonstrates, on the contrary, his ability to corroborate and appeal to the unformed desires of others" (144). A further irony, however, is that the adaptive faculty Anderson deprecates furnishes, after all, the key to Teddy's success. For that matter, it is the key to the success of anyone who makes a living through mass marketing. As Parrinder says, "Edward's exploitation of rubbish is his exploitation of the whole society" (Huntington 42), but for the exploitation to work the exploiter had best share his society's taste for rubbish. Musing on his uncle's coup in managing a prodigious stock flotation, George exclaims: "£150,000 – think of it! – for the goodwill in a string of lies and a trade in bottles of mitigated water! Do you realize the madness of the world that sanctions such a thing?" (128). George may find it outrageous, but it is above all Edward's intuitive grasp of the world's madness – he is a "Mad Man" *avant la lettre* – that enables his meteoric rise. As George says, "One felt that he was silly and wild, but in some way silly and wild after the fashion of the universe" (113). Edward's "way of drawing air in at times through his teeth" (48), regularly notated by George with multiple zeds – "Zzzz" – is more than a mere Dickensian tic; it links to the steady expansion of Teddy's ego, and, above all, it mimics the tendency to self-inflation distending British society as a whole. It also, incidentally, prefigures George's experiments with manned balloons. One such aircraft, with ironic aptness, will waft the disgraced Teddy to his deathbed in France. Edward's long-suffering wife Susan laments, unwittingly invoking the balloon trope, that the great commercial venture has "puffed him up and smashed him – like an old bag – under my eyes" (300).

The image evokes pathos, but one's sympathies with the punctured magnate, though real, have their limits; the smashed balloon has never been full of anything but hot air. In a book not always marked by subtlety, one of Wells's subtler touches is to make Edward, the great manipulator of signs and slogans, brazenly manipulative in his relations with others. He has little trouble managing his wife, since Susan is throughout a paragon of long-suffering compliance. A more resistant but still susceptible subject is his nephew, George. His early misappropriation of George's small legacy from his mother, which he loses through a hare-brained gamble with stocks, bids fair to ruin the youth's future career. As usual, Teddy dodges accountability: "I'm not the sort of man to be careless with trust funds, you can be sure. I kept that aspect in mind. There's some of it left, George – trust me!" (65). Rather than trusting, George soon sees through the false advertising: "By this time I had really grasped the fact that my uncle had, in plain English, robbed me; the little accumulations of my mother, six hundred pounds and more, that would have educated me and started me in business, had been eaten into and was mostly gone" (66). Later, Edward compensates George by enlisting him in the lucrative Tono-Bungay scam, but even here he remains manipulative, luring George away from his purposed (and for Wells more legitimate) scientific pursuits. Where in James's *The Ambassadors* advertising is a sinister force seducing a promising young man away from his allegiance to the august European past, in Wells advertising deflects a gifted young man away from a scientific future transcending nation. For the older writer promotion betrays a world that has long and beautifully existed, for the younger it betrays a brilliant world that is just about to be born.

For both worlds – that of the past and that of the future – Edward Ponderevo substitutes a present world of deceitful discourse. His "creation" of Tono-Bungay boils down to the invention not of a product (the ingredients are commonplace) but of a name, and both the act of naming and the name itself testify to Edward's understanding of promotion as practical magic. Andrew Wernick's formulation defines the process succinctly: "Naming a product both facilitates the pinning of a borrowed meaning to it, and fixes its association as a sign" (33). Judith Williamson explains how the mystique operates: "Our act of buying, and saying the product's name, is thus a spell which provides a short cut to a larger action, performed not by us but by the product" (142). "Tono-Bungay" as a signifier may be humbug, but for commercial ends it possesses a spellbinding resonance, lending a specious credibility to the larger action – miraculous transformation – that it promises. And if the product does not in fact transform the lives of its users, the name, like a magician's "abracadabra," does utterly transform the lives of its makers. It is, George says, "that mystic word ... that was to alter all the world for us"; "[I]t roused one's attention like the sound of distant guns. 'Tono' – what's that? And deep, rich, unhurrying,–'*Bun - gay!*'" (104). An apt disciple of his "imaginative" uncle, George displays a keen sensitivity to the "poetry" – the affective charge – of the nonsense syllables. Wells here strikingly anticipates Baudrillard's view of advertising as tautology: "The mode of 'self-fulfilling prophecy' is the tautological mode. So it is with magical formulas, so it is with simulations and so also with advertising, which ... plays – for preference – on the tautological. Everything in that discourse is a 'metaphor' for one and the same thing: the brand" (128).

The vacuousness of "Tono-Bungay" as brand name matches the hollowness of the society Wells depicts. The novel establishes multiple links among its governing motifs of incantation, inflation, and infection. In an early essay, David Lodge called attention to the frequency of disease imagery, and Lucille Herbert extends Lodge's insight by connecting the idea of disease firmly to promotion, arguing that "advertising is a disease of language in just the sense that investment capitalism is the cancer in the Bladesover system" (148).[2] In fact, the overall effect of the narrative is to erase the boundary between the two sources of infection, capitalism and advertising.

In an Edwardian novel, a dominant male character named Edward is apt to have a typological significance. George thinks of his uncle in retrospect as "the symbol of this age for me, the man *of luck and advertisement*, the current master of the world" (221, emphasis added). Wells is clearly anxious to ensure that Edward's rise to unearned privilege and wealth be perceived as characteristic of modern British society; it may depend on luck, but it is no mere aberrant quirk of fate. As Lodge contends, Edward's history is "an effective parable of modern capitalism." Lodge resists seeing the parable as "the organizing principle in the design of *Tono-Bungay*" (219), foregrounding instead the "disease and decay imagery." And yet there seems no good reason to disjoin parable from imagery: both point to a morbid distortion in the social system that fosters the accumulation of vast wealth through chicanery, most notably the chicanery of advertisement. An early member of the Fabian Society and a lifelong socialist, Wells was persistently critical of capitalism as the prevailing order, and his novel is designed to highlight the importance of advertising as a handmaid of that order. In a letter of March 1907 to the editor of *The Nation*, Wells calls opportunism "of course, the very antithesis of the Socialism idea" (*Correspondence* 145). Edward Ponderevo is Wells's portrait of the patent medicine huckster as opportunist and, by extension, sworn foe of socialism.

Obviously, the nature of the product being promoted has a decisive bearing on the view of promotion the novel enforces. George may be struck by the mystic charge of the name Tono-Bungay, but he harbours no illusions about the mixture's properties: "The stuff was, I perceived, a mischievous trash, slightly stimulating, aromatic and attractive, likely to become a bad habit and train people in the habitual use of stronger tonics, and insidiously dangerous to people with defective kidneys" (112). Edward's rationale for marketing such rubbish is a euphemistic sophistry – "Tell me a solitary trade nowadays that hasn't to be – emphatic. It's the modern way! Everybody understands it – everybody allows for it" (111) – but it is altogether in character and all too identifiably "modern." (His corollary, that if he were not to market Tono-Bungay "'Mong other things, all our people would be out of work" (111), has a depressingly familiar ring in today's world of self-congratulating "job creators.") Ewart produces a vulgar send-up of the "Beach scene" poster clinching the image of Teddy as a posturing fraud: "a quite shocking study of my uncle, excessively and needlessly nude … engaged in feats of strength of a Gargantuan type before an audience of deboshed and shattered ladies. The legend, 'Health, Beauty, Strength' below, gave a needed point to his parody" (131–2). The nudity is in fact neither excessive nor needless; Ewart has portrayed the would-be Napoleon of commerce wearing the emperor's new clothes. Stripped of his wrapping, the entrepreneur, like the stuff he peddles, is exposed as a shameful fake. *Contra* George, the point of the parody is plain even without the legend. Ewart's invention is a far more pointed representation of the truth than any poster of Edward's devising.

 Misrepresentation, in fact, figures as a controlling motif in *Tono-Bungay*. Building on the unscrupulous marketing of a worthless tonic, Edward becomes the head of a financial colossus, but the colossus too is fraudulent.[3] Thriving on the promotion of fiction as truth, he ends, with poetic aptness, indicted for forgery. As Lodge and others have suggested, the "quap" that is the goal of George's frantic prospecting raid is dense with symbolic meaning: a mineral that decomposes over time and rots any materials it touches, it mimics the hazardousness of the structures Edward fabricates. Lears, speaking of early twentieth-century business history, comments that "managerial values were, in a fundamental sense, imperialistic: they sanctioned a dualistic pseudoscientism and systematized an anxious, driven mode of personal conduct" (138). Edward typifies the imperial self obsessively intent on commercial expansion and, like the national empires proliferating in his time, doomed sooner or later to implode.

In *Tono-Bungay* advertisement, the prime mode of misrepresentation, refuses to stay confined within the workaday limits of business affairs; it infects intimate personal relations. The "anxious, driven mode of personal conduct" characterizes the behaviour of all the leading characters, first and foremost Uncle Teddy. In this psychological arena, gestures of self-presentation shade into compulsive performance. Edward, a prime exemplar of Veblenesque conspicuous consumption, is given to gauging his belongings and actions by a promotional yardstick. Fretting over his and his wife's gaucheness in society, where they are baffled by fine wines and caviar and by niceties of dress, he protests: "We can't go on in that style, George – not a proper ad'" (196). (As Veblen with his signature ponderousness remarks, "[T]he value of manners lies in the fact that they are the voucher of a life of leisure. Therefore, conversely, since leisure is the conventional means of pecuniary repute, the acquisition of some proficiency in decorum is incumbent on all who aspire to a modicum of pecuniary decency" (49).) Again, vexed by Ewart's tardiness in delivering a chalice he has pledged to an East End church, Edward responds testily to George's remonstrance ("It's art ... and religion") by saying: "That's all very well. But it's not a good ad' for us, George, to make a promise and not deliver the goods" (212). Teddy is, in effect, continually conducting an operation of self-branding. In his fixation on image and performance, George's uncle finds it increasingly difficult to separate the personal from the promotional. He crassly acquires a trophy mistress to publicize his own standing as a virile magnate. The other commodities he consumes conspicuously, as if rehearsing for the role of Gatsby – larger and larger houses, more and more powerful motorcars – similarly serve as placards of his personal grandeur.[4] To adopt the terms of the British report *Think of Me as Evil?*, he is obsessed by the pursuit of "extrinsic" values at the expense of "intrinsic" ones. Even George's quizzical Aunt Susan is conscripted for the garish window-display. Contemplating her reflection wearing her first dinner-gown, "'A ham,' she remarked reflectively, 'must feel like this'" (199). Half a century ahead of schedule, she presciently anticipates Margaret Atwood's conceit of the edible woman.

While George does not share his uncle's appetite for "extrinsic" consumption, his personal affairs too are warped by misrepresentation. As Lears observes, "To Wells, all social relations in a commodity civilization seem shot through with fraudulence" (350). From first to last, George's marriage to Marion Ramboat (inauspicious name) is a tissue of deceptions. By reflex action, George projects onto the girl an aura akin to the mystic glow Edward's posters shed upon Tono-Bungay: "[M]y imagination endowed her with infinite possibilities" (101). Not that Marion is devoid of possibilities, but by attributing limitless potential to an ordinary young woman George replicates the "emphatic" work of advertising, performing a mystic transfiguration of the humdrum into the superlative. The operation recalls one of Ewart's barbs: "Your modern commerce ... takes all sorts of fallen commodities by the hand and raises them. Cana isn't in it. You turn water – into Tono-Bungay" (131). George similarly "raises" Marion, but here too the mystic wine reveals itself as a "fallen commodity." When he wins her consent to marry him by announcing that his uncle has increased his salary to five hundred pounds – well beyond the three hundred Marion had stipulated as a sine qua non – George confides wryly, "I forgot that she had raised her price two hundred pounds a year and that I had bought her at that" (139). In a world governed by money and promotion, sexual trafficking lurks even amid the chaste bowers of domesticity.

The wedding itself is a promotional charade, publicizing a "blissful union" that is at best delusionary. Beforehand, George protests: "A marriage is too sacred a thing, too private a thing, for this display" (139). In retrospect, he is forced to acknowledge that there is nothing either private or sacred about matrimony with Marion. The ceremony, with its air of frayed gentility, strikes him as a "mere indecent *advertisement* that I had been passionately in love with Marion" (147, emphasis added). Once again, advertising configures the occasion, which becomes imbued with the same lurid pretence that lies behind Edward's Tono-Bungay slogans.

And yet, ironically, it is precisely the dynamism embodied by Teddy's ads that Marion lacks. Her class-bound mentality, instead of spurring George on to bold action, returns him to the dingy stagnation of Bladesover: "She had no faculty of growth or change; she had taken her mould, she had set in the limited ideas of her peculiar class" (151). Lodge claims that "throughout the novel, *change* is associated with *decay*" (238, emphasis in original); yet a condition more closely allied with decay is stasis. Teddy's complaint that "there's no Development – no Growth" in the town of Wimblehurst is confirmed by Wells's chilling evocation of the place. Similarly, George's passionate affair with Lady Beatrice Normandy, another involvement founded on misrepresentation, brings no development or growth. Eventually it transpires that Beatrice "belongs" like an item on a shelf to the sinister, elderly Lord Carnaby; the upper class, like the middle, is stuck in a miasma of money and dissimulation. Poignantly, at the eleventh hour, Beatrice discloses to George that she is addicted to chloral hydrate – a sedative commonly found in nostrums of the Tono-Bungay sort (Lears 157).

But if in *Tono-Bungay* Wells's implied critique of advertisement is comprehensive, it is also conflicted. A question that needs to be answered is whether Wells's exemplar of promotion is called upon to carry a heavier symbolic burden than his case warrants. In a provocative essay, Paul A. Cantor raises a related issue apropos of Griffin, the protagonist of Wells's earlier (1897) novel *The Invisible Man*:

> Wells's portrait of Griffin confirms all the common man's suspicions of the businessman: that he is unproductive, that he is secretive in his dealings, that all he does is move around money that belongs to other people, that essentially his acquisition is a form of theft, that he lives off the work of others. Like many people, Wells cannot understand or appreciate the special contributions that the entrepreneur makes to the good of the economy as a whole. (Bloom 106)

While opinions may differ as to the "special contributions" of the entrepreneur, one could reasonably level a similar criticism of short-sightedness against Wells's portrayal of Edward Ponderevo. In its broad outlines it is a caricature of the capitalist as shameless swindler, with advertising the linchpin of the swindle. Even granted that capitalists, by and large, are aiming chiefly to make a profit, they are not invariably out to enrich themselves through deception at the expense of the credulous. Granted, too, that most ads depend on adroit suggestion for their persuasive effect, the cynical purveying of a worthless and even noxious product can be considered a deviant abuse of the mode. Beecham's Pills did, after all, bring relief from the specified disorder, and even Cadbury's cocoa was soothing, tasty, and nonaddictive. Wells could thus be charged with using Uncle Teddy's commercial rapacity and underhanded advertising methods as straw men fatally easy to smear, reducing complex social phenomena to a simplistic target. Misrepresentation may thus be more than a theme in *Tono-Bungay*; it could also be a conceptual failing of the work itself.

And yet such a critique could itself be called an oversimplification. Whatever the contributions of "good" entrepreneurs, there were enough unscrupulous operators of the Teddy type, and enough deceptive advertising, to exert a dangerously warping torque on the British society of Wells's time. Besides, Edward himself comes across as more than a stock figure of the rogue profiteer; as early notices remarked, he has a surprising power to engage readers' sympathies. The *Daily Telegraph* reviewer observed that Edward "is an absolute impostor, of very narrow wits, but of inveterate opportunism, who so thoroughly deceives himself into crediting his own lies that the reader ... finds his sympathy compelled to take the impostor's side against the very world he wrongs" (Parrinder, *Critical Heritage* 148–9). Charles Graves, in the *Spectator*, sees not only the character but the commercial profligacy he represents as inviting ambivalent judgment: "The romantic side of the mad game of modern commercial and journalistic adventure; the dodges of forcing worthless wares on a gullible public and getting rich quick, – all this is described with the utmost verve and a strange mixture of contempt and tolerance. Without justifying these methods, Mr Wells conveys the impression that they may prove a valuable school for sharpening one's wits" (*Critical Heritage* 153). George himself, whose wits may not be sharpened by attendance at his uncle's school but whose pockets are certainly lined, feels divided between censure and sympathy: "My feelings towards my uncle were extraordinarily mixed" (77). The mixedness communicates itself to readers, to whom Edward may appear a paradoxical Quixote of materialism. His "quest" is wholly self-serving but, like the fabled Spanish knight's, it includes a visionary dimension.[5] His huge though fleeting success implies a harsh judgment on the society that enables it and the methods that contrive it, yet on its own terms it is remarkable; it is "the story of a man of imagination" not among windmills but "among figures" (176).

In *Tono-Bungay* literature offers a repository of values at once antithetical to advertising and menaced by it. When Edward, seeking to purchase "culture" with his hastily amassed wealth, takes over an "important critical organ" (187) called *The Sacred Grove*, the title strikes an immediate false note because the deluge of advertising imported by the new owner desacralizes the essays devoted to literature and the arts. The wrapper of one issue, reproduced by George/Wells, announces essays on subjects ranging from "Charlotte Bronte's Maternal Great Aunt" to "The Genius of Shakespeare," along with "A Hitherto Unpublished Letter from Walter Pater," but is surmounted by an ad for "Twenty-three Pills" – "Not a Drug But a Live American Remedy" (188). The table of contents is fringed by miniscule effigies of the pill. While the "serious" items listed may look less live than the American remedy, George is right to call the "combination of letters and pills" "incongruous" (188). As Kupinse observes, Edward's *Sacred Grove* takeover embodies "one of the anxieties that *Tono-Bungay* expresses ... the possibility that the disinterested space of art, which might be idealized as affording a privileged site from which to voice social critique, would itself be co-opted by capitalism or an economically-centered nationalism" (67).

The anxiety Kupinse mentions is justified. In *Tono-Bungay* literature does not in fact offer a viable corrective to the onslaught of commodity promotion. Even the books the young George covertly reads in the Bladesover library – *Gulliver's Travels*, *Rasselas*, Gibbon "in twelve volumes" (23) – while doubtless more stimulating than essays on Charlotte Bronte's maternal great aunt, belong like such essays to the past and thus participate in the Bladesoverian stasis. George may, like Wells's Mr Polly, find in the "World of Books [a] happy asylum, refreshment, and refuge from the world of every day" (*History of Mr Polly* 130), but if one hopes to engage actively with the world of every day, an asylum may not be the ideal starting point.

What is more, while Wells gestures toward a clear opposition between charlatans like Teddy and creators of literature like himself, the wall dividing advertising from literary works is, as I have noted, porous. Books, too, are marketable commodities; booksellers were pioneers of modern advertising techniques. According to the Hindleys, "Book publishers were among the first to employ advertising on a large scale, together with the merchants of patent medicines, and their 'puffs' gave a new name to the English language" (93). Wells himself, in a letter of 3 October 1907 written during the composition of *Tono-Bungay*, scolds the publisher Frederick Macmillan, "I don't think you advertise well and I think you're out of touch with the contemporary movement in literature" (*Correspondence* 161). (Nevertheless, Macmillan's first (1909) edition of *Tono-Bungay* included at the back eight pages of advertisements for the publisher's own books, among them two by Wells – *Kipps* and *In the Days of the Comet* – and novels by such popular contemporary writers as Edith Wharton, Rhoda Broughton, and Ouida.) In Wells's mind, promoting books energetically and being *au courant* with the latest literary trends were tightly linked.

Complaints about literary "puffing" date back well into the nineteenth century. Nevett quotes a tirade by Macaulay in an 1830 issue of the *Edinburgh Review*: "The puffing of books is now so shamefully and so successfully practised, that it is the duty of all who are anxious for the purity of national taste, or for the honour of the literary character, to join in discountenancing it" (111). The discountenancing evidently had little effect; more than a century later, in a 1935 number of *Time and Tide*, A.A. Milne was lamenting that "[b]ooks are now being sold and advertised in just the way that other commodities are sold and advertised – by engaging a special shooter-down to shoot down the other man." The author of the *Pooh* books goes on: "And why not, it may be asked? Because books are not like other commodities. That the sale of cheap cigarettes is in the hands of a few big firms does not matter; one cheap cigarette, I imagine is very much like another. ... But the books of a little firm, with little money to spend in advertising, are not like the books of any other firm, whether big or little. They have a personality of their own and should be given a chance of survival" (Nevett 160–1).

Wells would surely have concurred with Milne. He would have justifiably resented any move to equate him, as a producer, with Uncle Teddy; he was, after all, no raffish purveyor of what might be termed "patent literature." His books have, in Milne's apt phrase, a personality of their own, and they have survived. Still, as a man whose livelihood depended on his writings Wells had to be much involved with promotional business. While he never aspired to financial preeminence, his commercial success in his own line of endeavour was as spectacular as Edward Ponderevo's and more durable. This veiled affinity may hint at why, for all the scorn *Tono-Bungay* lavishes upon Teddy's adventurism and its flouting of socialist ideals, some readers detected a covert identification between author and character. Indeed, later in his career Wells displayed a noteworthy measure of receptiveness to the lure of modern advertising. As Lears recounts,

During the 1920s, Harrod's, the London department store, asked three literary luminaries – George Bernard Shaw, Arnold Bennett, and H.G. Wells – to write testimonials for the store. They declined for a variety of reasons but took the proposal seriously, sympathetically, and at such length that their refusals were ultimately printed as advertisements. These writers all approved of modernizing tendencies: the hegemony of technical expertise and bureaucratic organization, the mass production of goods. (299)

Granted that Wells as a social reformer had to deplore Edward Ponderevo's shameless machinations, the dynamism of the character and even the crude opportunism of his advertising methods would seem to have fired his imagination. Wells may have been horrified by the waste and futility of his own society, but he was seldom tempted to look backward. If his treatment of Bladesover has a faint air of nostalgia, the novel is not, as critics sometimes seem to suggest, a full-throated lament for the loss of a static, organic order predating what James had called "our roaring age."

Rather than art and literature, it is the pursuit of scientific inquiry that, in *Tono-Bungay*, is offered as an antidote to the great promotional swindle. Edward himself is given to claiming "scientific" expertise, but his claims as usual turn out to be risible. While at Wimblehurst he develops an investment scheme he grandly calls "stock-market meteorology" (64) which he asserts to be "absolutely scientific. It's verifiable" (65), but which predictably leads to ruin. The pseudoscientific claims he later makes for Tono-Bungay are likewise mere mockeries of authentic science. They conform to the model of the ad for Vichy skincare products cited by Judith Williamson, featuring "a 'scientific' diagram showing a cross section of the skin magnified." As Williamson observes, "While seeming to be an explanation, [the diagram] is really a *symbol*: it denotes the skin, but connotes *science, facts, seriousness*: it represents the whole miraculous system of science but is empty of meaning in itself" (118, emphasis in original). Edward's happy, hungry phagocyte poster is an equivalent shady dodge. Such misrepresentations are set off against George's scientific studies and his later engineering achievements. George himself resents being diverted from real science by what he deems his uncle's absurdities. For George, scientific truth is "the one reality I have found in this strange disorder of existence"; as he roundly declares, "You cannot change her by *advertisement* or clamour, not stifle her in vulgarities" (226, emphasis added).

But despite George's high-sounding rhetoric, scientific truth does not seal him off hermetically from his uncle's clamorous, vulgar world of advertisement. In his introduction to a recent edition of *Tono-Bungay* Bryan Cheyette says, "Throughout the novel George attempts to find another kind of language which would beyond question distinguish him from his uncle. What is intriguing is that he continually fails to achieve this task" (xxii). For Cheyette, "However hard he tries to articulate his ideal of the future, George Ponderevo remains implicated in the worst aspects of Britain's Imperial plutocracy" (xli). George's actions support Cheyette's thesis. His involvement in the quap venture transparently reenacts the history of Britain's rape of its colonies' natural resources. What is more, whatever technological breakthroughs George achieves are funded by the spoils of Edward's advertising-based, oligarchic empire. And, most dramatically, his madcap flight to France with his dying uncle in his experimental balloon, the Lord Roberts β, does not free him from the impasse of his own and Edward's affairs. Indeed, the aircraft itself – named after a military commander renowned for his exploits in imperial outposts like South Africa and Afghanistan – serves as a reminder of George's lingering connections with empire's unsightly filaments.

So vis-à-vis the publicity-driven, late-imperial capitalist world over which Edward briefly towers, George can fairly be pictured as facing both ways. The same could be said – and has been said – of the author who created him. One might view this as a virtue rather than a flaw, pointing to a dialogic complexity in Wells's treatment of his two Ponderevos. As V.S. Pritchett remarked, "Wells as an artist thrived on keeping the seeds of his self-contradiction alive" (Foot 93). Cheyette too finds the dividedness a saving grace: "*Tono-Bungay*, to its credit, is Wells's most two-eyed novel. ... In the end, George is unable to dissociate himself from the overwhelming social forces which gave rise to Tono-Bungay in the first place" (xl). Arguably, the book's contradictions help to keep it from becoming merely a tendentious polemic.

Still, the author's Janus posture can sometimes blur the reader's vision rather than enrich it, and can seem more cross-eyed than two-eyed. A case in point is the state-of-the-art destroyer, the X2, which George has developed and, in the book's final pages, is testing. George regards it as the apex of his disinterested scientific accomplishments, but critics have by and large balked at this estimate. The warship represents, after all, not the contrary of advertisement but rather its apotheosis: a display-model touting the violent momentum cherished by the whole modern technology- and commodity-based establishment. Bladesover, the epicentre of Victorian obsolescence, may have been mired in stagnation but the destroyer stands for headlong technological change, conceivably leading to the Armageddon Wells had recently adumbrated in *The War in the Air* (1908). In that book Wells makes it frighteningly clear that the "scramble for a living in an atmosphere of advertisements and individual enterprise" (82) leads inexorably to the aerial holocaust that obliterates enterprise.

Near the end of his account George muses that, instead of *Tono-Bungay*, a more apt title for his book might have been *Waste*. "It is all one spectacle of forces running to waste, of people who use and do not replace, the story of a country hectic with a wasting aimless fever of trade and money-making and pleasure-seeking" (311). Here again, Wells prefigures a thinker like Baudrillard, who argues that in our society "wasteful consumption has become a daily obligation, a forced and often unconscious institution like indirect taxation, a cool participation in the constraints of the economic order" (47). But an equally apt title for George's narrative might have been *Advertisement*. Edward's promotional campaigns are the *ne plus ultra* of waste: they entail a misdirected prodigality of energy and imagination and entice thousands of consumers to squander their wealth, and possibly their health, on worthless trash. For the older, disillusioned George, the whole wildly successful Tono-Bungay venture has been an inexcusable fraud: "the giving of nothing coated in advertisements for money" (180). He concludes: "It was all a monstrous payment for outrageous fiction, a gratuity in return for the one reality of human life – illusion" (181). George's cynicism has a Swiftian ring, perhaps a faint echo of his furtive juvenile reading. What it elides is the intertwining of illusion with the complexities of the very society George and his uncle exploit for profit.

Both James and Wells perceived, with signal clarity, the looming dominance of promotion in their world. Their prophetic insights are embodied memorably, though in different registers, in two of their most important works. What neither man, however clairvoyant, could have been expected to predict was the enormity of advertising's proliferation in the decades following the appearance of those fictions. It was left to writers of that more promotionally saturated age to confront, and to endeavour to comprehend, the implications of this remarkable eruption.

3

Battles of the Bookshops:
Christopher Morley and George Orwell

"Of course you've read Wells already! Everybody has."
                    Christopher Morley, *The Haunted Bookshop* (129)

Christopher Morley's short novel *The Haunted Bookshop*, published a decade after Wells's *Tono-Bungay*, nods deferentially toward
the older writer's massive presence on the cultural horizon. Over the
intervening decade the sensibilities of people both literary and non-
literary had been shaken by a global upheaval that Wells's own writings had presaged. During the war years the tide of advertising had
been largely rechanneled into conduits of national propaganda. That
diversion itself, however, was to give a new impetus to the promotional surge. According to Stuart Ewen, "the [American] Committee
on Public Information, the propaganda bureau established during
the First World War," explains "how a national persuasion industry
was jump-started and why advertising specialists of the 1920s were
so at ease with the idea of molding other people's minds" ("Memoirs"
447). In fact, the postwar years saw a burgeoning of promotional
activity beyond the dreams even of a Teddy Ponderevo. Both Morley
and his younger contemporary, George Orwell, registered this phenomenon in their work. But where Morley's regard for Wells was
hardly more than *pro forma*, Orwell's awareness of Wellsian precedents had a far-reaching impact on his work.

"Christopher Morley" is not nowadays a name to conjure with,
but amid the early twentieth-century American literary landscape
Morley was a towering eminence. Mark Wallach and Jon Bracker
call him "one of the best-known and most influential figures of his
time in the world of American belles letters" (7), while biographer

Helen Oakley goes further: "During the Twenties and Thirties he was America's leading 'man of letters'; internationally, his reputation was exceeded only by that of George Bernard Shaw" (xi). Morley's acclaim owed much to promotional initiatives, many of them his own, yet his attitude toward advertising was equivocal. That ambivalence is amusingly conveyed in a piece of light verse:

When I die
I shall miss the ads.
There will be plenty of ads in Heaven –
Car-cards, billboards, double-page spreads,
All the delightful old favorites,
Such jolly folderol,
Such appealing bunkum.
But in Hell
There will be no ads –
It is too honest. (Wallach and Bracker 102)

Morley's fancied fiery destination will replace advertising with the wan consolations of truth. Yet the celestial billboards he foresees himself regretting are as suspect as they are seductive; they are "folderol" and "bunkum." As Philip Larkin was to point out in "Sunny Prestatyn," the choice between the allure of commercial fantasy and the astringency of sober fact is a painful one.

Morley's own literary career had one foot in a promotional Heaven and one in a more austere Hell. On the one hand, as novelist, journalist, and critic, he was seriously committed to the cause of *belles lettres*. Wallach and Bracker speak of his "predominant interest in the relationship between literature and life, which expressed itself clearly in most of his novels" (8). But along with that, he was a tireless booster of his own writing and of other people's: "This passion for promotion was constant throughout Morley's career, and it can be traced in virtually all of his literary activities" (Wallace and Bracker 20). His most popular novel, *Kitty Foyle* (1939), "was assisted by an intelligent advertising campaign that was based on copy supplied by the author" (69). Morley also wrote "a series of advertisements" for a subsequent work, *The Man Who Made Friends with Himself* (77); when it came to encouraging sales Morley was his own best friend. He served for many years on the selection panel for that lavishly successful marketing venture, the Book of the

Month Club. And his copywriting activities were not limited to the literary; "[I]n 1938 he wrote, anonymously, a series of advertisements for the Schlitz Brewing Company, employing his flair for promotional writing with considerable craftsmanship" (68). Still, Joan Shelley Rubin's dismissal of Morley as a "twentieth-century adman cum journalist" (138) seems unduly harsh. Among other things, it fails to acknowledge the complexity of Morley's evolving attitudes toward the promotional industry itself.

Morley's often mocking attitude toward advertisement emerges in "The Story of the Ginger Cubes" (1923), labelled by its author "a business satire" (Rubin 136). The satire is aimed primarily at the guild mystique of the resurgent postwar advertising business: its reliance on bafflegab, its posture of brash importunity. The tone throughout is whimsically facetious. Nicholas Ribstone, the proprietor of the Ginger Cubes (an innovative form of cure-all lozenge), coins a slogan worthy of Uncle Teddy Ponderevo to tout the Cubes' digestive benefits: "Why not invest in / A new intestine?" (*Powder of Sympathy* 155). Ribstone's penchant for infectious rhyme is not the sole token of his literary leanings; he instructs his advertising manager (such functionaries were by now becoming common): "What I want you to do is tell me what the resources of literature are in the way of quotations about Ginger" (157). Should such in-house expedients misfire, Ribstone has at hand an offer of professional help from George W. Gray, technical director of the Gray Matter Advertising Service. This agency proclaims its own merits in an enclosure replete with the trade jargon of its time ("The commodity must be (1) Institutionalized (2) Publicized (3) Distributionized (4) Internationalized" (167)). Morley also includes an encomium from the fictitious periodical *Lozenge and Pastille* extolling the unique cubical shape of the product. Ultimately Ribstone turns down Gray's high-minded offer of "an opportunity to cooperate in the public educationalization which is the real satisfaction of the advertising profession" (178). Morley's story itself clearly means to debunk any such "satisfaction" the profession has up its shifty sleeve.

Morley's treatment of advertising as a pursuit was not, however, invariably caustic. His short novel of 1919, *The Haunted Bookshop*, begins by positioning literature and advertising as adversaries but ends by suggesting that their fusion can hold unexpected promise. Completed just months after the Armistice, the novel draws on President Wilson's mission to the Paris Peace Conference as a political backdrop. The contest between bookishness and promotion is semifarcically embodied in two broadly sketched characters. Roger Mifflin, the proprietor of the titular bookshop, personifies biblio-philia and erudition verging on pedantry; the other, younger man, Aubrey Gilbert, is employed by the Grey-Matter Advertising Agency and epitomizes promotional zeal.[1] Of the two, Mifflin is granted far more time in Morley's pulpit. Although he comes across as some-thing of a comic crank, his opinions (copiously imparted) about books and public affairs demand serious attention. (The spirits that "haunt" the bookstore, he explains, are those of the great authors of the books lining its shelves.) On the other hand, Gilbert and his enthusiasm for the advertising business are treated with, at best, a flippant indulgence.

Yet the contrast between the two men – between the dedicated and the venal – is not absolute. While Morley classes Mifflin among those "men who have forsaken worldly profit to pursue a noble calling" (38), the bookseller unblushingly acts as an archpro-moter, mainly of works and authors Morley himself favours. Mifflin embraces the role of disinterested agent of enlightenment as distinct from mercenary tradesman: "I thank God I am a bookseller ... rather than some mere huckster of merchandise" (177). He assures Gilbert that the book business is unlike other trades and that he carries out a timely social mission: "Do you know why people are reading more books now than ever before? Because the terrific catastrophe of the war has made them realize that their minds are ill" (9). The goods he deals in are therefore not mere commodities but medicaments; he deems himself a "practitioner of bibliotherapy" (13). When advised that "bookselling must obey the ordinary rules of commerce," Roger explodes, "A fig for the ordinary rules of commerce!" (42). But despite his quixotry, the fact remains that Mifflin must sell his stock for profit to maintain his wife and himself. While he rejects the label of huckster here, in the antecedent (1917) *Parnassus on Wheels* he is called a "literary huckster" (58), and his future wife Helen muses, "That man was surely a born salesman" (44).

Being a born salesman implies a gift for persuasion of the sort normally ascribed to advertising. With that business, however, Mifflin wishes to have nothing to do. He snubs Gilbert's offer to "prepare snappy copy" for him (7), growling sententiously, "A man who is impassioned with books has little time or patience to grow rich by concocting schemes for cozening his fellows" (12). Even his

toast to Gilbert's vocation – "I pledge you prosperity to the black art
of advertising!" (18) – is backhanded. He tells the young man, "I
understand the value of advertising" (10) but insists that the most
trustworthy promotional method is abstinence: "In these days when
everyone keeps his trademark before the public, as you call it, not to
advertise is the most original and startling thing one can do to attract
attention" (11).

Nevertheless, even while protesting that the "'amazing future
ahead of the book business'" lies in regarding it as a profession
rather than a mere trade (10), Mifflin cherishes his association with
the great prune magnate Mr Chapman, whose name itself denotes
trading. Big business and book business coalesce in Chapman's
scheme to foster the education of his literarily named daughter
Titania, while enhancing her grasp of business, by apprenticing her
to Mifflin. At the end of the novel, business comes to the rescue of
letters when Chapman acts as an angel for the rehabilitation of
Mifflin's bookshop, devastated by a German terrorist bomb. As the
title of the final chapter – "Mr. Chapman Waves His Wand" – intimates, the tycoon plays the part of a fairy godfather, underwriting
the fortunes of Roger's literary enterprise. Thanks to this prune-
based subvention, Mifflin will be able to hold himself aloof from the
common ruck of commerce and, indeed, to dispense with infra dig
advertising campaigns.

On the surface, Morley's treatment of promotional work makes it,
by contrast, appear frivolous. Aubrey Gilbert, the eager young Grey-
Matter employee, displays the hidebound professional mentality
Morley would soon mock in "The Story of the Ginger Cubes." He
gloats about what his agency has accomplished for Chapman's
business: "I myself devised that slogan, "'We preen ourselves on our
prunes'" (26–7). Like Wells's Teddy Ponderevo, Gilbert proves to be
inordinately susceptible to the force of his own inspirations: "Having
himself coined the advertising catchword for [a brand of cigarettes]
– *They're mild – but they Satisfy* – he felt a certain loyal compulsion
always to smoke this kind" (100). His business mind-set even maps
onto his romantic infatuation with Chapman's winsome daughter.
He constructs Titania as "after all, the creature and offspring of
the science he worshipped – that of Advertising. Was not the fra-
grance of her presence, the soft compulsion of her gaze, even the
delirious frill of muslin at her wrist, to be set down to the credit of

his chosen art?" (104). Later he judiciously appraises the girl as a flesh-and-blood ad: "He admired the layout of her face from the standpoint of his cherished technique. 'Just enough "white space,"' he thought, 'to set off her eyes as the "centre of interest"'" (154–5). In his professional view, there is a grating disharmony between such a "layout" and the bookish dungeon in which Titania works; "She's as out of place here as – as a Packard ad in the *Liberator*" he tells himself (211), juxtaposing an iconic luxury sedan of the era against that era's most bellicose left-wing magazine. Having thus imagined the object of his desire, he is naturally led to conceive of his courtship in terms of a promotional challenge, an exercise in self-branding: "How am I going to sell myself to her?" he wonders. "I've simply got to deliver, that's all. I've got to give her service that's *different*" (217, emphasis in original). The narrator reflects wryly, "Thus, in hours of stress, do all men turn for comfort to their chosen art" (217).

Understandably, in view of such ironies, Rubin draws a black-and-white distinction between the two leading men, arguing that "*The Haunted Bookshop* counterpose[s] Roger Mifflin, the wise but unworldly bookseller, to Aubrey Gilbert, a naïve copywriter for the Grey-Matter advertising agency who almost lets the crooks get away" (135–6). Some scraps of dialogue do support the idea of a contest between bookish sage and bumbling commercial simpleton, as when Aubrey rashly accuses Roger of collusion with the German agents: "'In the name of Gutenberg,' said Roger, calling upon his patron saint, 'explain yourself or I'll hit you.' 'Who's he?' sneered Aubrey. 'Another one of your Huns?'" (244). The fist Mifflin imprints on Gilbert's chin seems an instrument of divine retribution. But that is not the whole story. Thoroughly though his mind is crammed with promotional claptrap, the younger man comes across as a well-meaning ingénu who carries forward the novel's romantic plot, such as it is, and his ardent solicitude for Titania wins the reader's sympathy. (Morley confesses in his preface "To the Booksellers" that the two *jeunes premiers* "rather ran away with the tale" (v).) During the war Gilbert served, appropriately, on the Committee on Public Information, where his expertise would have been put to patriotic use cementing the American public's adherence to the Allied cause. Although he occupies himself with trade journals, he is not devoid of literary taste; he prizes the stories of O. Henry, a writer Morley admired. He foolishly mistakes Mifflin's allegiances and gets thrashed for his blunder, but his suspicions of the local Germans turn out to be well founded, and despite some minor fumbling he shows pluck and resourcefulness in thwarting their fiendish scheme. He is, as his prospective father-in-law Chapman authoritatively concludes, "certainly the hero of this film" (283).

Morley engineers the tale's denouement to display Gilbert and Mifflin – promotion and *belles lettres* personified – joining their oddly coupled forces to foil the "Huns." Those treacherous aliens commit the deadly sin of wrenching literature from its proper uses. Mifflin's copy of Carlyle's *Cromwell* figures in the narrative as a talismanic prop; meant to serve as an aid to reflection for President Wilson on his mission to France, it is perverted by the Germans into a terrorist weapon, a shell for a bomb intended to stop the president from attending the Peace Conference. Contrary to their plans, the book explodes prematurely inside Mifflin's shop: "The floor rocked and sagged, shelves of books were hurled in every direction" (266). As Roger has observed earlier, "Printer's ink has been running a race against gunpowder these many, many years" (127); the sensational plot turn literalizes Roger's metaphor. And printer's ink ends up winning the race as far as Roger is concerned, since his stock shields him from the blast. "Thanks to that set of Trollope ... I think I'm all right. Books make good shock-absorbers" (268). The stand off between Mifflin's disinterestedness and Aubrey's imputed venality fades in importance once the two adversaries collaborate to shield Helen and Titania and unmask German skulduggery. Morley himself had a warm affection for Germany and its people; he generally adhered to principles of benign cosmopolitanism and would doubtless have seconded Roger's generous wish: "God help us – let's love the world, love humanity – not just our own country!" (124). Nevertheless, in drawing out the plot-intrigue of his novel he found it convenient to disregard such sentiments, falling back on "Huns" as suitable fodder to feed his American readers' patriotic ire. His inconsistency is unlikely to have harmed sales.

While Morley was not, like Wells, a militant socialist, his political views were on the whole left-leaning; toward socialism he was "benevolently accepting" (Wallach and Bracker 71). What the denouement of *The Haunted Bookshop* enacts, however, is a cheerful *entente* between literary culture and business – Aubrey's advertising included – at a precarious historical juncture. Whatever Woodrow Wilson and his peers may decide in France, all hostilities are amicably settled in Morley's Brooklyn. Gilbert gets taken under Mr Chapman's nurturing corporate wing, where he will hone his skills at creating "snappy" ads for prunes, presumably with Titania as his fairy muse and with Roger Mifflin's blessing. Ultimately, what haunts Morley's bookshop is not the spirit of bygone literary giants but the highly contemporary genius of promotion.

Morley's novel *Thunder on the Left* of 1925 – the year of *Gatsby* – offers a more nuanced account of promotion as a pursuit. As Ewen explains, "In the 1920s, advertising played a role of growing significance in industry's attempt to develop a continually responsive consumer market" (*Captains* 32), and Morley shows an incipient awareness of this historic shift. Here the representative of the industry is a more mature man, George Granville, employed by a railway company to write copy vaunting the charms of local Connecticut tourism. George is divided, much like Morley himself, between the contrary pulls of promotion and art. Although married to the beautiful, worldly society matron, Phyllis, he is passionately in love with Joyce Clyde, an artist and visionary. Phyllis finds publicity "such a crazy kind of business" (26); she pettishly resents George's "always thinking of his business first and her convenience afterward" (21). But George, in fact, is by no means always thinking of his business. He also has literary and aesthetic leanings that enrich his work while pointing beyond it. These interests, unfortunately, are no more to Phyllis's liking: "He found words entertaining, a habit that often annoyed her" (28). One is hardly surprised to learn that George has composed a brochure celebrating the Joys of the Separate Bed (46).

Joyce, by contrast, is able to identify with the "artist that lay printed like a fossil in George's close-packed heart" (137). Sadly, however, her artistic sensibility clashes with the other, unfossilized components of George's heart. Joyce singles out, with a Thackerayan pun, four Georges: "George the Husband, George the Father, George the Publicity Man, and then George the Fourth – *her* George, the troubled and groping dreamer, framed in an open window" (110, emphasis in original). But while Joyce feels connected only to the fourth layer of George's splintered personality, George himself likes to believe that the third – the publicist – gives some scope to his fourth, more creative self. His brochure praising the bucolic charms of Dark Harbour, where the Granvilles are vacationing, evokes

in "thick, treacly prose" (227) the harbour's appeal for visitors, especially artists: "There is a brilliance in the air, an almost Italian richness of colour, in the Island's landscape" (226). George takes "a
rational pride in this composition. It was in the genially fulsome vein
esteemed by railroad companies. Even if people weren't tranquil,
in a place so competently described, they ought to be" (226). Such a
corporate stamping of wish upon reality might be considered a
Wellsian act of misrepresentation; more charitably viewed, it could
qualify as a leap of creative imagination. Whenever Phyllis tells him
he might have become a famous fiction writer, "These are my fictions, he always replie[s], pointing to his private shelf of advertising
pamphlets, neatly bound and gilded as his Works" (226).

George's pride in his work – or "Works" – suggests that Morley
recognized some affinity between literary art and promotional arti-
fice. Wallach and Bracker observe that Morley "firmly rejected any
hierarchy that separated the 'artist' from those whose work was
equally essential if art were to be made real and alive – if it were to
find an audience to enjoy and appreciate it" (28). But their reading
of the cited passage as "Morley's defense of George's – and by implication his own – publicity work" (54) misses Morley's irony; it over-
estimates his indulgence toward his protagonist. The detail "neatly
bound and gilded" drily insinuates the narcissism of George's literary pretensions. One can imagine the smirk Wells's Ewart might
have bestowed on such a claim to artistic status.

George has, in fact, suppressed the artist latent within him in order
to produce banal simulacra of art. He is a grown up but stunted version of his alter ego, the perennial child Martin Richmond, who is
misidentified by Phyllis as an artist. Phyllis's assumption is factually
groundless but figuratively correct; Martin has managed to retain
over the years an artist's wide-awake freshness of vision. George, by
contrast, has withered into an incoherent jumble of discrepant
psychological shards. He enacts within himself the unresolved
conflict between disinterested creativity and the instrumental publicizing of the scenery he peddles. It is this deeper exploring of the
adman's *interiority* that marks an advance over Morley's earlier
work and arguably over Wells's generally external portrayal of
Edward Ponderevo, whom we see only through his nephew's eyes.
George's passion for Joyce rekindles his creative impulses and even,
ironically, renews his feeling for his wife, Phyllis, but in the end it is
the huckster who emerges triumphant.

In a disconsolate, lucid moment George recognizes that "[l]ife had gone by him, while he was fretting over paltry trifles, and left him a drudge" (208). He finds "[h]is absurd vision of being an artist in living, of knowing the glamour and passion of some generous fruitful career, of piercing into the stormy darkness that lies beyond the pebbly shallows of to-day – all risible!" (251). According to the novel's epigraph, "[W]hen men heard thunder on the left … [t]hen did the prudent pause and lay down their affaire to studye what omen Jove intended." Instead of piercing into the stormy darkness, George is too firmly wedded to his mundane "affaire" to avoid becoming risible, however poignant his fate. In *Thunder on the Left* advertising may aspire to the condition of art, but it remains a *pis aller*. All the same, it was a *pis aller* to which the book's author was himself powerfully drawn, a fact that no doubt made his protagonist's dilemma all the more resistant to resolution.

"Up to 1914 Wells was in the main a true prophet," wrote George Orwell in 1941. "In physical details his vision of the new world has been fulfilled to a surprising extent" (*CEJL* 2, 171). In his 1936 novel *Keep the Aspidistra Flying*, Orwell projects his own portentous vision of a "new world" dominated by promotion. Like *Tono-Bungay*, *Aspidistra* hinges on the tight linkage between the power of advertisement and the power of money. The book's epigraph immediately introduces the latter motif; it is a profane parody of 1 Corinthians 13, substituting "money" for the King James version's "charity": e.g. "And now abideth faith, hope, money, these three; but the greatest of these is money." Orwell shared Wells's view of capitalist society as governed by financial cupidity, along with his estimate of advertising as a major channel for that cupidity. Both men would have endorsed Max Horkheimer's perception of "the rule of economy over all personal relationships, the universal control of commodities over the totality of life" (Ewen *Captains*, 59). Like Morley's George Granville, Orwell's protagonist, Gordon Comstock, is torn between his creative impulses and economic necessities. But while Orwell's novel is comic in manner, it delivers an angry protest against a social order that stifles creativity and wastes talent – an ideological severity alien to Morley. For Orwell, advertising was not to be benignly shrugged off as "jolly folderol."

In Morley's *The Haunted Bookshop* the world of bookselling and the world of advertising square off, come to blows, and finally clasp hands. In *Keep the Aspidistra Flying* a contrary dynamic prevails.[2] Comstock flees his detested job with the New Albion advertising agency to take refuge in bookselling, but finds no relief from the stresses of his hemmed-in life. The alternatives of literature and promotion are not, as in Morley's novella, reassuringly balanced; they cannot be harmonized – indeed, they are not even real contraries. True, Gordon does initially find the shop liberating. "But how happy he had been, just at first, in Mr McKechnie's bookshop! For a little while – a very little while – he had the illusion of being really out of the money-world. Of course the book-trade was a swindle, like all other trades, but how different a swindle!" (*Aspidistra* 62). But his tempered euphoria soon gives way to revulsion: "At this moment he hated all books, and novels most of all. Horrible to think of all that soggy, half-baked trash massed together in one place" (8). Here any Mifflinesque notion of literature as a sovereign cure for a war-ravaged world becomes laughable. Condemned to be a purveyor of soggy, half-baked trash, Gordon might as well be publicizing prunes or Tono-Bungay.

Gordon aspires to be a poet (he has already published a slim volume morosely entitled *Mice*) and "They wanted literary talent in the New Albion" (58), but the advertising world recognizes his talent only by prostituting it to mean and mendacious ends. Yet McKechnie's bookshop offers no refuge from mendacity. Orwell himself, who held "the outmoded opinion that in the long run it does not pay to tell lies" (CEJL 1, 332), learned from his brief stint as clerk in a Hampstead bookshop that "[a] bookseller has to tell lies about books, and that gives him a distaste for them" (CEJL 1, 277). What is more, by keeping him on meagre wages, the job at McKechnie's does not even allow Gordon to pursue his literary ambitions. Orwell's fictional bookshop is haunted not, like Morley's, by the august literary giants of the past but by all-too-present spectres of penury and depression. As Gordon sourly reflects, "In a country like England you can no more be cultured without money than you can join the Cavalry Club" (*Aspidistra* 13). On his puny income, the only imaginable cavalry charge is a plunge into the valley of intellectual death. According to Raymond Williams, "[M]ost of Orwell's important writing is about someone who tries to get away [from an oppressive normality] but fails" (*Orwell* 39), a paradigm that perfectly fits *Aspidistra*.[3]

Gordon's employer, McKechnie, is no gallant champion of literature like Morley's Roger Mifflin but a hack scrambling to make a profit. As for the owner of Gordon's next and worse bookshop, the slyly named Mr Cheeseman, "To him a book was as purely an article of merchandise as a pair of second-hand trousers" (219). Gordon, rather than spurring and instructing his clients like Roger, holds them in contempt and at best grudgingly humours them. (In his essay "Bookshop Memories" Orwell recollects: "Many of the people who came to us were of the kind who would be a nuisance anywhere but have special opportunities in a bookshop" (CEJL 1, 273).)

Rather than bookselling, however, it is advertising that is Orwell's main occasion for outrage; he treats the subject with an animus utterly unlike Morley's genial mockery. Differences of sensibility and personal style apart, this contrast is best explained by social and economic shifts that had occurred between the immediate postwar years and the mid-thirties. As Ewen notes, "The 1920s emerge as a watershed, the beginnings of a new social order codified by corporate developments" (*Captains*, 192). The outlines of the new order, and the prominence within it of a vastly expanded promotional apparatus, would inevitably have been more apparent to Orwell than they could have been to Morley, writing early in the preceding decade. The agency Gordon Comstock flees, the New Albion, is "one of those publicity firms which have sprung up everywhere since the War" (*Aspidistra* 56). (It is, of course, a loaded name; the agency stands for a whole altered conception of England that is obliterating the old.) Commentators regularly cite a line from the novel, "Advertising is the rattling of a stick inside a swill-bucket," as Orwell's own considered judgment. (James Twitchell, for example, quotes the sentence without providing any context (12).[4]) Actually, the line conveys not even Comstock's personal verdict, let alone Orwell's, but Gordon's impression of the view held by his coworkers: "They had their cynical code worked out. The public are swine; advertising is the rattling of a stick inside a swill-bucket" (*Aspidistra* 57). Orwell in his own voice might not have put it so brutally. However, he might well have concurred with Gordon's feeling that "publicity – advertising – is the dirtiest ramp that capitalism has yet produced" (57). As Gordon Bowker suggests, in *Aspidistra* "it is the power of advertising, the handmaiden of capitalist greed, which is his prime target" (170).

What Comstock detests in the advertising business is its intrinsic dishonesty, entailing the telling of lies to abet the functioning of a corrupt and exploitative system – a Wellsian act of misrepresentation. For Gordon, the mind-numbing conformity on which that system depends is epitomized by the posters visible from McKechnie's shop:

> He looked again at the ad-posters. He really hated them this time. That Vitamalt one, for instance! "Hike all day on a slab of Vitamalt!" A youthful couple, boy and girl, in clean-minded hiking kit, their hair picturesquely tousled by the wind, climbing a stile against a Sussex landscape. That girl's face! The awful bright tomboy cheeriness of it! The kind of girl who goes in for Plenty of Clean Fun. (19)

Gordon's loathing here is unpleasantly tinged with misogyny. Still, he reacts even more abrasively to an ad for Bovex, featuring a male patron seated in a restaurant:

> "Corner Table enjoys his meal with Bovex". Gordon examined the thing with the intimacy of hatred. The idiotic grinning face, like the face of a self-satisfied rat, the slick black hair, the silly spectacles. Corner Table, heir of the ages; victor of Waterloo, Corner Table, Modern man as his masters want him to be. A docile little porker, sitting in the money-sty, drinking Bovex. (19)

It is the aura of bovine or porcine complacency – the animal images reecho – that most enrages Orwell's impoverished clerk and aspiring poet.

The theme is taken up later in a pivotal conversation between Gordon and his affluent but ostensibly socialist friend, Ravelston. Gordon struggles to explain why he takes promotional atrocities like the Bovex poster so much to heart:

> "Look at that bloody thing up there! Look at it, just look at it! Doesn't it make you spew?"
>
> "It's aesthetically offensive, I grant. But I don't see that it matters very greatly."
>
> "Of course it matters – having the town plastered with things like that."
>
> "Oh, well, it's merely a temporary phenomenon. Capitalism in its last phase. I doubt whether it's worth worrying about."

"But there's more in it than that. Just look at that fellow's face gaping down at us! You can see our whole civilization written there. The imbecility, the emptiness, the desolation!" (91–2)

It is a confrontation between orthodox Marxian theory, dutifully trotted out by Ravelston, and the pulse of pragmatic experience, voiced by Gordon with Orwell's implicit endorsement. For Ravelston, the ads are to be dismissed as a mere unaesthetic clutter incidental to capitalism, destined soon to be swept away by the revolution. (We are later informed that Ravelston's "favourite table" at the posh restaurant he frequents is "the corner table" (170), a sly hint that the "revolutionary" remains complicit with the whole Bovex-sipping establishment that has nurtured him.) Gordon insists on *scanning* the poster as the testament of a mass mentality that is rotten and doomed. Nothing in Morley's treatment of advertising at all resembles such a perception. It recalls some of George Ponderevo's darker pronouncements but extends and refines on them, anticipating Williams's analysis in *Problems in Materialism and Culture*: "We shall not understand advertising if we keep the argument at the level of appeals to taste and decency, which advertisers should respect. The need to control nominally free men, like the need to control nominally free consumers, lay very deep in the new kind of society [emerging after World War One]" (180). The imbecility Gordon perceives in the figure of Corner Table is already symptomatic of such corporate hegemony.

While Gordon's literary prowess had warmed his welcome at the New Albion – he soon got promoted to copywriting, for which he "show[ed] a remarkable talent" (*Aspidistra* 59) – the novel insists that copywriting and poetry are mutually inimical. The reason for this derives from Orwell's most passionately held convictions. In Orwell's view, the value of literature hinges on the writer's fundamental honesty. As he declares in "Literature and Totalitarianism," "The first thing that we ask of a writer is that he shall not tell lies, that he shall say what he really thinks, what he really feels. The worst thing we can say about a work of art is that it is insincere" (*CEJL* 2, 161). An aphorism from "The Prevention of Literature" sums up his objection to the subverting of authorial sincerity by political or commercial pressures: "A bought mind is a spoiled mind" (*CEJL* 4, 95). Since for Orwell advertising "buys" the minds of its devisers, it excludes sincerity and can thus be considered only a shoddy travesty of autonomous literary art.

It is therefore appropriate that at the end of *Aspidistra* Gordon should preface his return to the New Albion by trashing the manuscript of "London Pleasures," the long poem on which he has been toiling: "The sole fruit of his exile, a two years' foetus which would never be born. Well, he had finished with all that. Poetry! *Poetry*, indeed! In 1935" (255, emphasis in original). He aborts the untimely "foetus" by shoving it down a sewer: "He doubled up the manuscript and stuffed it between the bars of the drain. It fell with a plop into the water below. *Vicisti, O aspidistra!*" (256). The Latin sardonically parodies Swinburne's "Hymn to Proserpine": "Thou hast conquered, O pale Galilean, the world has grown grey from thy breath." The aspidistra, that unpoetic fixture of domestic decor, is the novel's talismanic emblem of bourgeois conformity. Junking his cherished manuscript is the one terminal act of sincerity Gordon can perform to solemnize the selling back of his mind, and his twisted allusion to a famous poem signals his embrace of the grey, prosaic world of aspidistra-keepers and copywriters. For Swinburne's dour, life-denying Jesus he substitutes the triumphant, poetry-denying contemporary Mammon. The fetus of his own poem must be immolated on the altar of domesticity – sacrificed to the literal fetus gestating in his girlfriend Rosemary's womb.

Since its publication, the novel's ending has been widely denigrated as contradictory or implausible. According to Nicholas Guild, "[C]ritics of the novel frequently cite this ending as its greatest fault" (Oldsey and Browne 144). Reviewing the novel in 1956 on its first American appearance, Dorothy Van Ghent argued that "at this point the wild truth that the book has so far had becomes a liability, for the action winds up as a romantic comedy of manners" (*Critical Heritage* 83). Rita Felski finds that "[w]hile *Keep the Aspidistra Flying* concludes with a final epiphany, whereby the erstwhile rebel Gordon Comstock comes to recognize the vitality, honor, and decency that dwell in suburban souls, this conversion is largely unmotivated and singularly unconvincing" (38). What such readings overlook is the likelihood that the supposed "epiphany" asks to be taken not solemnly but ironically. The vitality, honour, and decency that may henceforth dwell in Gordon's soul hardly balance the moral and artistic collapse that his return to advertising entails, a collapse the whole thrust of the novel makes palpable.

Orwell's personal history sheds some light on his treatment of Gilbert's retrogression. His aversion to advertising may seem perverse in a writer who was to rebrand himself by substituting for the commonplace-sounding "Eric Blair" the more resonant "George Orwell," but it was deep-seated. At the age of twelve, "he played practical jokes on crooked advertisers, in one case pretending to be a woman troubled by obesity and anxious for a cure. Having haggled the fee down from two guineas to half a crown he then announced that the problem had been cured by a rival firm" (Bowker 42). Later, in his mid-twenties, "he began a play ... attacking fraudulent advertisers" (Bowker 102). As Bowker says, "[t]he focal issue of intentional misuse of language to deceive ... was an issue to which he would return again and again" (109), and he was especially alert to newfangled techniques of cajolery. Like his character Gordon Comstock, and like his eventual critic Raymond Williams, Orwell came to see artful manipulation as a key element of the capitalist "swindle." For him, as for Wells, the swindle was aggravated by influences from across the sea. In a London Letter to the *Partisan Review* of 1942 he observes: "One periodical reminder that things *have changed* in England since the war is the arrival of American magazines, with their enormous bulk, sleek paper and riot of brilliantly-coloured adverts urging you to spend your money on trash" (CEJL 2, 270, emphasis in original). What is most flagrantly new about the "new Albion" is its garish American tinge.[5]

The obvious model for Orwell's exposé of the menace of profligate advertisement was Wells. When George Bowling, narrator of *Coming Up for Air* (1939), recalls that "Wells was the author who made the biggest impression on me" (122), he could be speaking for Orwell, who believed that "[t]hinking people who were born about the beginning of this century are in some sense Wells's own creation" (CEJL 2, 170–1). While he grew disillusioned with Wells's prophetic, utopian vein – "Wells wears the future around his neck like a millstone," he complains memorably in his essay on Dickens (CEJL 1, 488) – he never lost his esteem for Wells's earlier novels: "We value H.G. Wells ... for *Tono-Bungay, Mr Polly, The Time Machine*, etc.," he writes in 1946 (CEJL 4, 293).

In unmistakable ways, the example of *Tono-Bungay* stands behind Orwell's treatment of advertising in *Keep the Aspidistra Flying*. But there are significant differences. Above all, Orwell dwells less than Wells on the process of creating promotional copy and, therefore,

includes less searching analysis of the mechanisms whereby ads contrive to manufacture preference – to persuade consumers to "spend
their money on trash." The posters Gordon views from the bookshop are static emblems of mindless compliance rather than dynamic
agents of persuasion. The emphasis falls heavily on *visual* outrage
("Look at that bloody thing up there!"). Only after Gordon's final
return to the New Albion are we given a fuller account of the scheming inventiveness that generates successful copywriting: "Gordon
had a big job on hand at the moment. The Queen of Sheba Toilet
Requisites Co. were sweeping the country with a monster campaign
for their deodorant, April Dew" (*Aspidistra* 258). (The name of the
toiletry wryly evokes the lyric tradition Gordon has forsaken.)
Gordon's superior, Mr Warner, comes up (on the analogy of "BO")
with a happy inspiration: PP, standing for "pedic perspiration," the
basis for a scaremongering campaign akin to Teddy Ponderevo's
browbeating posters. Gordon contributes ably to the effort, leading
Warner to report, "There was no doubt about Gordon's literary ability," a pronouncement that drives home the irony with a dishearten-
ing thump.

Taking issue with Warner's estimate, critics have repeatedly voiced
doubt about Gordon's literary ability. According to one early reviewer, Isaac Rosenfeld, "[Gordon] chooses the life of poverty and
failure in preference to a career in copywriting (for which, unfortunately, he has more talent than for poetry)" (*Critical Heritage* 85).
Terry Eagleton, objecting to the novel's ending on the grounds that
it "obscure[s] the issue, trying to salvage the value of social rejection
while simultaneously affirming the merit of social settlement," observes, "We do not ... know how much Gordon has lost by his abandonment of poetry, and so how truly detrimental his re-integration
might be, since neither we nor he can decide whether he is a good
poet or a bad one" (Oldsey and Browne 126). Waiving the fact that
it is hardly up to Gordon to decide how good a poet he is, such perplexities are finally beside the point. *Keep the Aspidistra Flying* is not
the tale of a budding Milton, or even Swinburne, doomed by cruel
hardship to remain mute and inglorious. What counts is that Gordon
evidently has *some* talent; he has published a volume of verse, albeit
with puny sales, and he produces a poem of nine quatrains during
the course of the narrative. That text, which begins "Sharply the
menacing wind sweeps over/The bending poplars, newly bare,"

evolves by accretion at intervals; the full version is given at the end of chapter seven. Is it a great poem? Hardly, but it *is* a poem, showing some facility with verse composition. (Orwell, whom few would deem a great poet, saw fit to publish it as a free-standing work entitled "St Andrew's Day, 1935" (Rodden 42).) What Gordon sacrifices by his promotional backsliding is not the assurance of fame, but the imponderable glimmer of possibility.

The clear precedent for Gordon's poem-in-process is to be found in Joyce's *A Portrait of the Artist as a Young Man*. Writing in 1933 to Brenda Salkeld, Orwell observes that *Portrait*, though "a commonplace book compared with *Ulysses*," nevertheless "has good bits in it" (CEJL 1, 153–4). Some of the "good bits" may have been those in the final section of *Portrait* where Stephen Dedalus is shown composing *seriatim* a villanelle, "Are You Not Weary of Ardent Ways." Here too, since Stephen does not create a certifiable masterpiece, it might be tempting to infer that he is doomed to failure in his artistic vocation. Again, however, Joyce's strategy is simply to establish, through concrete example, that his fledgling poet has at the very least shown proficiency in managing an exacting form. He has not arrived, but he has embarked. The same can reasonably be assumed about Gordon's effort, which if nothing else transmits a candidly glum impression of modern urban life: "flicked by whips of air,/ Torn posters flutter, coldly sound/The boom of trams and rattle of hooves,/And the clerks who hurry to the station/Look, shuddering, over the eastern rooves" (*Aspidistra* 161).[6] The clerks in Gordon/ Orwell's poem brood upon humdrum but pressing anxieties ("They think of rent, rates, season tickets,/Insurance, coal, the skivvy's wages,/Boots, school-bills, and the next instalment/Upon the two twin beds from Drage's" (161)) far removed from the phantasmal terrors, "pedic perspiration" and the like, Gordon is paid to conjure up in his postbardic role as copywriter. Whatever the magnitude of his literary gifts, as an aspiring poet Gordon maintains an alertly critical posture toward the life around him. As a New Albion functionary, he debases his talents by concocting fantasies designed either to scare or hoodwink a gullible public. Orwell has built into his narrative a telling contrast between poetic composition as representation and copywriting as misrepresentation.

We know little about Gordon's projected long poem, "London Pleasures," except its inglorious end. But at least as envisioned it is

an ambitious stab at seriousness, whereas devising slogans about
"PP" is a manifestly trivial misuse of imagination. Gordon's surren-
der to such banality may afford him dependable creature comforts
and family life; it may integrate him into the great guild of the bour-
geoisie. His reflection, "Our civilization is founded on greed and
fear, but in the lives of common men the greed and fear are myste-
riously transmuted into something nobler" (255), is more than a
mere alibi for craven retreat. However, his compromise is also an
enforced abandonment of artistic challenge in favour of mendacious hackwork, an unfortunate fall from lyric to jingle. He may
force himself to the conclusion that "[t]he aspidistra is the tree of
life" (255), but the whole narrative confirms that it is a blighted
tree, one on which his fairest hopes are crucified. As Rosenfeld says
of Gordon's eleventh-hour purchase of the emblematic plant: "This
house-plant had always been to him the abhorrent symbol of middle-class domesticity – as much as to say, 'He loved Big Brother'"
(Critical Heritage 85). The implied connection with Nineteen Eighty-
Four, as we shall see, is very much to the point.

At the close of Aspidistra Gordon, turning his back on the Call of
the Wild, hearkens to the Coo of the Domestic. When the pregnant
Rosemary (whose unpromising Wellsian surname is Waterlow) urges
him to go back to the agency, Gordon reflects that leaving the New
Albion "had been the sole significant action of his life" (207) but one
he cannot follow through. Because family life spells enlistment in the
ranks of shoppers, householders, and aspidistra fanciers, Gordon's
reversal of his grand action is presented as a flight from a "manly"
mode to a "feminine" one. It is appropriately preluded by his drunken
nocturnal visit to a zone of prostitutes, where the "appalling faces of
tarts, like skulls coated with pink powder, peered meaningly from
several doorways" (177–8). Prostitution, one infers, makes a fitting
prologue to a return to advertising; the linkage of ideas becomes
almost automatic. Gordon himself has long been aware that women
breathe out a "powerful wordless propaganda" (106) urging compliance with the conventional norm. This helps to explain, if not excuse,
the gender bias rightly detected by Daphne Patai, who observes that
"the interlocking themes of Gordon's rebellion against the money
god and his anger at women can never be disentangled" (120). The
evidence suggests that Orwell himself shared such a bias; his "As I
Please" column from late 1946 concerning ads in American fashion
magazines (CEJL 4, 273–4) maintains a derisive tone, as witness his

comment on one magazine's cover photo of a man kneeling at a woman's feet: "[T]o a casual glance he looks as though he were kissing the hem of the woman's garment – not a bad symbolic picture of American civilization, or at least of one important side of it" (274). Gordon, swallowing the toxic twinned bait of advertising and domesticity, has been at once Americanized and feminized.

Increasingly after *Keep the Aspidistra Flying*, Orwell's concern with promotional matters shifted from commercial advertising to political propaganda. It is a development responsive to the course of public events. According to Jackson Lears, "The rise of totalitarian social movements in the 1930s had persuaded many observers to erase the progressive aura surrounding 'publicity' and redefine the shaping of public opinion as 'propaganda'" (236). For Orwell, who found little that was progressive in publicity, there could never have been much to redefine, but after his exposure to Soviet policy in revolutionary Spain, his sensitivity to propaganda in the usual sense became keener. What remains constant is his Wellsian insistence on the kinship between promotional agency and calculating misrepresentation. The classic model is embodied by Squealer, the propaganda-pig in *Animal Farm*: "The others said of Squealer that he could turn black into white" (16).

Small but telling details link *Keep the Aspidistra Flying* with *Nineteen Eighty-Four* (1949), where it is the prerogative of the ruling clique to turn black into white. In the first novel one of the posters Gordon loathes, proclaiming the merits of QT Sauce, "was torn at the edge; a ribbon of paper fluttered fitfully like a tiny pennant" (10). Early in *Nineteen Eighty-Four* Winston Smith observes "[d]own at street level another poster, torn at one corner, [which] flapped fitfully in the wind, alternately covering and uncovering the single word INGSOC" (6), a detail repeated some pages later: "Down in the street the wind flapped the torn poster to and fro" (25). In both books the tear subtly implies a sinister abrasion of the social fabric, deriving in the first instance from commercial cajolery, in the second from political brainwashing. Again, in *Nineteen Eighty-Four* Winston, crushed after his ordeal at O'Brien's hands in Room 101, is shown sitting in a café where "his corner table was always reserved" (232); when he encounters his similarly stultified lover Julia, he has a "nostalgic vision of his corner table, with the newspaper and the chessboard and the ever-flowing gin" (235). Here, as in Gordon's detested Bovex poster, the specified table is equated with the anaesthetic cancelling of authentic personhood. Orwell may not have consciously intended these resemblances, but they suggest a convergence between the underlying structures of imagination in the two books. Bowker lists more general parallels, going so far as to consider "*Nineteen Eighty-Four* a grotesque parody of his earlier novel – as if Orwell thought 'I can tell this story better second time around'" (388).

And yet it is not, after all, the same story. The central focus of *Nineteen Eighty-Four* is remote from posters for Bovex and Vitamalt. According to Andrew Wernick, while commercial advertising resembles propaganda, "there is a difference. The effectiveness of promotion is not measured by the extent to which its claims and perspectives are actually believed. What matters is simply the willingness of its audience to complete the transaction promotion aims to initiate. And in this, the casualty is not so much 'truth' as the very meaningfulness of the language material (whether verbal, visual or auditory) which promotional messages mobilize to that end" (189). Orwell would normally have rejected the notion that truth is not a casualty in commercial advertising, but by the 1940s he seems to have gravitated toward a position nearer to Wernick's. He introduces a 1943 review of a book on Indian independence by stating: "If you compare commercial advertising with political propaganda, one thing that strikes you is its relative intellectual honesty. The advertiser at least knows what he is aiming at – that is, money – whereas the propagandist, when he is not a lifeless hack, is often a neurotic working off some private grudge and actually desirous of the exact opposite of the thing he advocates" (CEJL 2, 349). Note that the "honesty" Orwell attributes to advertising is *contingent*, and that its object is venal. Still, on Orwell's ladder of undesirables advertising no longer occupies the bottom rung.

Orwell's personal relation to the making of propaganda was by no means simple. In 1941 he became an English language producer for the Indian section of the BBC. As Bowker says, "The job on offer, as he must have known, involved producing the very 'foreign propaganda' he had already judged 'stupid'" (281). Orwell "worried that he was expected to broadcast an imperialist line to his Indian listeners, but was able to avoid this mostly by producing programmes specifically for Indian university students" (287). He did, however, advance the (not implausible) official line that Indian nationalists would be better served by the British rulers than by the usurping

Japanese (287). By 1943, chafing at the B B C's attempts to restrict his extramural literary activities and doubtful about the usefulness of his service, Orwell was ready to give up the post. Although he claimed that the years he had spent there were "wasted" (291–2), his experience of the B B C bureaucracy and his direct involvement with propaganda fed into his later creation of the ideology of Ingsoc in *Nineteen Eighty-Four*.

For Orwell, propaganda might be called advertising run amok, like the elephant he recounts having shot in his famous essay. Oceania is a society from which commercial advertising has been purged because the economy is one of planned scarcity rather than abundance, and the place of such publicity has been taken by whole-sale promulgation of the state's fantastic version of reality. Some techniques used by the authorities actually resemble modern commercial advertising more closely than anything to be found in *Keep the Aspidistra Flying*. An example is the sequence of images flashed on the screen during the Two Minutes Hate:

> The Hate rose to its climax. The voice of [Emmanuel] Goldstein [the demonized dissident leader] had become an actual sheep's bleat, and for an instant the face changed into that of a sheep. Then the sheep-face melted into the figure of a Eurasian soldier who seemed to be advancing, huge and terrible, his sub-machine gun roaring, and seeming to spring out of the surface of the screen, so that some of the people in the front row actually flinched backwards in their seats. But in the same moment, drawing a deep sigh of relief from everybody, the hostile figure melted into the face of Big Brother, black-haired, black-moustachio'd, full of power and mysterious calm, and so vast that it almost filled up the screen. (16)

Through a cunningly contrived sequence of filmic dissolves, the appalling Goldstein is revealed to be a fearsome bullet-spraying wolf in sheep's clothing, promptly to be liquidated by an image of Big Brother as Good Shepherd. The basic technique of suggestion-through-juxtaposition is readily recognizable to twenty-first-century television viewers, though normally it is put to the service of selling not totalitarian ideology but automobiles or hairsprays.

Winston's job is to devise propaganda to sustain the rule of the possibly fictitious Big Brother, whom he secretly hates, like the neurotic propagandist of Orwell's 1943 review. But if he despises the propaganda he is obliged to churn out, Winston feels a fascinated curiosity about another, half-remembered sort of publicity. When the faux-dissident O'Brien pours wine for him and Julia, the gesture sparks in Winston a faint recollection:

> It aroused in Winston dim memories of something seen long ago on a wall or a hoarding – a vast bottle composed of electric lights which seemed to move up and down and pour its contents into a glass. Seen from the top the stuff looked almost black, but in the decanter it gleamed like a ruby. (139)

The flashback spotlights two linked attributes of the Ingsoc regime: the unsparing deprivation of sensory stimuli and the proscription of commercial advertising. The effect inevitably produced is that of a poignant nostalgia for the less austere, more colourful free market past, the "heaven" that Morley had flippantly imagined plastered with garish ads.[7]

It does not follow that Orwell's own attitude toward advertising had, by the time he wrote his most celebrated novel, greatly mellowed. It is startling, however, to find in a writer so steadfastly averse to capitalist modes of promotion a tension between distaste and tolerance. The narrative positions commercial publicity as the relic of a past that is at least more humane than the projected totalitarian, postcapitalist hell of the future. According to Marshall McLuhan, "The misleading effect of books like George Orwell's *1984* is to project into the future a state of affairs that already exists" (*Bride* 93), but such a stricture holds good only on the most broadly general level. A more pertinent criticism has been voiced by András Szántó, who points to the narrowness of Orwell's model of publicity: "What Orwell knew well was the threat of Totalitarianism: the horror of Fascism and the creeping shadow of Communism. What he didn't know – what he couldn't really know – was how modern consumer society would mold propaganda to its own form. Contemporary methods of persuasion are subtle, insidious, sugarcoated, focus-grouped, and market-tested – and comparable in their effectiveness to anything served up by despots and demagogues of the past" (xii–xiii).

Yet whatever the validity of such a critique, it does not cancel Orwell's unique grasp of promotional manipulation and its relevance to modern means of social control. For Morley, advertising was an amusing, if suspect, novelty of modern life; for Orwell, it was the symptom of a frightening, pervasive modern malaise. It was Orwell's capacity to see promotion within a broader social context and to come to grips with its darker implications that gives even an immature work like *Keep the Aspidistra Flying* its enduring urgency.

4

Radio Days:
Wakeman's *The Hucksters*
and Wouk's *Aurora Dawn*

The advent of commercial radio dramatically extended advertising's outreach. By the 1940s the title of the flagship industry journal, "Printer's Ink," had become an anachronism, although it was not to be updated until 1967.[1] According to James Twitchell, "What happened with radio is the crucial step in the development of Adcult and in the modern carnival culture that followed" (82). As Twitchell notes, "By 1938 radio had surpassed magazines as a source of advertising revenue" (89). This was, however, a uniquely American phenomenon. During World War Two George Orwell became personally involved with radio broadcasting, and in *Nineteen Eighty-Four* he anticipated some disturbing potential applications of television. But in Orwell's Britain commercial messages on the BBC were proscribed, as they generally were on the Continent. These restrictions explain why the new medium of publicity became an eligible subject for literary treatment in 1940s America but seldom elsewhere.

The enhanced visibility (or audibility) of advertising as a major fact of American cultural life encouraged the production of popular fictions about the adman as hero.[2] Two representative examples appeared just after the close of the Second World War: Frederick Wakeman's *The Hucksters* (1946) and Herman Wouk's *Aurora Dawn* (1947). Fascination with promotion as a lucrative, even glamorous, pursuit contended with growing public concern about the powerful and possibly dangerous control advertising had come to exert over consumer preference. Such suspicions were over time reinforced by studies probing new and highly manipulative techniques of persuasion, most notably Vance Packard's best-selling 1957 exposé of corporate subterfuge, *The Hidden Persuaders*.

What made radio advertising unprecedented was its invasiveness; it resembled not Orwell's Corner Table so much as that worthy's Foucauldian sibling, Big Brother. "A newspaper or magazine ad can be totally ignored, quickly scanned, or thoroughly read ... but the audio and audio/visual commercials are more obtrusive, more abrupt, more jarring" (Book and Cary 1). As the authors of a 1938 how-to manual on radio advertising note,

> When advertising agencies entered the radio field, they found that they were dealing with a medium which, if not entirely new, was at least quite different from anything that they had experienced. Radio required them to deal with actors, musicians, writers, arrangers, literary and music rights experts, engineers, sound effect technicians, and musicians unions. They found it necessary to change their style of copy to meet the demands of the ear rather than the eye. (Hettinger and Neff 275–6)

But if radio brought novel challenges, it also looked backward, recalling the unruliness of an earlier era. As Lears observes, "Radio advertising brought a return of oral performance and snake-oil style," and "the impact of the Depression intensified the hysteria of product claims" (194). For many in the big agencies, "the radio announcer embodied not intimacy but pseudo-intimacy, a return to the repressed past of advertising. ... Radio advertising offered a revised version of the patent medicine appeal – smoother, more technically sophisticated, more wedded to emergent mass culture formulas, but still dependent on narratives of transformation and 'sophisticated hokum'" (335). During and just after the Second World War, a time of national sacrifice when austerity had shrunk the range of commodities on offer, the "hard sell" may have struck many as otiose. But the postwar years marked the start of a period when Americans would plunge into an unexampled buying frenzy, a will-to-possess that in turn encouraged advertising's aggressiveness. According to Erik Barnouw the "consumer goods explosion ... increased the number, length, and stridency of commercials, and brought back much of the 'pawnshop' atmosphere of the early 1930's" (42). Barnouw describes how, as a result, "the ascetic war years were replaced by a frontier boom town atmosphere, with a scramble for stakes large and small" (44).

Both *The Hucksters* and *Aurora Dawn* achieved robust sales in this heady climate. Both were boosted by their status as Book of the

Month Club selections; they presumably garnered the imprimatur of Christopher Morley, a doyen on the panel of judges. *The Hucksters* was promptly made into a successful Hollywood film. Both authors had worked in advertising, and Wouk had done some script writing for radio before joining the American military.

Both novels aspire to the status of parables for the times. In each, the protagonist – Victor Norman in *The Hucksters*, Andrew Reale in *Aurora Dawn* – is an attractive and ambitious young man with a promising future in promotion. The two face the common obstacle of propitiating an intemperate, despotic sponsor. Barnouw calls the sponsor "a potentate of our time" (4), and the imaginings of Wakeman and Wouk flesh out his judgment. As Barnouw observes, "In the sponsor-controlled hours [of broadcasting], the sponsor was king. He decided on programming. If he decided to change programs, network assent was considered *pro forma*. ... In 'Radio City' – completed in 1933 – every studio had a sponsor's booth" (33). Barnouw, summoning the standard metaphor, claims that "[s]ponsored broadcasting ... was often in danger of sliding into prostitution" (32). In Wakeman and Wouk echoes of just-concluded global trauma obliquely but pressingly intrude (though the action of *Aurora Dawn* is nominally situated several years before America's entry into hostilities). The domineering sponsor-figures, constantly demanding to be appeased yet chronically unappeasable, come across as homegrown corporate versions of the imperious Italian *Duce*.

In Wakeman's novel, and possibly in Wouk's, the potentate in question was modeled on a fabled, recently deceased figure: George Washington Hill, president of the American Tobacco Company. Hill was, according to William Meyers, "the most demanding client in Madison Avenue history" (27); at Lord & Thomas, the agency Hill used, "[e]mployee turnover was high" because nobody could manage to placate Hill for long. Both novels make the careers of the protagonists, ultimately driven to quit their jobs through their reluctance to grovel, reflect such insecurity. In each, the young leading man is offered a choice between the values of the metropolis, New York (coupled with Hollywood in *The Hucksters*), and the verities of the American "heartland," where integrity may still flourish and where prostitution is no more than a naughty rumour.

In *Keep the Aspidistra Flying* Gordon Comstock had been faced with a Hobson's choice between a penurious bohemian/artistic life and a career as an advertising copywriter, which ensured a comfortable domestic existence while vetoing any allegiance to artistic values. In the two American books the picture gets turned upside down. Advertising is constructed not as enabling the sanctities of family life but rather as ravaging them; it may bring a sumptuous level of affluence, but it is conjoined with rampant philandering, heedless of the constraints of marriage or formal engagement, and with a species of occupational vagrancy. As a career, advertising is hyperurban and rootless; the rewards of genuine family togetherness become possible only through a stoical renunciation of the job. And yet, for all that, the job has its insistent glamour.

Victor Norman, the male lead of *The Hucksters*, stands among the earliest exemplars of what was to become a familiar type of modern hero: the Madison Avenue man as cynical but supremely "cool" adventurer. His chosen career involves him in a style of life that is driven, materialistic, and shallow, but also opulent, exhilarating, and sexually enterprising. Wells's Teddy Ponderevo, in the equivocal response he tends to elicit, dimly prefigures the type, but Teddy is more comical and pathetic than glamorous, and his promotional dealings do not unfold within a fully articulated institutional framework. Rather than glancing backward, Norman's type looks ahead to *Mad Men*'s mad, bad, and dangerous Don Draper.

The opening tableau of *The Hucksters* establishes the basic *mise en scène*. The recently demobilized Norman awakens in a Manhattan hotel room after an assignation with a woman who, if not a prostitute, is plainly a casual flame: "Marguerite came out of the bathroom in her slip, looked around for her dress, and began to put it on" (3). Vic is staying in the Waldorf, in the "Louis XVI suite" (5), and is looking forward to a job interview at the Kimberly and Maag advertising agency, located appropriately in Radio City. The first actual advertisement we encounter is one Vic has placed in the *New York Times*. It begins: "VICTOR NORMAN who arrived in New York from Paris last week, today announced his resignation from the Office of War Information, Overseas Radio Division, and stated his plans to return to commercial radio work" (5). The cornerstone of promotion is self-promotion.

In both Wakeman's novel and in *Aurora Dawn*, Manhattan office towers stand for the idea of personal "verticality," the soaring career trajectory pursued by the protagonist and his colleagues, most of whom yearn to ride on an elevator going endlessly upward. This iconography had a basis in fact; according to Lears, the practitioners of advertising "came to constitute an extraordinarily privileged elite, increasingly elevated above and isolated from the concerns of ordinary Americans" (196). Copywriters and executives of the J. Walter Thompson Company occupied offices located aloft in the Graybar Building; as Lears remarks, "No wonder their outlook on their audience seemed to reflect the view from the thirty-sixth floor" (197). Kimberly and Maag, situated on the sixty-seventh floor of the RCA Building, nearly doubles the JWT altitude, with a correspondingly lofty disregard for the huddled masses far below.

In both novels this arrogant verticality is set off against the horizontal and more "democratic" vastness of the American heartland. Vic, for his part, has in his youth forsaken the level plain to go in search of altitudes, a route to be retraced years later by *Mad Men*'s Draper: "Like many a midwesterner [Vic] had long ago chosen to ignore his birthplace, and to forget, literally, the home soil in which his roots had once been deeply planted" (5). Such willed amnesia has grave consequences for the moral bearings of the forgetter. The decadence of the Manhattan advertising milieu is personified by Kimberly, who indulges in binge drinking and, though married, consorts with call girls. In an early scene he invites Vic over for drinks, asking whether it would disturb him "to have a couple of ladies present" and adding grandly that one of them is "all yours. Bought and paid for" (70). The young recruit, however, "could never understand the necessity for a man to use them [i.e. prostitutes], amateurs being a dime a dozen, these days" (71); it all boils down to a matter of price tags. Even when Kimberly later directs his amorous urges toward his wife the event takes on a bordello aura. After gulping some anaesthetic scotch Maggie "put down the glass and her fingers felt for, found and slowly removed the diamond brooch from the Hattie Carnegie dress. They placed the brooch silently on the table and then reached slowly but unsurely for the side zipper that made the dress fit so well over her hips" (155). Performing a striptease on demand is the price of being a handsomely accoutred Madison Avenue wife.

Performing on demand, as Vic later explains, is also the price of leading an affluent life as an adman, but it hardly brings more stability than Mrs Kimberly enjoys: "It is … a life of insecurity, as ad men float from one agency to another, just as they float from New York to Hollywood and back again, making different sets of sounds for the different groups from whom they extract their livings" (129). Feeling "so homeless, so rootless" (66) living in the Waldorf, he attempts to secure a more settled mode of life by renting a Manhattan apartment and furnishing it with costly antiques, but this arrangement can provide nothing better than a sham domesticity. It achieves no solider a connection with history than does his "Louis XVI" Waldorf suite.

Vic's gift for "making different sets of sounds" to appease the appropriate people should by rights guarantee him a brilliant future. His strategy for success hinges on the principle of "sincerity," a motif whose use provides some of the most assured satiric touches in Wakeman's uneven book. Sincerity, that moral and literary touchstone dear to the Englishman Orwell, also has long roots in American cultural history. According to Lears, "The middle and upper classes in the antebellum United States ... created an ideal of unified, controlled, sincere selfhood – a bourgeois self – as a counterweight to the centrifugal tendencies unleashed by market exchange" (75). In the nineteenth century, Lears notes, "the bourgeois home" became "the nursery of sincere human relations" (75–6). The novelty introduced by Vic and his like involves grafting sincerity onto the "tendencies unleashed by market exchange." According to Simone Davis, the early advertising mogul Bruce Barton, in his 1922 tract *The Man Nobody Knows*,

> points out again and again that nothing persuades like sincerity. This tenet, proffered repeatedly in many advertising manuals as well, opens up a conundrum, for how can sincerity itself be maintained once its benefits have been tabulated and are being strived after? Ultimately, the resolution of this quandary involves a shift in the way truth value itself gets figured and talked about. The notion of a fixed essence or inherent nature that shapes much discussion of authenticity and truth, whether absolutist or metaphysical, is not of use in this context. Instead, the truth value of a claim or performance resides in its bottom line impact, its effects on other people. (60)

In their 1938 advertising handbook Henninger and Neff stipulate: "Above all, it is absolutely necessary that the audience be convinced of the speaker's sincerity" (9) – but, it goes without saying, less necessary that the speaker *be* sincere.

For Vic Norman, sincerity means precisely the contrary of what it meant to Orwell: not a "fixed essence or inherent nature" but a studied disposition of appearances. Priming for his interview with Kimberly, Vic puts on a pair of shoes he has bought in London, that accepted mecca of sartorial refinement: "Those shoes were the goddamnedest sincerest looking shoes in all of New York" (5). En route to the agency he decides, though low on funds, to purchase a costly necktie: "It was hand-painted, rich, and very, very sincere, being priced at thirty-five dollars" (6). Rather than the customary meanings of "honest" or "heartfelt," to Vic the word "sincere" signifies *energetically projecting an image* of wholehearted commitment to the values of the managerial class. We are immersed in Guy Debord's "society of the spectacle." Above all, Vic's "sincerity" signifies obeisance to the primacy of money as the measure of all things. ("But the greatest of these is money," as Orwell's epigraph had sardonically put it.) Large numerical figures, usually denoting salaries, ricochet throughout the book; Kimberly, for example, offers Vic a starting salary of thirty-five thousand dollars a year (12), a princely sum in 1945. Effective self-promotion hinges on the adroit performance of "sincerity," a point Wakeman drives home by harping on the word as a running gag. After confiding to Vic that he is respected by Dave Lash, on whose talent agency Vic has practiced a shifty ruse, Kimberly's partner Maag asks in astonishment, "How do you do it, son?" Vic replies on cue, "It's because I'm so sincere" (165). The narrative loosely follows the structure of a *bildungsroman* in which Vic's journey toward maturity is measured by his progress from acting "sincere" to being – in the usual sense – sincere.

From the start, however, Vic harbours one feeling that can be called sincere as commonly understood: his chagrin at not having participated in active military service: "You know ... the real tragedy of my life is that I missed that war they're fighting out there. Calling all men" (201). Not having been called, he feels less of a man; his galling self-image as a noncombatant threatens his masculinity and whets his need to hold his own in civilian competition. "'I feel guilty about those guys'" (52), he tells his secretary after interviewing a job-seeking serviceman. His own service has been with the Office of War Information, "only halfway in war" (9) as he wryly puts it, where (like Morley's Aubrey Gilbert in an earlier conflict) he has applied his professional expertise to the making of propaganda. (As Lears notes, the OWI was from its inception dominated by members of the advertising industry (248).) Again like his televisual off-spring, Don Draper, Vic compensates for the ingloriousness of his military career with his zeal to prove himself in the combat zone of advertising.

Vic's new job with Kimberly Maag affords him a rare opportunity to vindicate his threatened manhood: going head-to-head with the soap magnate Evan Llewellyn Evans, a corporate bully who exacts servile obedience from his minions and especially from the Beautee soap account manager. In radio, as Lears observes, "the advertiser (through the agency) controlled the entertainment as well as the messages about the product. The result was a complete subordination of art to commerce" (334). As a consequence of this dictatorial system, according to Barnouw, "[t]he folklore of sponsor meddling fills volumes of radio and early television history" (3). Along similar lines, Hettinger and Neff warn: "In choosing a program for his campaign, a business executive can make no greater mistake than to base his choice on his and his friends' preference" (111), but this is precisely the mistake the egomaniac Evans persists in making (little though he cares about the preference of his friends, if any). The task of containing the damage while seeming to propitiate Evans – a dilemma that supplies the mainspring of the plot – falls to the embattled Vic Norman.

For Evans, the secret of successful advertising is repetition. Kimberly advises Vic: "'All the other advertisers want you to change ideas every six months because they get tired of them. Mr. Evans knows the public is just beginning to be aware of ideas by then ... so he keeps repeating, repeating, repeating them until everybody goes crazy. That's why Beautee soap is top dog'" (78–9, ellipsis in original). Kimberly is in fact exaggerating Evans's singularity; repetition had early become a selling standby in commercial broadcasting. The handbook *Successful Radio and Television Advertising* counsels: "*Utilize Repetition*. Significant copy points, such as the brand name, the keynote idea, and the primary appeal, should be repeated several times in each commercial" (Seehafer and Laemmar 186, emphasis in original). Evans does admittedly push this approach beyond the bounds of normal business expediency. He exacts obsequious repetition of his own taglines from his underlings; the catechistic echo "Check?" "Check!" becomes an inevitable tic punctuating the dialogue. It seems only fitting that Evan Evans's very name enacts repetition.

Vic asserts his contested manhood by withholding the subservient echo that Evans peremptorily awaits. Rejecting the role of clockwork acolyte, he declines to pretend that the soap *Duce* is invariably right. He baulks at Evans's order that he fire a negligent office worker, even though Evans considers his resistance "cavalier." More daringly still, he successfully flouts Evans's bigotry by including a black maid in a dialogue spot for Beautee soap. When his secretary, Miss Hammer, nervously warns him, "Mr. Evans doesn't care for – you know – colored people" he replies disarmingly, "Now you're being too sincere, Miss Hammer" (16). The glance at censorship has a firm basis in broadcasting history; Barnouw notes that the du Pont company banned from its *Cavalcade of America* series any mention of "government projects such as the TVA, which the sponsor considered socialistic; labor history; and, for a long time, the Negro" (34). Despite Hammer's qualms, Vic prevails by dazzling Evans with his commercial, which repeats its "Love that soap" tag relentlessly enough to make the tycoon forget his racial bias.

Nevertheless, Vic's sponsor-defying bravado is fragile. It is severely tested by his anxiety to cement a lasting relationship with Kay Dorrance, a charming married woman whom he has met, along with her two children, on the train to California. (Kay is traveling to join her husband, a high-ranking military officer now demobilized from active duty in the Pacific.) After arriving in Hollywood, by fudging his high-minded liberal principles Vic betrays his incipient failure of nerve. Early on he impresses his superiority to prejudice upon Jean Ogilvie, a Jewish nightclub singer with whom he is having a fling: "I have no hatred, nor love for Jews, Irish, Welsh, Abyssinians, Seven Day (*sic*) Adventists or any other group," he blusters. "I only hate or love individuals." (94). But now, desperate to secure for Evans the services of the lacklustre comic Buddy Hare, he bullies the Jewish talent agent David Lash, who has signed up Hare with a rival sponsor, by playing the race card: "They're going to say a Jew did it. They're going to say that you, Dave Lash, a Jew, pulled this fast one" (189). Vic is quick to realize that "he had done a bad thing," but the incident raises doubts about his ethical fibre.

We are therefore unsurprised when, fearful of losing Kay, he at last consents to kowtow to the bullying Evans. Before a crucial meeting he tells Kimberly ominously, "I'll be so goddam sincere that the Old Man will quote take off his hat to me unquote" (286). At the meeting he is appalled to hear himself echoing Evans's "Right"; he recognizes that he has succumbed to The Fear (290), a prey to terminal "sincerity." What follows is a "narrative of transformation" akin to those in vintage commercials. Vic undergoes a convulsive change of heart, causing him to decline with a flourish Kimberly's generous offer of a partnership: "There's not that much money in the world" (303). His painstakingly furnished apartment "suddenly became distasteful" (304); he now sees that consumerism, rather than paving the road to belonging, only aggravates the anomie to which ad men are prone. And not stopping there, he abjures his relationship with Kay, whose husband's military heroism makes him a "real man" with a claim upon her that a mere huckster like Vic cannot match. Vic makes this gesture even while knowing that Kay is ardently in love with him and not with Dorrance. As Lears remarks about the scene, "It is the climax of *Casablanca*, the moment when authenticity is realized as stoical renunciation" (368). One might add that, as in the Bogart film, the moment of "authenticity" comes across as creakily stagey.

The basis of the love affair itself, however, has little to do with routine Hollywood romance. The moving force behind Vic Norman's attraction to Kay Dorrance is, from the outset, Vic's need for *rootedness*, ideally in domestic form. Before he even encounters Kay on the train he is smitten with her painfully adorable children; "Your two," he assures her, "It was love at first sight" (117). Despite Kay's physical appeal, "[i]t was a sexless feeling Vic had about her" (118). This immediately sets the relationship apart from his casual amours, though it becomes steamily sexual later. By a piquant irony, it takes an adulterous liaison to offer Vic what his life has sorely lacked: *home* and *family*. One descries here the early tremors of the family-worship that would dominate the oncoming fifties. If Kay comes to represent for Vic a wholesome counterweight to the turbid whirl of advertising, she nonetheless remains a figure dear to the promotional heart: a maternal icon ensconced within the normative nuclear cluster. Vic's notional "rebellion" against the business of advertising masks a deeper compliance with some of advertising's most cherished assumptions.

Vic's rootless alienation is objictified by his shuttling on fast trains between the complementary poles of Manhattan and Hollywood, the latter place abounding even more than the former in "sincere" poseurs. A major effect of this to-and-fro is to emphasize Vic's detachment from the "train-through" states he traverses and the people who inhabit them, a denial of his own origins in exactly that region. As he whizzes through miles of Arizona he reflects sententiously, "I wish I could have a more profound feeling for my country, my people, and myself. I do not, in all truth, seem part of you, or do you seem part of me" (139). His love for Kay in effect "naturalizes" his psyche, ushering in a change of heart towards "my country, my people" and a revulsion from metro-centric life. On the train back to Manhattan, solitary and missing Kay, he sentimentally broods on this change: "Looking out at the land, the land that had always seemed so barren and desolate, so unfamiliar and undesirable, he now felt that it must be good because it was loved by people who spent their lives on it and with it" (277). It is an irony – though likely not a deliberate one – that Vic's patriotic "conversion," his bonding with the "real" America, is enabled by his cuckolding of an authentic American military hero.

The seedy Los Angeles hotel where the two have their trysts seems oddly incongruous: "It's a place called the Mapleton," Vic tells Kay. "Unquestionably filled with whores, drunks, and small crawling objects. We couldn't go there" (234). They end up going there, but instead of being tainted by the squalor, their love transcends it; though intensely physical, it is more than that. It transmutes the Mapleton from bordello to love bower; the true locus of prostitution is not a Californian flophouse but the tall towers of Madison Avenue. In the end, instead of opting, like Gordon Comstock, for a secure and remunerative job, Vic turns down a five-figure salary and professional stardom. Here, too, the spoils of hucksterism might have made matrimony (with a divorced and doting Kay) feasible, but not on terms Vic deems honourable. Whatever may happen in the world of prosaic factuality, in Wakeman's romantic universe family values and advertising do not mix.

The Hucksters implies as well that advertising is unmixable with true art, a stance more nearly resembling Orwell's. Vic's intimacy with Kay stirs him to look askance at his chosen career path. "Oh, everyone in the ad game is intelligent," he tells her when they meet on the train. "They have to be. You see, ad men are half-creative. For example, disappointed novelists do very well in what I call the ad game" (129). His pronouncements anticipate the cynicism of *Mad Men*'s Roger Sterling, but they do not convince Kay. "I think you're an artist and don't know it," she fondly counters. "A writer, maybe" (132). Vic demurs: "You see, Kay, a real honest-to-god artist has an easy out – his ivory tower. It's we characters who haven't any ivory tower to run to that are really trapped. And we find out too late that a thousand dollars a week won't help us much either" (132). Here, as in *Aspidistra*, the line dividing art from advertising is impregnable. What Orwell would not, of course, countenance is Vic's coupling of genuine artistry with ivory towers – with a hermetic isolation from the life of the lowly streets.

Wakeman's book presents itself as an exposé of the advertising industry and its prizing of consumerism, commodification, and financial gain: the golden jackpot of a thousand a week. But the critique it mounts is ultimately facile. Evan Llewellyn Evans, the moving force behind the madness of advertising, is an amusing caricature but too idiosyncratic to justify the symbolic weight assigned to him. True, he personifies a defining feature of this era of promotion: the iron grip of the sponsor on broadcasting. He also illustrates the unscrupulousness with which the listening public is routinely gulled into opting for branded products. To Vic he confides, "I'll tell you a secret about the soap business, Mr Norman. There's no damn difference between soaps" (23). Yet despite such revealing touches, the colourful figure of the bullying tycoon deflects attention from the systemic nature of modern marketing; it *personalizes* an increasingly impersonal regime of mass persuasion for profit. The psychological mainspring of Wakeman's narrative is Vic Norman's need to redeem his manhood, called in doubt by his noncombatant war status; Evans provides him with a formidable Axis-style autocrat to take on, and vanquish, in single combat. The manipulative mendacity of the ads he produces becomes, inevitably, a secondary issue.

More awkwardly still, despite its revisionist pretensions, the novel dwells dotingly on the rewards accruing from an upper-echelon advertising job like Norman's. While Vic's relationship with Kay supposedly impresses on him the triviality of money, during his California sojourn he takes her to dinner at "the second finest and most expensive restaurant in America" (193). The reader is assured that "[f]or both of them ... this exotic, for California, café might just as well have been a hamburger stand" (193); but the fact remains that it is all too palpably *not* a hamburger stand.

Vic ends up disenchanted with both Manhattan and Hollywood; one imagines him, having quit his job at his apogee of triumph, returning to his native American plains, for which his reverence has been rekindled. But this projected pastoral reversion inspires scant confidence; it has too much the air of being a flight from unmanageable issues into pastoral evasion. Wakeman's bid to set "family values" antiseptically apart from the spreading virus of commercialism is patently naïve. Should Vic indeed decide to revisit the flat hinterlands, one wonders how long he will linger there before returning to the lofty, wicked pinnacles of Adland.

The figure of the Madison Avenue man as dashing reprobate proved ripe for cinematic treatment, and Vic Norman was soon appearing on screens across the continent, played by the seasoned matinee idol Clark Gable. Along with Gable, the 1947 film featured the veteran character actor Sidney Greenstreet as Evan Llewellyn Evans and Deborah Kerr as Kay Dorrance. The screenplay (not by Wakeman but by Luther Davis) modifies the novel in ways that reveal much about popular attitudes towards promotional matters.

Some relatively minor changes stem from the production code in force in the Hollywood of the 1940s. Instead of "There's no damn difference between soaps," Evans/Greenstreet says tamely, "There's absolutely no difference between soaps." Kimberly's dealings with prostitutes are excised, presumably also for reasons of "wholesomeness." Other "uncomfortable" topics, like those dealing with race, are likewise excluded; in effect, Evans's racial squeamishness trumps Vic's tolerance. Evans's aversion to black people goes unmentioned, though Vic's pilot Beautee soap commercial still includes an African-American sounding maid. Instead of using Dave Lash's Jewishness to shame him into compliance on the Buddy Hare impasse, Vic now, improbably, relies on his knowledge of Lash's early years – he was a reform school inmate, born on "the other side of the tracks" – to blackmail Lash. Nor is Jean Ogilvy (played by a young Ava Gardner) identified as Jewish.

Other changes have more serious repercussions. The affair between Vic Norman and Kay Dorrance is here no longer adulterous. Kay is now a general's widow; as played by the emphatically British Kerr, she is of English birth – the daughter of a lord, no less. Her two children are (perhaps fortunately) given only walk-on roles, though some sense of her appeal to Vic as representing a "family alternative" to the lonely debauchery of advertising is still transmitted. Crucially, Vic himself, instead of working the propaganda mills at the Office of War Information, has served gallantly in the American military; he has seen active combat during the Allied invasion of Normandy. The prominent motif of Vic's haunting guilt as a noncombatant thus vanishes, along with the opprobrium of his cuckolding an American war hero. The intent of these sanitizing moves was no doubt to avoid tarnishing the leading man's lustre and to minimize moral ambiguities film audiences might have found unsettling.

Most interestingly, the satire aimed at the advertising industry is appreciably muted. The novel's wry play on the use of "sincere" is given only a token showing; to the clerk who sells him the thirty-five-dollar tie Vic explains leadenly that he only means to *seem* sincere. There is some brisk mockery of radio commercials, such as Vic's "Love that soap!" creation or the mortuary spot that Jean Ogilvy hears at a moment of dramatic stress. The dialogue also incorporates some strictures against advertising excesses; the point is made that radio now delivers not what the public desires but what the sponsor happens to like. In general, the film gives even more prominence than Wakeman's book to the war of nerves between the sponsor-potentate Evans and the long-suffering Norman. At the climactic meeting Vic, having won over the domineering tycoon, intrepidly denounces him as a fear-monger; calling him all wet, he suits the deed to the word by pouring a pitcher of water over his head. When Vic, now of course jobless, tells Kay that he cannot marry her because he will no longer be able to support her, she reproves him fetchingly, "Stop being a breadwinner and kiss me." She exhorts him to forget about making *big* money; there are alternate career paths to advertising – ones in which he could "sell things he believes in and sell them with dignity and taste." What these might be is left unspecified.

In Hollywood's version of *The Hucksters*, advertising makes a convenient target; audiences enjoyed indulging in complacent laughter at obnoxious commercials, and movies enjoyed laughing at radio. But what the film version of *The Hucksters* reveals most strikingly is the limited capacity of Hollywood – certainly the Hollywood of that age – as a vehicle for contentious critiques of popular culture. Whatever provocative tensions are to be found in Wakeman's book the film softens or expunges in the interest of inoffensive blandness. In fairness, one should add that the novel itself offers no trail-blazing critique of advertising as an increasingly portentous social presence.

––––––––––

Herman Wouk's novel *Aurora Dawn*, like *The Hucksters*, takes the form of a contemporary parable tracing an aspiring young adman's progress toward disillusionment and integrity. Where Victor Norman advances from spurious "sincerity" to the genuine sort, Wouk's

Andrew Reale moves from being "Reale" to being simply real. To accomplish this, Andrew, too, must abandon his involvement in promotional deviltry and his allied dreams of wealth and status. Andrew works in the sales department of a major network, the Republic Broadcasting Company; he has undertaken a mission which may reward him either with "a leap close to the top of RBC's executive hierarchy, in the thin, intoxicating ozone of twenty-five thousand a year, or possible ignominy and dismissal" (57–8). Once he manages his great leap upward he will, like Vic Norman, be offered a lucrative partnership in an advertising agency, and he too will turn it down. The alternative he will prefer is cattle ranching in the "unspoiled" West.

As in Wakeman, this life-decision pivots on a choice of female partners, and here again a career in promotion entails sexual infidelity. On one hand stands the coquettish, rich Carol Marquis, daughter of yet another soap magnate, Talmadge Marquis; "[S]he seemed an embodied fashion rather than a person" (26), as Wouk all too bluntly sums her up. On the other hand is the fresh and spontaneous Albuquerque belle Laura Beaton, to whom Andrew is engaged. But even Laura, having gravitated to Manhattan to work as a super-model, seems less fresh than before. Her professional given name has been sweetened from Laura to Honey by busy toilers in the New York public relations hive; the girl of the golden West has been pasteurized into a consumable commodity. The crotchety artist Michael Wilde advises her unkindly that she is "selling [her] body – in photographs" (76). The firm that has come up with her new name is called, pointedly, the Pandar Agency (Wouk has a weakness for ponderous puns; compare the name of the advertising agency that works for Marquis: Grovill and Leach). Marketable as Laura is, however, Andrew, a champion of the bottom line, is prompted to jilt her for the more remunerative Carol.

Although completed a year after *The Hucksters*, Wouk's novel is set a decade back in time so that the action occurs prior to the outbreak of war. But a more important difference between the books is marked by the literariness of Wouk's, as the Pandar allusion indicates. The novel abounds in urbane asides by the narrator, a loquacious commentator in the vein of such classic precedents as Fielding and Sterne. There are mock-solemn references to earlier literature and (especially) philosophy, which Wouk had studied at Columbia. Through the narrator's asides and the characters' words and actions,

Aurora Dawn canvasses a cluster of briefs pro and contra advertising as a force in modern society. This interplay of positions looks promisingly dialogic; certainly, Wouk makes a more strenuous attempt than Wakeman to scrutinize from varied angles issues connected with the growing sway of promotion. Unfortunately, the final result is to blur rather than to enrich what the novel wants to say about its central concerns; the narrator's elaborate neutrality finally registers as question-begging indecision.

The brutal side of modern commercial promotion is personified by Talmadge Marquis, president of the Aurora Dawn soap company and a near twin to Wakeman's soap ogre Evan Evans. Marquis is obsessed with marketing his product, about which he knows nothing. His imperial headquarters is perched high in the recently completed Empire State building. The major action stems from Marquis's whim of securing a popular backwoods preacher, Father Calvin Stanfield, along with his flock, as a vehicle for promoting his soap brand on the radio. Religion is thus made to minister to profane commercial greed; godliness is suborned by cleanliness. While Stanfield does agree to appear on radio (his congregation needs funds), he strives to insulate the broadcasts from any taint of commercialism. Andrew Reale, as mediator, ostensibly addresses Stanfield's concerns, but covertly circumvents them. By slotting a promotional "message" just prior to the start of the preacher's program, when listeners are already tuned in, he proposes to "'tie an old-fashioned, double-barreled, two-and-a-half minute straight commercial into Father Stanfield's broadcast; and he will never object to it, and probably never even know it!'" (94). Ironies abound; Andrew brashly justifies his scheme as a "'uniquely unselfish act on the part of a soap company'" (94).

Here, as in *Tono-Bungay,* it is an artist-figure, Michael Wilde, who voices the most vehement critique of promotional finagling. Like Wells's Ewart, Wilde views advertising as an unseemly web of deceptions. Addressing a Manhattan dinner party where several of the company are involved in the production of Stanfield's radio show, Wilde delivers his "famous Oration against Advertising" (143). He entreats "all these gentlemen to redeem the strange, bittersweet miracle of their lives, while there is yet time, by giving up the advertising business at once" (144). His utterances are dire to the point of burlesque; they sound, in fact, like parodies of Frankfurt School invectives against modern mass culture. (Horkheimer and Adorno's

Dialectic of Enlightenment had appeared a few years before Wouk's novel.) In Wilde's view, advertising "has tarnished Creation. What is sweet to any of you in this world? Love? Nature? Art? Language? Youth? Behold them all, yoked by advertising to the harness of commerce!" (145). Untrammelled venality has debased the currency of discourse: "[Y]ou are cheapening speech until it is ceasing to be an honest method of exchange" (146). For Wilde "the ultimate outrage" is to have "the people's yearning toward God harnessed to make them yearn toward a toilet article" (147). He sums up advertising as "an occupation the aim of which is subtle prevarication for gain, and the effect of which is the blighting of everything fair and pleasant in our time with the garish fungus of greed" (147–8).

Wilde's jeremiad has appreciable rhetorical force, so that initially one is tempted to identify it as voicing the novel's settled ideological stance: a vindication of the truth of Art against the lying subterfuges of Commerce. Any such inference, however, soon proves premature; Wilde is no Ewart-style *raisonneur* – Wouk reserves that function for a quite different character. The stunned silence following the "Oration" is broken by a wisecrack from Mr Stephen English, a suave and judicious banker: "Mike, it's a pity that talk doesn't register on canvas. If piffle were painting, you'd be Michelangelo" (148). The quip prompts from the audience a cathartic burst of grateful merriment: "The frail jest broke the tension like a lightning spark. A deluge of laughter followed" (148). English caps his witticism by producing a well-turned apologia for promotion:

> What [Mike] said was true enough about certain unsavory
> details of the business, but he missed the real point. Advertising
> exists because it creates demand, and demand is the solar energy
> of the American system. He also missed the obvious fact that our
> people like advertisements. They like to look at pretty girls' pic-
> tures, they like to be promised the moon in a bottle of mouth
> wash, and they enjoy the pleading for patronage implicit in all
> advertising copy. (151)

Despite its patrician condescension, English's line of argument has its own persuasive power. His measured manner humorously sets off Wilde's anathemas, and his defence of advertisements as socially beneficent fictions seems prima facie plausible. But now a different perspective is introduced by Andrew, who, though shaken by Wilde's talk, offers for Carol Marquis's benefit his personal rebuttal: "The burden of his rapid lecture to the girl was that advertising was just his way of getting to the top, and that it was no better or worse than any other way, so far as he could see. If he could get ahead faster in advertising because he had the knack of pleasing people and making ideas convincing, what was wrong with that?" (156–7). The self-serving casuistry backfires; in the reader's eyes, if not in the young woman's, it damages Andrew's credibility rather than Wilde's. What does damage the artist's is Andrew's offhand remark that "there was nobody in America more successful in advertising his own self than Michael Wilde" (157). In this worldly ambience, even those who most stridently denounce promotion turn out to be carriers of its virus.

The dinner crowd's chorus of laughter at Wilde's expense is patently glib. But at the same time the very wildness of Wilde's discourse (the name is of course another pun) saps its force. The condemnation of advertising sounds too febrile, too extreme to be taken to heart. Wouk teasingly confounds judgment further by placing a narratorial thumb on every scale; "the sole purpose of this chapter," he confides, "being to illustrate the proposition in its first sentence, that there are as many opinions as there are people in every event" (160). The doctrinaire relativism destabilizes firm conclusions regarding the issues the novel engages. Still, despite the elaborate show of neutrality, one begins to suspect that some opinions have a claim to be considered more equal than others.

What undoes one opinion – Andrew's – is the young man's behaviour toward his fiancée. The blithe defender of his own calling convinces himself that he is "trading up" in exchanging Laura for Carol, "for all the world as though he were about to make a daring bid at contract bridge" (159). He approaches the task of cashiering the girl as a promotional hurdle, happily hitting on a "Unique Selling Proposition": "He did not fail with great tact to bring in the name of Stephen English, and to acknowledge humbly that that patrician was much more worthy of her charms and could give her more happiness than himself, a poor, struggling advertising man, and noting ... that this point went home, he dwelt on it with considerable 'selling power'" (164). To quote Morley's aside in *The Haunted Bookshop*, "Thus, in hours of stress, do all men turn for comfort to their chosen art." When Laura predictably but embarrassingly asks him whether he loves Carol, Andrew falters, prompting from the narrator a taunting apostrophe: "Come, Andy, speak up! ... Speak, Andy, and meet the challenge of this sentimental question. You've parried thousands of harder thrusts before! ... You can't lose countenance, man, or you lose the sale!" (164–5). Reale's hypocritical punting of emotional realities confirms a point Wilde has made in his "Oration": language itself is being cheapened in the interest of material gain.

An unexpected backer of the artist's cause turns out to be the guest of honour, Calvin Stanfield. "You was worryin' them folks fer the hell of it," the preacher advises Wilde in his rustic idiom, "but you was worryin' them with the truth, which is the best worrier they is" (154). Stanfield declares his intention of repeating the gist of Wilde's remarks in his weekly radio address, news that startles the assembled company and flabbergasts Marquis. At a follow-up meeting to stem the crisis, the soap potentate lays down commercial law: "Do you suppose I will permit a word of that communistic subversion to be uttered on my program?" (188). Once again, true to form, the sponsor feels no compunction about meddling with broadcast content.

In the event, Stanfield's talk turns out to be far from communistic; indeed the novel gingerly distances itself from actual communists, who are said to have an "affinity for public commotion" (225).[3] For Marquis, however, the risk that Stanfield's remarks will "[cast] reflections on the radio industry, on the advertising profession, and on my products" suffices to make them "scurrilous and subversive" (205). The address is entitled, provocatively enough, "The Hog in the House" (187); but while it purports to be a reframed version of Wilde's diatribe, Marquis's anxieties prove needless; Stanfield's embrace of the artist's opinions is carefully measured. Where Wilde had denounced advertising lock, stock, and barrel, the preacher pulls his punches. Indeed, he calls advertising "a punchin' bag in our own land that every highbrow and scribbler swings at sooner or later," thus disavowing the aesthetic elitism that Wilde embodies. Notwithstanding his ominous-sounding "hog in the house" metaphor, he declares remarkably that he "ain't even agin" advertising (237). At bottom, his quarrel is not with the general phenomenon but with its excesses and improprieties; with instances of it that flout religious values or common decency. He is really objecting to what Mr English calls "certain unsavory details of the business"; ultimately the homespun maverick's position replicates the well-groomed banker's. He complains that radio advertising has come to crowd out the entertainment it sustains: "readin' their signs in yer parlor until it's all signs and no pleasure – that's hog" (241).[4] His objection to the exploiting of young women for commercial purposes glances tellingly at Laura: "Leadin' yer prettiest daughters out o' yer homes into big cities, undressin' 'em and printin' pictures of 'em to sweeten up their products with the sweetness of Eve and Mary – that's a hog right in our laps" (241). Sacred womanhood, personified by the cited biblical figures, has, like Laura, been commodified into "Honey."

From his vantage point in the late forties the narrator comments wryly on the futility of Stanfield's complaints:

> In these nine years much has occurred, including a war, but nothing has happened to the harmless profession of advertising except that its prosperity has increased. Our citizens in the happiness of their lot ignored Stanfield, and to this day still ignore the whole matter, even as dancing picknickers disregard the gnats on a fine summer's day. (242)

The tone (e.g. "the harmless profession of advertising") is of course ironic; though Stanfield is implicitly compared to a mere troublesome gnat, the narrator plainly considers him a gadfly who deserves earnest attention. He is a voice crying in a wilderness of commercials.

Stanfield stands for the enduring verities of religion that are being eroded by the materialist concerns of a secular and mercantile world. When Andrew attends Laura's wedding to Stephen English (a union that proves happily ephemeral), he is struck by the prospect of the small church "surrounded by the stone sides of high office buildings and the immense windows of department stores": "Commerce had lapped around it, but still it stood, a quiet island of unprofitable sanctity amid the flooding tides of business" (213).[5] The accompanying drawing in the 1956 illustrated edition of the novel makes the point vividly (Figure 6). Reale's later, clumsy attempt to blackmail Stanfield (he has unearthed the preacher's youthful liaison with a British girl) marks his own betrayal of sanctity for the sake of profit. The supposed "harmlessness" of his profession is belied by his predatory ruthlessness.

For all the trappings of authorial neutrality, in Wouk's novel it is the Reverend Stanfield who assumes the role of *raisonneur*. The preacher gives the overbearing Marquis his comeuppance and helps

Figure 6

to persuade Andrew to reclaim Laura after her impulsive, but never consummated, marriage to Stephen English. (The banker, with lofty magnanimity, renounces his claims and indeed befriends the young couple. If Talmadge Marquis embodies the dark side of capitalism, there are more luminous sides to be found.) Like Vic Norman, Andrew is tempted to take a lucrative partnership in an advertising agency, but he too decides to wash his hands of the business. In a spasm of clairvoyance he recoils from the profession he had so ardently pursued: "'Why,' he concluded to himself, 'what are we but a crowd of well-kept slaves in golden chains, wearing out our lives in a devil-dance of lying, throat-cutting, sensuality, luxury, cheating, conniving, and fooling the public?' He loathed himself and his life. He felt a desperate urge to write a book" (263–4). With its theatrical exaggeration, Andrew's epiphany is the funniest moment of the novel. After his excitement subsides, however, Andrew wisely resists the urge to scribble his confession. Instead, he settles into an American idyll, united with his Laura (purged of her "Honey" coating) in the bucolic West, pursuing his life in an angel-dance of wholesome probity far from the tall satanic office towers and the fetid broadcast studios. His career there as a cattle rancher and family man reverses his earlier dreams of promotional glory. Nevertheless, in his rustic surroundings he continues to cultivate his native talent: "The advertisements of his prize bulls in the *Hereford Journal* still disturb orthodox cattlemen. He was the first client to order and pay for a back cover in four colors on that staid publication" (283). Although he is no longer trumpeting the merits of Aurora Dawn, even in his bovine surroundings he maintains his zest for "progress."

Wouk's novel is a clever, if brittle, period satire on promotional business. More urbane than *The Hucksters*, it deploys a wide range of literary and philosophical reference to place the social implications of mass advertising within a broader perspective than Wakeman's book provides. Both novels are framed as cautionary tales of commercial "sin" and pastoral "redemption," but Wouk's light-hearted, humorous treatment manages to avoid turgid melodrama. Even so, *Aurora Dawn* can hardly be said to explore in depth the complex cultural issues it raises. The anathema delivered by Michael Wilde is undercut by the identity of its source, a supercilious dandy, and by its own "wild" extravagance. The Reverend Stanfield's "Hog in the House" critique is more credible because Stanfield possesses the *gravitas* that Wilde lacks. However, while lamenting the excesses of advertising it fails to come to grips with a general problem like the social consequences of manipulative demand-creation, which the banker English lauds as "the solar energy of the American system." At the end of the novel the narrator warns readers against drawing from it the moral "Radio and advertising are the curse of our age." "Friends," he muses, "the old punch-and-judy show of Folly has been played against a thousand backgrounds, and the curtain will yet rise and fall on a thousand more. There are good people and bad people scattered through all the paths of the living" (276). Like most bromides, Wouk's contains its grain of truth. Yet it dismisses with a philosophical wink the complex and urgent social concerns on which the narrative has touched.

By the radio days of the 1940s, advertising had taken on a momentum and pervasiveness unknown to writers of the previous generation. Employment in the industry had grown in its scope and significance, and the novels by Wakeman and Wouk were timely in representing, more fully than Wells or Morley or even Orwell, the kinds of experience offered by such work. Yet both writers content themselves with targeting local abuses of commercial promotion – the "hoggish" arrogance of sponsors or the shallowness and vulgarity of some promotional techniques – rather than probing the systemic pressures behind those failings, such as, to adopt Michael Wilde's vivacious phrase, "the garish fungus of greed." There is an instructive parallel here with the following decade's most widely read exposé of promotional misrepresentation, Vance Packard's *The Hidden Persuaders*. While castigating innovative technical subterfuges – subliminal "messages" and the like – Packard goes out of his way to exempt the "normal" functioning of the industry: "Advertising … not only plays a vital role in promoting our economic growth but is a colorful, diverting aspect of American life, and many of the creations of ad men are tasteful, honest works of artistry" (Ewen *Captains* 188). This sounds like a reprise of the sage accommodations of Wouk's Mr English and Reverend Stanfield. As Ewen comments, "[S]uch a disclaimer … clearly misses the point. Whether or not the advertising industry has become the mainstay of artistry in American life is not the issue. *Why* and *how* and *to whose benefit* seems a more productive line of questioning" (*Captains* 188, emphasis in original).

Although it may well be more productive, it is not a line of questioning rigorously pursued by either Wakeman or Wouk. The only alternative to the established system either author envisions is an unlikely retreat from money-grubbing, urbanized modernity into a modest existence within an unspoiled American "heartland" – "Back out of all this now too much for us," to borrow Robert Frost's phrase in "Directive" (CP 520) – a pastoral vision as dated as the Raveloe of *Silas Marner*. Meanwhile, the energetic mass marketing of both Wouk's novel and Wakeman's harmonizes with the basically conservative nature of the fables they produced; the whole commercial logic of the bestseller works against a more searching or abrasive treatment of contentious issues. Well might Wouk have hesitated to brand radio and advertising the curse of our age; few writers have been more richly blessed by the gods of promotion.

The radio days of Wakeman and Wouk's novels were soon made a mere memory by technological advance. In his preface to the 1956 illustrated edition of *Aurora Dawn* Wouk asks: "Who would have dreamed, a mere ten years ago, that the money-crammed world of radio was a bubble about to burst?" (7). Despite the explosive impact of television, however, Wouk says, referring to "the abuses and follies pictured in *Aurora Dawn*": "None of this has changed. Aurora Dawn is a more rampant goddess than ever"(7–8). The decades that followed were to prove his words prophetic.

5

Doors of (Mis)Perception:
Margaret Atwood's *The Edible Woman*

Placed side by side, the writers discussed in the preceding chapters – James, Wells, Morley, Orwell, Wakeman, Wouk – comprise a rather oddly assorted men's club. This monochrome effect is not surprising; during the period so far addressed, advertising itself was a male-dominated industry, and those drawn to write about it (aside from the few exceptional women who chronicled their efforts to pursue a career in it) tended naturally to belong to the presiding sex.[1] By the 1960s, however, the gender balance had begun to change, in the promotional realm and beyond. Margaret Atwood's 1969 novel *The Edible Woman* responds to this evolution; it views promotional work from an angle reflecting its author's distinctive positioning as a woman. (Atwood's Canadian nationality, too, bears on her perspective; but in the present context gender trumps citizenship.)

The Edible Woman is notable for its exploration of female subjectivity, and for its exposure of the power of promotional forces to channel a woman's perceptions, matters at best gingerly skirted in the texts heretofore considered. Here the issue of misrepresentation, central in *Tono-Bungay*, undergoes a decisive shift, focusing now on *self*-misrepresentation. The novel's protagonist, Marian MacAlpin, is doubly exposed to distortions of the latter sort, both through her identity as a woman and through her job with a firm, Seymour Surveys, dedicated to promotional business. On the literal level, her work links her with "hucksters" like Vic Norman and Andrew Reale, but a still more important dimension of advertising here is as a metaphor, a convenient means of refracting the pressures promotional culture exerts on a vulnerable female subject. Marian's susceptibility manifests itself in her interactions with the people and objects surrounding her and, above all, in her precariously unfolding self-image.

Jean Kilbourne, author of *Can't Buy My Love: How Advertising Changes the Way We Think and Feel* (1999), argues plausibly that female consumers are peculiarly exposed to promotional influences. She maintains that, "advertising's messages are inside our intimate relationships, our homes, our hearts, our heads" (58). While Kilbourne's "our" is not gender-specific, the context implies that she has women chiefly in mind. She explains how the omnipresence of promotion feeds into sexual politics: "[A]t the very least, advertising helps to create a climate in which certain attitudes and values flourish, such as the attitude that women are valuable only as objects of men's desire, that real men are always sexually aggressive, [and] that violence is erotic" (290–1). *The Edible Woman* anticipates Kilbourne's insights and provides an articulated fictional frame for them, wittily puncturing commercially generated stereotypes of "real" women as well as "real" men, and debunking stock notions of the erotic appeal of male violence. Atwood profited from the lively public debate of such issues in the 1960s, a development stimulated by popular feminist texts like Betty Friedan's seminal 1963 *The Feminine Mystique*. Among numerous other concerns, Friedan's book highlighted the bearing of advertising on women's perceptions of their world and (especially) of themselves.

In her afterword to a 1989 reprint of *The Edible Woman*, Linda Hutcheon observes: "In all her writing, Atwood shows herself to be the tireless explorer and exposer of cultural clichés and stereotypes, in particular of those that affect women" (313). Clichés and stereotypes inevitably raise issues of perception, a subject in which Atwood has been interested throughout her career, both as poet and novelist. Hutcheon argues that, "[Atwood's] novels are all, in some way, novels about identity and perception" (Grace 27). In *The Edible Woman* these two ideas are fused; as Marian MacAlpin's perceptions become more acute, her sense of her own identity grows more confident. This process is inseparable from Marian's relation to advertising; to attain to a more trustworthy understanding of her world and her position in it, Marian must liberate her vision from promotional blinkers. The novel thus focuses more intently on personal interiority than do most earlier advertising fictions, a psychological move extended in the books by Morrison and Ferris examined in the next chapter.

There is nothing outré in the notion that advertising modifies the perceptions of those incessantly exposed to it. The Marxist critic György Lukács contended that in twentieth-century capitalism "the commodity had become a universal form. The very *perceptions* engendered within this process ... begin to reflect the priorities of capitalism: the primacy of the system of exchange, the destruction of craft, the fragmentation of work and social life" (Ewen, *Captains* 193, emphasis in original). Stuart Ewen claims that by the early twentieth century "the injection of corporate bonding into the interstices of existence was altering and attempting to safely standardize the common perception of daily life" (*Captains* 214–5); more recently Ewen has written of "the powerful role of perception management in today's society, and the steady commercialization of nearly every human experience" ("Memoirs" 447). And the effects of standardization ramify well beyond mere purchasing habits. To quote Kilbourne's summation: "Advertising often sells a great deal more than products. It sells values, images, and concepts of love and sexuality; romance, success, and, perhaps most important, normalcy" (74) – that is, it homogenizes the perceptions of the world available to those living within a consumer society, validating some and vetoing others.

Advertising typically aims at creating, by means of such hegemony, an uneasy self-consciousness in its targets. According to Ewen, the "notion of the individual as the object of continual and harsh social scrutiny underscored the argument" of many guides to advertising techniques in the 1920s (*Captains* 34); the "pedic perspiration" campaign of Gordon Comstock's New Albion agency is a fictional example of such premeditated surveillance. Because they are subject to culturally inscribed anxiety about their personal appearance and demeanour, women have long been prime candidates for this sort of commercial manipulation. Ewen documents that as early as the 1920s "[t]he real insecurity women felt about 'what a woman should be'" (*Captains* 179) was being cannily exploited by ads. Atwood deftly exposes the warping pressure exerted by promotional scrutiny, the force Karen Stein calls "the threatening aspects of the specular, the gaze" (45). A telling example of the linkage of observation, aggression, and promotion occurs in a poem from Atwood's early collection *Power Politics* (1971), "They Eat Out," in which the speaker says "The other diners regard you [her companion]/some with awe, some only with boredom:/they cannot decide if you are a new weapon/or only a new advertisement" (*Selected Poems* 114). The syntax hints that the supposed alternatives – weapon or ad – are interchangeable terms.

Marian's insecurity about her appearance illustrates the way in which advertising can function as a vector of conformity, enforcing on women a socially approved, "normal" self-image. As Simone Davis observes, "Cast by the [advertising] industry as the ultimate object of scrutiny, the [female] consumer must be read, interpreted, 'mimicked' ... and seduced" (2–3). A symptom of Marian's openness to such seduction is her urge to gaze at her own reflection in mirrors. (Ewen notes that even in magazines dating back to the 1920s "between eight and ten ads per issue depict a woman at or looking into a mirror" (*Captains* 239 note 121).) Primping for her engagement party, Marian stands in front of her two old dolls, one blonde and one dark: "She saw herself in the mirror between them for an instant as though she was inside them, inside both of them at once, looking out ... the blonde eyes noting the arrangement of her hair, her bitten fingernails, the dark one looking deeper, at something she could not quite see ... By the strength of their separate visions they were trying to pull her apart" (243). To quote Kilbourne again, "The culture, both reflected and reinforced by advertising, urges girls to adopt a false self, to bury alive their real selves, to become 'feminine'" (130). Kilbourne mentions a "Special Night Barbie that shows [girls] how to dress up for a night out" (132). If the dark doll represents Marian's authentic but submerged self, which she "cannot quite see," the blonde one embodies her socially approved Barbie image. Ewen cites a 1920s "booklet advertising feminine beauty aids [that] had on its cover a picture of a highly scrubbed, powdered and decorated nude. The message of the title was blunt: 'Your masterpiece – Yourself'" (*Captains* 179–80). Peering anxiously into her mirror, Marian becomes an "artist" of her own resplendent, fair-haired, unreal effigy. As Baudrillard aptly sums up the consequences of the "myth of Woman" in consumer culture: "[N]ot just one's relationship with others, but also one's relation to oneself becomes a *consumed* relation" (95, emphasis in original).

Atwood's interest in advertising dates back to her tender years. Rosemary Sullivan records: "Like most children, Margaret learned the singing commercials by heart: 'You'll wonder where the yellow went when you brush your teeth with Pepsodent'" (32). Later, Atwood herself "wrote singing commercials for the school dances"

(68). Already exhibiting her signature quirkiness, she "decided to compose an operetta about synthetic fabrics. She called it 'Synthesia: Operetta in One Act'" (68–9). As a student at the University of Toronto "[s]he even wrote a literary parody of [her instructor] Northrop Frye in which she applied his archetypal theory of literary criticism to the current Ajax [cleanser] commercial" (96). By the date of *The Edible Woman*, this youthful whimsicality had given way to a more mature understanding of the impact of promotion on individual psyches, above all women's. But over the years Atwood's fascination with advertising simply for its own sake has remained constant, palpable as a tension even between the lines of her satiric critique.

More even than Frye, another eminent Canadian academic contributed significantly to Atwood's understanding of promotion and its repercussions. In her recent book *In Other Worlds* (2011), Atwood writes of her discovery of Marshall McLuhan's work:

> The first of McLuhan's books was *The Mechanical Bride*, which analyzed such things as advertisements and comic books for their mythic and psychological content, and illustrated itself with reproductions of the ads, and thus got pulled from the market by soap flake companies and such for copyright infringement; but you could buy this book on the sly from McLuhan's basement, which I did. Due to my interest in cereal boxes, magazine ads, and comics, I of course found his book delectable. (45)

In a 2011 *Globe and Mail* interview ("Margaret Atwood, Uncensored") Atwood describes her first attempt at a novel, which "happily for myself and the rest of the world never got published": "It was influenced by Marshall McLuhan. There was a lot of advertisements in it." In the same interview she refers to *The Mechanical Bride* as "a piece of genius," adding that "it is very funny." Both judgments could fairly be applied to Atwood's first published novel, which, like her earlier, scrapped one, incorporates "a lot of advertisements," not to mention a lot of McLuhan.

In its mode *The Edible Woman* is comic, but as Hutcheon rightly says, "[T]he one thing Atwood never lets us forget is that we should not mistake humour or irony for lack of seriousness" (Afterword 318–9). Far from unserious, the book is, to quote W.J. Keith, "a passionately committed exposé of the world of packaging and consuming" (64). Marian MacAlpin's job with Seymour Surveys resembles one Atwood had held herself, vetting questionnaires for Canadian Facts, "a Toronto market-research company that farmed out and collected interviews on clients' products" (Sullivan 140). Marian's work of sampling consumer responses, not to a specific product but to publicity *for* products, represents a new phase of promotional culture that might be called meta-promotion: the systematic surveying of public perceptions of advertisements. McLuhan's critique of such expedients is vehement: "[A]s market-research tyranny has developed, the object and ends of human consumption have been blurred. Know-how has obliterated the why, what, and when" (*Bride* 31). It is a sentiment with which Atwood would have concurred. Tyrannical or not, however, market research could sometimes yield tangible results. As William Meyers reports, in 1970, the year after *The Edible Woman* appeared, the tobacco giant Philip Morris, having acquired the floundering Miller Brewing Company, "undertook an exhaustive psychological research study that revealed the inner needs of American beer drinkers" (65). The resulting campaign for Miller High Life – "Miller Time" – turned the enterprise around. Marian's canvassing for that *echt* Canadian product, Moose Beer, is meant to deliver a similar bounce.

Whatever its utility, for a young woman like Marian the job has its drawbacks. Her workplace is structured rigidly according to gender, as Marian explains in terms that harmonize wittily with the book's dominant metaphor of eating: "The company is layered like an ice-cream sandwich, with three floors: the upper crust, the lower crust, and our department, the gooey layer in the middle" (18). She adds: "Because our department deals primarily with housewives, everyone in it … is female" (19). The "upper crust" of managers and the "lower crust" of manual labourers are both exclusively male and presumably firm rather than "gooey." The whole structure can serve as a model for the pressures that "squeeze" Marian as a female employee of a male-heavy promotional firm. Essential to Marian's job is the euphemistic blurring of raw factuality. In responding to a customer who has found a squashed insect in her box of advertised cereal, "[t]he main thing, I knew, was to avoid calling the housefly by its actual name" (28). As Wouk's Michael Wilde might have pointed out, speech is being cheapened until it ceases to be an honest method of exchange.

Orwell, too, would have been unsurprised by such evasive juggling of language for the sake of profit. He would likely have endorsed Kilbourne's dictum: "Advertising is our *environment*. We swim in it as fish swim in water" (57, emphasis in original). Atwood shares this awareness of promotional discourse as an enveloping medium. Joan Foster, the protagonist of Atwood's third novel, *Lady Oracle*, admits: "I was a sucker for ads, especially those that promised happiness" (25). Marian displays a like susceptibility. Her "fascination with advertisements" (Keith 44) is, as noted earlier, a trait she has in common with Atwood, who has acknowledged that when on public transport "I always read the ads" (*Payback* 6). (Marian confides that, "I don't like talking on buses, I would rather look at the advertisements" (14).) Riding the bus after kissing her strange friend Duncan at the laundromat, she "stared for a long time at an advertisement with a picture of a nurse in a white cap and dress. She had a wholesome, competent face and she was holding a bottle and smiling. The caption said: GIVE THE GIFT OF LIFE" (110). Marian, still at this stage immersed in the enveloping promotional ether, can assent to the Madison Avenue conceit of life as an article that might be gift-wrapped and bestowed, possibly through a magical kiss. Later, however, when she begins to suspect that her gallant sexual "initiation" of Duncan has actually been no novelty for him, "[t]he starched nurse-like image of herself she had tried to preserve as a last resort crumpled like wet newsprint" (293). She is beginning to realize that promotional clichés are worse than useless for purposes of self-definition.

Such incidents suggest the extent to which Marian's perceptions have been skewed by ads and by the commodities they publicize. "I've always been influenced by appearances," she confesses (37). Over time, however, a contrary movement struggles to emerge within her psyche, an obstinate resistance to promotional "appearances." Early in the novel she has been assigned the task of gathering responses to a questionnaire for the new Moose Beer brand, but later, when ads for the product begin "to appear everywhere, in the subway trains, on hoardings, in magazines" (166), she feels troubled by their air of unreality: "The fisherman wading in the stream, scooping the trout into his net, was too tidy: he looked as though his hair had just been combed, a few strands glued neatly to his forehead to show he was windblown. And the fish also was unreal; it had no slime, no teeth, no smell, it was a clever toy, metal and enamel." Marian's recoil from such processed images recalls Gordon Comstock's loathing of posters featuring Corner Table and his fraudulent kin. The difference is that for Marian this revulsion is not a habitual response but a new and eye-opening discovery. Later, sampling some Moose Beer "out of curiosity," she discovers that "[i]t tasted just like all the other brands" (172). Browsing in the supermarket, she reflects: "She knew enough about it from the office to realize that the choice between, for instance, two brands of soap or two cans of tomato juice was not what could be called a rational one. In the products, the things themselves, there was no real difference" (191). As Evan Llewellyn Evans would have reminded her, there is "no damn difference between soaps" – or soups or brands of beer.

The illusionism of commercial discourse begins to control Marian's perceptions of her own body: "Marian gazed down at the small silvery image reflected in the bowl of the spoon: herself upside down, with a huge torso narrowing to a pinhead at the handle end" (161). The effect hints at the deforming forces impinging on Marian's ego, suggesting too that her body is taking precedence over her head or mind. Baudrillard contends that the body – "the finest consumer object," as he wryly calls it – "has today become an *object of salvation*. It has literally taken over that moral and ideological function from the soul" (129, emphasis in original). Responding to pressures from a market-driven society, Marian has come to experience her own body as such an object of consumption; little wonder if she begins to think of herself as edible.

As her wedding to her lawyer fiancé Peter draws near, Marian's visual distortions grow more alarming. Taking a bath before the engagement party, gazing at the two taps and the spout, "in each of the three silver globes she could see now that there was a curiously-sprawling pink thing. She sat up, stirring the water into minor tidal waves, to see what they were. It was a moment before she recognized, in the bulging and distorted forms, her own waterlogged body" (241–2). Understandably perturbed, she thinks, "She ought to have her eyes examined, things were beginning to blur" (241). As Shannon Hengen argues, however, "near the novel's end, Marian can begin to see herself ... signaling for her an emergent, independent sense of self" (52). Allied with that emergence is a new ability to see others, above all Peter, lucidly as well. Her history could thus be charted as a kind of cognitive Pilgrim's Progress. What Gloria Onley says of the protagonist of Atwood's second novel, *Surfacing* – that she attains to a "liberated naked consciousness, its doors of perception symbolically cleansed" (79) – applies equally to that heroine's precursor, Marian.[2] Atwood told an interviewer that "the ads in [*The Edible Woman*] are obviously chosen for the fact that the words that they contain resonate with other words in the book" (*Conversations* 28), but it is not just words the ads resonate with, it is Marian's whole perceptual gestalt.[3]

In *The Edible Woman* sexual relationships become configured by promotional groundswells. Atwood's resistance to commercialized "romance" accounts for her emphatic response to what might have seemed a tempting publishing opportunity: "I'm somewhat appalled that *Redbook* is considering (or has been given a chance to consider) [*The Edible Woman*], but it would be an irony of fate" (letter of 3 March 1968 to Pamela Fry, Atwood archive). *Redbook* magazine featured popular fiction interlarded with ads directed at female consumers; Atwood's "irony of fate" is self-explanatory. For Atwood, associating herself with the patriarchal models of the "feminine" featured in popular journalism would have amounted to a self-betrayal.

Nevertheless, her treatment of such conformity in *The Edible Woman* seldom lapses into caricature. Marian's roommate, Ainsley, does not snugly fit standard female stereotypes. Avid not for marriage but for the celebrity status of motherhood, she is less a husband-hunter than a sperm-gatherer. Still, in its offbeat fashion her behaviour betrays advertising's controlling grip on women's expectations. Keith sees Marian and Ainsley as moving along contrary paths ("Whereas Marian began as a 'respectable' young woman contrasting with Ainsley as independent rebel, Marian is now moving towards the officially abnormal while Ainsley is drawn back to the conventional" (46–7)), but actually Ainsley's conventionality is evident from the outset. She enters the scene as the enforcer of promotional norms: "She gave me a disgusted look. 'Every woman should have at least one baby.' She sounded like a voice on the radio saying that every woman should have at least one electric hair-dryer" (42). Her drive toward maternity never swerves from this doggedly consumerist groove. Having contrived to become pregnant, she urges the rewards upon Marian ("You really ought to try it sometime"), who wonders "how she could be so casual about it, as if she was recommending a handy trick for making fluffier pie-crust or a new detergent" (142). Later, after succumbing to "scientific" alarmism about the dire effects of fatherlessness on male offspring, Ainsley wails "If I have a little boy, he's absolutely *certain* to turn into a ho-ho-ho-homosexual" (201, emphasis in original). The panicky mother-to-be imagines her baby as a marketable product crying out for a paternal "sponsor"; she shuns homosexuality as an off-brand.

Ainsley's mode of self-presentation is a meticulously staged piece of self-branding. Scheming to lure Marian's friend Len Slank into impregnating her, she fashions an absurdly demure image to suit her promotional campaign: "[Marian] studied [Ainsley's] latest version of herself, thinking that it was like one of the large plump dolls in the stores at Christmas-time, with washable rubber-smooth skin and glassy eyes and gleaming artificial hair. Pink and white" (74). Such false advertising entails its own risks; once she has impressed her little-girl persona upon Len, Ainsley cannot easily unbrand herself: "And she couldn't even talk back: it was necessary for her mind to appear as vacant as her face. Her hands were tied. She had constructed her image and now she had to maintain it" (131).

Marian, too, risks entrapment within a constructed image, one that is different but that threatens to tie her hands just as tightly. While Ainsley prepares her for her engagement party "Marian sat passively, marvelling at the professional efficiency with which Ainsley was manipulating her features. It reminded her of the mothers backstage at public-school plays, making up their precocious daughters" (246). Afterward, "Marian stared into the Egyptian-lidded and outlined and thickly-fringed eyes of a person she had never seen before. She was afraid even to blink, for fear that this applied face would crack and flake with the strain" (246). Threatened with loss of control over her own image, she finds herself "experimenting, looking in the mirror, trying to find out which particular set of muscles would produce the desired effect" (247). Gazing at her reflection, she worries that she has mutated into a surreal replica of herself. The alienation stemming from compliance with norms of approved feminine "charm" could hardly be more arrestingly conveyed.

Peter is an unwitting party to the fashioning of Marian's self-estranging, marketable doll-persona. Yet Marian's fiancé is himself the captive of promotional clichés; Atwood makes it plain that such mental entrapment is by no means an exclusively feminine condition. As she remarks in a 1972 interview with Graeme Gibson, "Let's say that I think of society in two ways; one is simply the kind of

thing that Western Industrialism has done to people, and the other is
the Canadian thing, where men particularly have been amputated"
(*Conversations* 17). Peter may personify "the Canadian thing," but
his limitations transcend national borders; they are generically modern. They pertain above all to standardized products of Western
industrialism. Ainsley calls Peter himself "nicely packaged," an
ambiguous compliment; Marian initially finds the quality attractive
(161–2), but later has her doubts. The expert packaging extends to
Peter's personal space: "His refrigerator was so white and spotless
and arranged; [Marian] thought with guilt of her own" (255). A
devotee of strict personal hygiene, Peter has a "clean familiar soap-
smell" (230), no doubt because he takes frequent showers (62). His
social contacts apparently compose a fraternal order of ablution;
Ainsley refers to Peter's male business friends as "the Soap Men"
(195). Ewen describes "the Cleanliness Institute," an early promotional organization, as "push[ing] soap as a 'Kit for Climbers'"
(*Captains* 45). The well-scrubbed Peter is himself a confirmed
climber; he lives for the nonce on an upper floor of a building under
construction, while "rising [in his law firm] like a balloon" (60).

Peter's pneumatic cleanliness goes along with a daunting regular-
ity: "All his accessories matched" (70). After the crisis of Marian's
flight from their engagement party, he can only ask: "Why the hell
did you leave the party? You really *disrupted* the evening for me"
(294, emphasis added). The disorder that irks Peter is Marian's
instinctive gesture of protest against the sterile regime he strives to
impose, but he is too obsessively committed to that regime to read
the hidden message of her unruliness.

Like other men of his type and class, Peter inhabits a universe of
fetishistic objects. A prime example is his automobile, "perhaps the
archetypal commodity" (Ewen *Captains* 203). When Marian, on an
earlier occasion, impulsively flees his presence, he uses the car to
track her. Other items with which he is linked, guns and cameras,
likewise figure as instruments of macho assertiveness. He regales Len
Slank with an account of shooting a rabbit: "So I let her off and
Wham. One shot, right through the heart" (74). He goes on to revel
in the minutiae of evisceration: "'So I whipped out my knife, good
knife, German steel, and slit the belly and took her by the hind legs
and gave her one hell of a crack, like a whip you see, and the next
thing you know there was blood and guts all over the place'" (74).
As John Lauber remarks, "The story shocks not because the action

was cruel ... but because of the insensitivity of the teller to nature and to his audience. It's no wonder that Marian, listening, identifies herself with the female victim" (Moss 22). Marian is prompted to identify, of course, by Peter's pronouns ("took *her* by the hind legs"), which transmit his transparent glee in using a symbolically male implement ("good knife, German steel") to mutilate a feminized nature. As Veblen long ago observed, "It is, indeed, the most noticeable effect of the sportsman's activity to keep nature in a state of chronic desolation by killing off all living things whose destruction he can compass" (257), a description that fits Peter with deadly exactness. Marian understandably begins to wonder if she may be included in her sportsman-lover's catalogue of destructible natural objects.

What compounds the shock effect is Peter's mirth: "He paused to laugh" (74). Here, as often in comic novels, laughter itself becomes an infallible moral indicator, and Peter's follow-up comment confirms his tone-deafness: "God it was funny. Lucky thing Trigger [his aptly-named friend] and me had the old cameras along, we got some good shots of the whole mess" (74). "Good shots" – graphic mementos of cruelty – are cause for hilarity rather than compunction. Cameras in *The Edible Woman* are objects insistently associated with chuckling brutality, as is that other macho mechanism, Peter's car. Peter shows a chortling *sang froid* toward some shrubs he squashes with his Volkswagen: "'They're going to see an alteration in their landscape gardening when they get up in the morning,' he chuckled. He seemed to find willfully ruining other people's property immensely funny" (88). By treating his impact on the environment as a joke, Peter exposes the dark, unfunny underside of his psyche.

Peter is hardly a "rounded" character, but his "flatness" is not a defect of portraiture. The deficit that *defines* Peter's personality is precisely his lack of a further dimension. The lack is not, however, apparent to Marian, owing to her fiancé's conformity to accepted promotional prompts. "People noticed him, not because he had forceful or peculiar features, but because he was ordinariness raised to perfection, like the youngish well-groomed faces of cigarette ads" (65). As Ewen notes, "Through advertising ... consumption took on a clearly cultural tone. ... The mass 'American type,' which defined unity on the bases of common ethnicity, language, class or literature, was ostensibly born out of common desires – mass responses to the demands of capitalist production. Mass industry, requiring a corresponding mass individual" (*Captains* 42). Peter is a poster boy matching poster-circulated public expectations. And Marian's job itself dictates her ideas of suitability in a male partner: as McLuhan says, "[S]urvey techniques inevitably throw up images of normalcy that reflect the ways of those who make few demands of themselves" (47). Rather than making demands of herself, Marian internalizes the homogenizing assumptions of the surveys she is employed to take.

Just as Marian gradually comes to "see through" advertising, so it is "through" advertising that she comes to see Peter's deficiencies; she begins to perceive him as no more than the sum of his possessions, among which she herself is numbered. Ironically, she gains more knowledge from contemplating the things Peter owns than from looking steadily at their owner. At their engagement party, gazing at Peter's closet-full of outfits, she wonders: "How could they hang there smugly asserting so much invisible silent authority?" (254). Her harbouring of doubts about the trappings of male dominance is an important preliminary step toward challenging the authority of the man they adorn.

For the moment, however, aided by alcohol, she reconciles herself to Peter's cardboard-cut-out identity. Observing him taking snapshots of guests, she assures herself of his "normalcy":

> He reminded her of the home-movie ads, the father of the family using up rolls and rolls of film on just such everyday ordinary things, what subjects could be better: people laughing, lifting glasses, children at birthday parties ... So that's what was in there all the time, she thought happily: this is what he's turning into. The real Peter, the one underneath, was nothing surprising or frightening, only this bungalow-and-double-bed man, this charcoal-cooking-in-the-backyard man. (269)

What stands out is the *willed* nature of Marian's gratitude for her fiancé's banality. As Keith observes, "[T]he word 'normal' develops into a disturbing leitmotif as the book progresses" (31). The conjunction of the idea of normality with advertising clichés makes the leitmotif doubly disturbing; Atwood uneasily balances the "adnormal" against the supposedly "abnormal." Marian's fantasy of Peter benignly middle-aged quickly morphs from complacency to panic. The Peter she has calmly imagined tending a barbecue dissolves into an "unmoving figure, which she could see now held a huge cleaver in the other hand" (270); Peter the back-yard chef is only a cover for Peter the blade-wielding ripper. Locating the real-life Peter in an adjacent room, she finds the axe now posing demurely as a camera, but her newly sharpened perceptions penetrate the disguise: "Peter was there, dressed in his dark opulent winter suit. He had a camera in his hand; but now she saw what it really was" (270).

It is, of course, not the first time Marian has been unsettled by her friend's penchant for photography; one recalls the "old camera" Peter has used to memorialize the mangled rabbit. On this later occasion, taking snapshots prior to the party, Peter urges her to "look natural, come on, *smile*" (257, emphasis in original), but the self-negating command to "look natural" backfires; "[h]er body had frozen, gone rigid. She couldn't move, she couldn't even move the muscles of her face as she stood and stared into the round glass lens pointing towards her, she wanted to tell him not to touch the shutter-release but she couldn't move" (257). As critics have noted, the moment recalls the poem "Camera" from *The Circle Game*, in which the speaker protests: "Camera man/how can I love your glass eye?" (56). Several companion pieces evoke this petrifying, mechanical type of perception, like section four of the title poem: "and I am fixed, stuck/down on the outspread map/of this room, of your mind's continent/… transfixed/by your eyes'/cold blue thumbtacks (49–50). What is added in the novel is the promotional dimension; here transfixing photographic images merge into clichéd advertising freeze-frames, like the one Marian espies in Peter's photo magazine: "Beside the column of print there was an advertisement, a little girl with pigtails on a beach, clutching a spaniel. 'Treasure It Forever,' the caption read" (256).

Marian has been striving to ward off her fear of Peter's gaze as immobilizing, fixing her as a mausoleum icon to be lifelessly "treasured forever." At the party, she at last penetrates the true nature of the relationship. "[W]hen she felt behind her for the doorknob, afraid to take her eyes off him, he raised the camera and aimed it at her; his mouth opened in a snarl of teeth. There was a blinding flash of light" (270). The burst is, in literal terms, Peter's flashbulb, but figuratively the "blinding flash" signals Marian's sudden inward illumination, the end of her blindness to Peter's snarling emotional dominance. She sees herself, frighteningly, through Peter's eyes as a bedraggled billboard display: "She sensed her face as vastly spreading and papery and slightly dilapidated: a huge billboard smile, peeling away in flaps and patches, the metal surface beneath showing through" (270). In her letter of 3 March 1968 to Pamela Fry, written after having revised this episode, Atwood asks anxiously: "Do let me know what you think of the new version; especially whether you feel Chapter Twenty-Seven (the party chapter) is now a real revelation, given Marian's new attitudes towards Peter" (Atwood archive). She had no cause for concern; the scene in fact comes across powerfully as a "real revelation" for the abruptly disenchanted protagonist and for the reader as well.

Much later, after her final, valedictory talk with Peter, Marian takes her own conclusive mental snapshot of her (now) ex-fiancé:

> Already the part of her not occupied with eating was having a wave of nostalgia for Peter, as though for a style that had gone out of fashion and was beginning to turn up on the sad Salvation Army clothes racks. She could see him in her mind, posed jauntily in the foreground of an elegant salon with chandeliers and draperies, impeccably dressed, a glass of scotch in one hand; his foot was on the head of a stuffed lion and he had an eyepatch over one eye. Beneath one arm was strapped a revolver. (302)

The revolver is self-explanatory, but the eyepatch has an equally pointed significance. As several critics have noticed, it alludes to long-running ads in the *New Yorker* and elsewhere for Hathaway shirts.[4] What gives the reference its sting, however, is the emphasis on monocular vision. Now that her own field of perception has broadened, Marian manages at last to register the narrowness of her friend's perceptual range. Having achieved that clarity, she is free to escape from her own constricting tunnel vision of love.

Duncan plays the role of mentor for Marian's perceptual emancipation, though a mentor of an unprepossessing type. His character has provoked more than its fair share of critical distaste. Marge Piercy calls him a "sloppy, self-centered graduate student" who "strikes me as no great leap forward" for Marian (McCombs 55), a judgment seconded by George Woodcock, for whom Duncan "is a more insidious kind of parasite, a lamprey battening on [Marian's] compassion to feed his monstrous self-pity" (McCombs 93). But Keith accurately identifies the monstrous lamprey's saving grace: "Duncan exists as the opposite of all that Peter represents" (41). The opposition hinges on promotional motifs: where Peter is a walking advertisement, Duncan is an accomplished adbuster.[5]

Since the measure of Marian's personal progress is her growing disaffection both from advertisement and from Peter, her friendship with such a contrarian figure has a decisive importance. As Keith again argues, "Duncan's function in the novel gradually emerges as the voice of Marian's instincts and intelligence" (41). The young man's peculiar compliment to Marian when she is wearing his dressing gown – "Hey ... you look sort of like me in that" (159) – betrays his besetting narcissism, as does the quasi-erotic sequel: "[T]here was an uneasy suspicion in one corner of [Marian's] mind that what he was really caressing was his own dressing-gown, and that she merely happened to be inside it" (159). Still, the incident signals a real rapprochement between the two. Atwood's treatment of Duncan is happily unsentimentalized; he is a knight in shabby armour. He is routinely exasperating: he never says what Marian wishes or expects him to say, except perhaps at the end, when he concedes that her cake was delicious. From the start, he jolts her from her occupational and perceptual moorings; when she confronts him at his door with her Moose Beer questionnaire, the strange creature she takes for a child turns out to be a twenty-six-year-old graduate student. Yet his subverting of her professional composure is, little though she suspects it, what she most of all needs. His appearance – "He was cadaverously thin; he had no shirt on, and the ribs stuck out like those of an emaciated figure in a medieval woodcut" (51) – makes him the diametric opposite of a male model in a glossy fashion spread. He proceeds, as Keith says, "while ostensibly responding with fascination to the Moose Beer jingle, to subject it to the devastating critique which it so obviously deserves" (35). The critique is all the more devastating for being oblique, tongue in cheek rather than belligerent.

The encounter quickly shakes Marian's factitious aplomb. "The questionnaires I was carrying had suddenly become unrelated to anything at all, and at the same time obscurely threatening" (51). Marian's sense of threat may derive from subliminal qualms about the nature of her task. Noting that *Fortune* magazine conducted its first public opinion survey in 1935, Jackson Lears comments: "This was a key moment in the fine-tuning of managerial thought about mass society. Statistical sampling, whether sponsored by business or government elites, soon became an instrument for rendering public debate more manageable and predictable. The survey became *another threatening force* against which people had to struggle to maintain alternative visions of reality" (44, emphasis added). Unlike Marian, Duncan has no need to struggle to maintain an alternative vision; his perceptions by their very nature diverge from the promotional norm. After launching the interview, Marian discovers him on the phone listening to the taped beer commercial "with the receiver pressed to his ear and his mouth twisted in something that was almost a smile" (55). He has perversely switched his role from the expected passive subject to the undesired sceptical critic. Afterward, Duncan's Rorschach responses to the questions Marian recites farcically thwart the project's normalizing bias:

> "First, what about 'Deep-down manly flavour'?"
> "Sweat," he said considering. "Canvas gym shoes. Underground locker-rooms and jock-straps ..."
> "Now what about 'Long cool swallow'?"
> "Not much. Oh, wait a moment. It's a bird, white, falling from a great height. Shot through the heart, in winter; the feathers coming off, drifting down." ...
> "What about 'Healthy hearty taste'?" ...
> "I know the pattern, there's one of them in the Decameron and a couple in Grimm's; the husband kills the wife's lover, or vice versa, and cuts out the heart and makes it into a stew or a pie and serves it up in a silver dish, and the other one eats it. Though that doesn't account for the Healthy very well, does it?" (55–6)

Duncan's free-associating is, of course, funny, but it is also beguilingly individual, even in its way *poetic*. Marian has sometimes been read as a semi-autobiographical figure, but it is really Duncan whose quizzical imagination gives him an affinity with Atwood herself. Delving into paradigms drawn from folktale and classic literature, he rebuffs the expectations of programmed response called for by the barrage of weary (and beery) slogans. His riff on "deep-down manly flavour" hilariously defeats the normative bow to masculinist swagger. But his most masterly inspiration comes in reply to "Tang of the wilderness": "'Oh,' he said, his voice approaching enthusiasm, 'that one's easy. ... It's one of those technicolour movies about dogs or horses. "Tang of the Wilderness" is obviously a dog, part wolf, part husky, who saves his master three times, once from fire, once from flood and once from wicked humans'" (57). The archetypal film scenario Duncan invokes is of course clichéd, but that makes it all the more apt a comment on the banality of the beer catchphrase. As Marian tells herself later with comical understatement, Duncan "definitely wouldn't fit" at a place like Seymour Surveys (106).

While Marian's job may be what Lauber calls it, "an outrageous invasion of personal privacy" (Moss 20), it does not foster personal connection. Duncan, paradoxical as always, manages to turn impersonal intrusion into a startlingly personal encounter. Accused by Marian with giving inconsistent and misleading answers, he replies, "I was bored; I felt like talking to someone" (57). Marian's pity turns to resentment: "I had been feeling compassion for him as a sufferer on the verge of mental collapse, and now he had revealed the whole thing as a self-conscious performance" (58). Performance like Ainsley's little-girl act is tiresome, but performance can have more positive uses and Duncan's follows a richly literary script, drawing on sources ranging from Boccaccio to animated cartoons to Shakespeare. (Duncan's name – his last is withheld – contains a Shakespearean echo, and he discourses learnedly about the status of the text of *Titus Andronicus*.) Here, as in Orwell, literature and advertising are at loggerheads; wielded by Duncan, the literary tradition acts as a weapon with which to stymie the importunities of promotion.

This does not mean that formal literary studies are spared the rod of Atwood's satire. Duncan's roommate Fisher's flatulent ruminations about womb symbols in D.H. Lawrence and the hermetic subtexts of *Alice in Wonderland* are wickedly sent up. However, Lauber's claim that "[t]he 'intellectual' world of Duncan and his roommates Trevor and Fish offers no real alternative to the consumer society" (Moss 26) is too sweeping; it applies to the roommates, but not to Duncan. The latter's disillusionment with academia derives precisely from his belief that the study of literature has become as venal as the flogging of material commodities, offering only a highbrow version of the "magical transformation" promised by ads: "Production-consumption. You begin to wonder whether it isn't just a question of making one kind of garbage into another kind. The human mind was the last thing to be commercialized but they're doing a good job of it now; what is the difference between the library stacks and one of those used-car graveyards?" (158). What Atwood calls "the kind of thing that Western Industrialism has done to people" is, for Duncan, the kind of thing being done to books.

Duncan speaks for an impromptu approach to reading as opposed to the assembly-line regimen of "literary studies." He dismisses colleagues like his roommates with a Wildean quip: "[T]hey're all too literary, it's because they haven't read enough books" (210–11). Duncan himself, though not doggedly bookish, brings his reading vividly to bear on the life around him. Even his literary fun with "Tang of the Wilderness" deconstructs the stock responses demanded by Madison Avenue. No wonder Marian reflects that it would be "disastrous if this man were to encounter either Peter or Ainsley" (147); those two, though not close friends, are twinned by their kindred lack of originality. The contents of Peter's bookcase – "his law books on the bottom shelf, his hoard of paperback detective novels on the top shelf, and miscellaneous books and magazines in between" (63) (some of these, we later learn, are "books and magazines on cameras" (165)) – tell us all we need to know about his taste in literature.

Next to Peter, with his macho drive, Duncan can seem effeminate. His view of his own orientation is cryptic. "Well, maybe I'm a latent homosexual," he confides to Marian. "He considered that for a moment. 'Or maybe I'm a latent heterosexual. Anyway I'm pretty latent'" (210). Where Peter plays the roles of hunter and photographer, Duncan's pet pastime is, as one might have guessed, *sui generis*. In the laundromat, their favoured meeting-place, he explains to Marian: "I watch laundromat washers the way other people watch television, it's soothing because you always know what to expect and you don't have to think about it" (102–3). His enjoyment of the random kaleidoscope of garments seems, if nothing else, preferable to Peter's annihilation of small animals; it does not serve him as a pretext for callow self-congratulation.

The laundry "show," anomalous and fluid (and commercial-free), epitomizes its viewer's temperament. "That's the nice thing about me," he tells Marian. "I'm very flexible, I'm the universal substitute" (160). More even than a substitute, he fancies himself a changeling: "I got switched for a real baby when young and my parents never discovered the fraud" (155). Rather than a "normal" character, Duncan seems an extraterrestrial visitant untouched by the commonplaces of bourgeois routine. The unearthly scene of his childhood harmonizes with such an identity: "It's a mining town, there isn't much of anything in it but at least it has no vegetation. ... [I]t's barren, nothing but the barren rock, even grass won't grow on most of it, and there are the slag heaps too" (158–9). The earthly model for Duncan's home asteroid is probably Sudbury, a northern Ontario mining town important in Atwood's formative years: "Sudbury was another magic place of my childhood. It was like interplanetary travel ... With its heaps of slag and its barren shoulders of stone, it looked like the moon" (Sullivan 27). For both author and character, the "magic" of such an austere locality resides in its remoteness from a cluttered, inventoried supermarket civilization.

Though he may be at best a "latent" lover, Duncan's ability to read Marian and to reorder her perceptual field makes him a uniquely valuable guide. Meeting her in her street clothes instead of her work attire, he says "I didn't place you at first. Without that official shell you look sort of – exposed" (101), intuiting the gap between Marian's hard occupational armour and her vulnerable core. Like her, he is beset by conundrums of perception and image. He confides that he has smashed the bathroom mirror with a frying pan: "I got tired of being afraid I'd walk in there some morning and wouldn't be able to see my own reflection in it" (153). What his "deviant" behaviour reveals is not at all, as his concerned room-mates think, his need of psychiatric help, but rather his awareness of the ego's frailty and malleability.

Laughter, here again, defines character. Where Peter's might be called the laughter of control, often triggered by mechanisms – cars, guns, cameras – Duncan's is the laughter of dispassionate critique. His characteristic response to what he finds absurd or pretentious is the subversive snicker. Thus, when Marian feebly remarks that being a graduate student in English would be "sort of exciting" he responds: "'Exciting.' He snickered briefly. 'I used to think that'" (104). He snickers most crushingly when he arrives at Marian and Peter's engagement party to find Marian bedecked in gaudy finery: "'You didn't tell me it was a masquerade,' he said at last. ... Duncan began to snicker. 'I like the ear-rings best,' he said, 'where did you dredge them up?'" (265). As T.D. McLulich observes, "Marian's [red] dress acts as an advertisement of her sexuality" (McCombs 187), and Duncan's role here, as usual, is that of adbuster, puncturing Marian's flaunting billboard facade. When she later turns up at the laundro-mat, he teasingly greets her as "the Scarlet Woman herself" (273); self-advertisement, he implies, is a mode of prostitution. When they seek out a hotel for their sexual tryst and are told by the clerk, eyeing Marian's attire, "it isn't that sort of place," Duncan snickers at her discomfiture (278), enjoying the salacious innuendo. Though he is no puritan, before having sex Duncan stipulates that Marian "peel that junk [her make-up] off your face" (280–1); he recoils from intimate contact with a promotional placard.

Peter's perceptions of Marian miniaturize her self-concept. When he proposes, she sees herself "small and oval, mirrored in his eyes" (89). Later, when they are dining out, "He was sizing her up as he would a new camera, trying to find the central complex of wheels and tiny mechanisms, the possible weak points, the kind of future performance to be expected: the springs of the machine" (165–6). Duncan's gaze has the reverse effect; he enlarges Marian's own perceptual lens, not through mechanical inventory but through empathy. When she exits an office party and takes refuge in the park near a concrete pool, a symbolically apt "*calm open eye* of silence" (189, emphasis added), she shows oddly little surprise at meeting Duncan, and he tells her that he has been expecting her. The two seem drawn together by an occult magnetism, a shared connoisseurship of open, unsponsored vistas.

Duncan unseals Marian's eyes to prospects beyond homogenizing surveys and self-promoting masquerades. She has begun to fear that she is turning into a zombie-like consumer: "These days, if she wasn't careful, she found herself pushing the [supermarket] cart like a somnambulist, eyes fixed, swaying slightly, her hands twitching with the impulse to reach out and grab anything with a bright label" (190–1). She intuits that it is "dangerous to stay in the supermarket too long. One of these days it would get her. She would be trapped past closing time, and they would find her in the morning propped against one of the shelves, in an unbreakable coma" (193). Her dread of retail narcolepsy extends to other areas of her life – above all, her personal relationships – that demand reflexive acceptance of the "products" on offer. But she discovers another, liberating space when Duncan escorts her to the museum. "'Come on,' Duncan said, almost in a whisper. 'I'll show you my favourite things'" (202). He conducts her reverently to his "favourite mummy case" (206): "Marian looked through the glass at the painted golden face. The stylized eyes, edged with dark-blue lines, were wide open. They gazed up at her with an expression of serene vacancy" (206). Marian's stance here is far removed from that of the comatose supermarket browser or that of the cosmeticized idol with "the Egyptian-lidded and outlined and thickly-fringed eyes" that Ainsley assembles. What Marian confronts here is not an array of ephemeral goods on a shelf but the gaze of the immemorial past. She experiences a sudden shock of recognition utterly foreign to her workaday experiences.

Another outing further extends Marian's perceptual scope. Here, Duncan accompanies her on an "escape" to his pet city ravine, a site that "provides an ideal realistic-yet-symbolic setting for Marian's final and decisive lesson from her mentor" (Keith 58). (The "lesson" gains additional force from the site's contrast with the enclosed urban spaces favoured by Peter.) Like the museum, the ravine is a locale long cherished by Duncan, though now threatened by the detritus of the throw-away supermarket society: "They're beginning to fill this place up with junk too, you know, beginning with the creek. I wonder why they like throwing things around all over the landscape ... old tires, tin cans" (290). Eerily, Duncan's voice comes "as though from nowhere," as if from the genius of the place itself. "They tell me I live in a world of fantasies," Duncan confides. "But at least mine are more or less my own" (292). "They" may be room-mates or else the chorus of "serious" people like the aspiring lawyer Peter. It is the poet's prerogative to dwell with dreams that are improvised and marginal instead of mass-produced and mass-marketed. The ravine is Duncan's advertisement-free, life-enhancing theatre of imagination, and for Marian too it becomes a place of perceptual liberation.

Meanwhile, in the all too solid world of shelves and supermarkets Marian flirts with literal starvation. While her behaviour may appear erratic, it makes sense that a woman whose engagement and whose job both weld her to commodity culture should be driven to reject consumption *tout court*. As Kilbourne observes, "While men are encouraged to fall in love with their cars, women are more often invited to have a romance, indeed an erotic experience, with some-thing even closer to home, something that truly does pump the valves of their hearts – the food we eat" (108). (One television commercial Kilbourne cites urges women: "Bake a Comstock pie ... they'll love you for it" (109).) Marian's growing revulsion from her erotic rela-tionship with Peter takes its toll on her relationship with food. Figuratively speaking, her fiancé has regarded her all along as a Comstock consumable. As Lears points out, such a construction of femininity has a lengthy history: "The newer corporate advertising contained almost nothing but sweet young things." Lears quotes one *Printers' Ink* contributor who in 1909 endorsed the suitability of such "pretty girl advertising" to products like candy: "Woman is in her realm here and her smiling countenance will at once give the impression of a sweet, delicate, pure, dainty, luscious and winning bonbon" (187). Someone made to feel like a bonbon may show a natural aversion to the act of eating. After the omnivorous Peter exits the scene, Marian's own appetite magically revives.

Duncan's relation to Marian has been at bottom prosthetic; he acts as a psychological crutch or, better, as a lens through which to see more widely and sharply. The function of the cake Marian bakes is instead emetic: it enacts a catharsis of her own constructed, etiolated image. With its red tinge recalling Marian's "masquerade" dress, the cake is, as Lauber notes, "a caricature of Marian at her most artificial, as she prepared herself for the party" (Moss 28). It is a parodic advertisement of Marian's laboriously fabricated sex appeal. By baking, eating, and sharing it she celebrates a communal rite of self-purgation, a culinary bonfire of vanities.

At the end of the novel Duncan tells Marian: "[Y]ou're back to so-called reality, you're a consumer" (311). This is literally true. As Keith says, "[L]ife, like politics, is the art of the possible, and ... if one is to live in a society at all, compromises are inevitable" (68). And yet such compromises derive their character from the nature of the society in which they occur, and some are bound to be more palatable than others. Marian may be back to "so-called reality," but she still must face the dilemma of how to live in a consumer society without being herself consumed – how to negotiate a world of advertisement without becoming a billboard for herself. One can see this as a curious premonition of the dilemmas Atwood herself has had to face as a literary celebrity, though the twenty-something Atwood who wrote the novel could hardly have foreseen this irony. Like Christopher Morley in a prior generation, Atwood has been extensively involved in the promotion of her own work, and she has increasingly relied upon the resources of modern technology for that purpose.[6] (In a recent interview, speaking of the pressures placed on authors by new media like Facebook and Twitter, Atwood has said: "The term 'relentless self-promoter' used to be an insult in publishing circles. Now it will be a necessity" (Adams, *Globe and Mail*).)

Yet even amid the promotional whirl, Atwood has, like Marian in her more private sphere, striven to preserve her own integrity. What is more, she has never forgotten the ironic disparity between the lives of women as they are blazoned in ads and the unsung, unglamorous reality. As recently as 2006, in a poem from her collection *The Tent* sardonically entitled "Bring Back Mom: An Invocation," she conjures up a retrospective vision of

> Mom, her dark lipsticked mouth
> smiling in the black-and-white
> soap ads, the Aspirin ads, the toilet paper ads,
> Mom, with her secret life
> of headaches and stained washing
> and irritated membranes –
> Mom, who knew the dirt,
> and hid the dirt, and did the dirty work,
> and never saw herself
> or us as clean enough. (107)

The lines could be read as an inverted prophecy of the life Marian has avoided by renouncing marriage with a soap-scented, monocular Hathaway man.

In a 1976 interview with Linda Sandler, Atwood says, "The tone of *The Edible Woman* is lighthearted, but in the end it's more pessimistic than *Surfacing*. The difference between them is that *The Edible Woman* is a circle and *Surfacing* is a spiral ... the heroine of *Surfacing* does not end where she began" (*Conversations* 45). One can grant that *The Edible Woman*, however comic in tone, projects a darkly disenchanted vision of a woman's life in the modern consumer society. But is Marian helplessly caught in a circle game? Elsewhere, in an interview for the *Guardian*, Atwood has said that "[t]he book is about someone who does not know what to do with her life" (quoted Sullivan 241). Atwood's characterization of her protagonist accurately describes her disorientation throughout much of the narrative, but it overlooks her state of mind at the end. Marian will still make purchases at the supermarket, surveys will still get conducted (though not by her), magazine ads and TV commercials will still saturate the environment, while junk of a more concrete sort will still choke Duncan's precious ravine. And yet the conclusion leaves Marian not back at square one but, arguably, at square one-point-five. She has gained knowledge of what *not* to do with her life or allow others to do with it. Her wariness vis-à-vis advertising and its correlative values has a more credible basis than the tergiversations of the leading men of *The Hucksters* and *Aurora Dawn*. In "Notes Towards a Poem That Can Never Be Written" Atwood identifies as an arduous but inescapable poetic imperative "To see clearly and without flinching/without turning away" (*Selected Poems* 265). By the end of her not-quite-closed spiral orbit Marian has made detectable progress toward lucid, unflinching, unsponsored seeing.

6

Creative Creatives: Blake Morrison's *South of the River* and Joshua Ferris's *Then We Came to the End*

The decades following Atwood's *The Edible Woman* did not transform the essential nature of promotional culture. Influenced by the groundbreaking Doyle Dane Bernbach campaigns for Volkswagen, mentioned in chapter 1, advertisements in general tended to become more sophisticated in their approach, a fact sometimes reflected in fictional representations of the industry. A television commercial like the mid-sixties spot publicizing Benson and Hedges 101 millimeter cigarettes – "A silly millimeter longer" – could entertain with its witty self-mockery. The wit, admittedly, did not render the product marketed any less hazardous to users' health.

Beyond this increasing self-consciousness, the period witnessed another development of great consequence: an exponential growth of promotional culture's magnitude and diffusion. As Stuart Ewen comments, "In the 1980s, commercialism mushroomed into a vehement global religion. Where advertising once inhabited circumscribed arenas – television, radio, newspapers, magazines, billboards – today nearly every moment of human attention is converted into an occasion for a sales pitch, while notions of the public interest and noncommercial arenas of expression are under assault" ("Memoirs" 447). Two accomplished novels published in 2007, Blake Morrison's *South of the River* and Joshua Ferris's *Then We Came to the End*, bear the impress of this promotional deluge. The novels are set on opposite sides of the Atlantic, Morrison's in Britain and Ferris's in the United States, but their main concerns overlap. Both investigate advertising as a livelihood and illuminate the frustrations and rewards such employment brings to its practitioners. Both adopt a nuanced approach to the evocation of character, avoiding the

overheated melodrama of popular treatments of the industry like
The Hucksters. Finally, both show advertising personnel conducting
business as usual, and yet both convey an ominous sense of the
unusual; of things coming, in Ferris's phrase, to an end.

One cause for growing literary interest in the life-experiences of
promotional workers derives from the sheer fact of numbers. Wells's
depiction of Uncle Teddy Ponderevo as a lone wolf of mass marketing is exaggerated for dramatic effect, but in turn-of-the-twentieth-
century Britain the ranks of such pioneers were sparse enough to
make the portrait credible. Recent figures, however, bear out Ewen's
claim of rampant growth. According to the US Bureau of Labor
Statistics, in 2012 the number of Americans employed in advertising,
public relations, and related services was more than 430,000. A
2011 report places the number so employed in Britain at more than
120,000, not counting "just under 164,000 employees who consider
themselves to be undertaking advertising type jobs outside of the
advertising industry itself" (*The Contribution of Advertising to the
UK Economy*). Such figures explain why writers might wish to
explore the subjectivities of advertising's many servitors, not to mention the impact of such a "vehement global religion" on society as
a whole. An issue probed by both writers is whether this form of
employment, along with the imaginative flair it entails, can legiti-
mately be called "creative." Neither of the two novels attempts to
settle this question definitively; both balance indulgence against
sceptical critique.

Libby Raven, a central figure in *South of the River*, is a well-paid
executive in a London advertising agency whose work affords her
much satisfaction but who nevertheless undergoes severe stress from
the combined pressures of her job and marriage. Morrison's novel
and Ferris's alike present lives lived on the edge of desperation; in
both, the action gravitates toward crises of depletion and dispersal.
By the end of *South of the River* three of the five major actors have
either left England or are about to do so. Libby and her friend Harry
are both off to the United States, she to amplify her agency's operations, he to take a promising job in local broadcasting. Anthea,
Libby's ex-husband Nat's ex-lover ("ex"s proliferate here), is guiding the humanitarian efforts of aid workers in the Third World. Nat's
uncle Jack Raven, an elderly and disaffected provincial businessman,

is straying in an unfamiliar London neighbourhood, suspended in a haze of disorientation. Only to Nat does England appear to offer promise, yet Nat, who has long nursed ambitions to write for the stage, is by now an ex-playwright and must settle for a routine if comfortable job as a college teacher. By the end of *Then We Came to the End* most of the characters are still in the city, Chicago, where they start out, but they have almost all left the struggling advertising agency that has been their home base, most through dismissal – or, as the colourful trade patois has it, being obliged to "walk Spanish down the hall." Lynn Mason, the formidable chief of agency operations, has succumbed to cancer. Here too, one encounters an oppressive sense of diminishment and closure.

In both books, as in Orwell and Atwood, the cause of literary art is posed against the more remunerative calling of commercial copywriting. The French theorist Pierre Bourdieu's frequently cited distinction between economic capital and cultural capital is relevant to this contest. According to Bourdieu, the relations between the two species of capital are too complex to be expressed as an absolute either/or polarity: "Because the fields of cultural production are universes of belief which can only function in so far as they succeed in simultaneously producing products and the need for those products through processes which are the denial of the ordinary practices of the 'economy', the struggles which take place within them are ultimate conflicts involving the whole relation to the 'economy'" (82). Bourdieu is referring specifically to the "disinterested" production of works of "high" culture, literary or artistic, as distinct from frankly commercial works aiming at mass sales. But the distinction can also be applied to the sphere of advertising, which affirms rather than denies "the ordinary practices of the economy" but which also obviously endeavours to "produce a need" both for itself and for the products promoted. As the choral narrator of *Then We Came to the End* declares, "We informed you in six seconds that you needed something you didn't know you lacked. We made you want anything that anyone willing to pay us wanted you to want. We were the hired guns of the human soul" (234). This sounds more like the idiom of underworld extortion than staid commercial discourse. Yet since the manufacturing of desire is a feature of both the artistic "upper" world and the promotional "under" world, the two realms share appreciable common ground.

Both novels are permeated by confusion and conflict, elements that become identified both with promotional and with literary endeavour. Three of the five focal characters in *South of the River* (Nat, Anthea, and Harry) engage in writing either as a vocation or an avocation; all three have abandoned it by the end in favour of other pursuits. In *Then We Came to the End* a number of the characters are so-called "creatives" (copywriters or graphic designers), and some practise freelance writing on the side. Of these, only Hank Neary ("our own poetaster" (68)) succeeds in producing a published work. Neither book could be called a polemical exposé of advertising as a controlling force in modern society. While neither takes a blandly uncritical stance, overall both acknowledge the industry as an inextricable thread in the fabric of contemporary life and both depict work in the industry as at least fitfully rewarding. In *Then We Came to the End* the narrator concedes that "buried beneath all the bitching, there were parts of the job we loved" (359). If the job involves absurdities, that fact only confirms its congruence with an absurd surrounding universe. (The list of "some of Joshua Ferris's favourite books" appended to the paper edition of the novel includes Samuel Beckett's absurdist trilogy.) Oddly, reviews of both books seldom identify their treatment of advertising as a key narrative strand; they tend instead to see the characters' activities simply as generic specimens of life in the contemporary business milieu.

Important managerial figures in both novels – Libby Raven in Morrison, Lynn Mason in Ferris – are female. This represents a striking shift from the gender-specific, "layer-cake" hierarchy of Marian MacAlpin's workplace. By the early years of the twenty-first century such highly placed female operatives had become much less of an anomaly than in Marian's day. Nevertheless, Libby and Lynn alike still have to contend with patriarchal friction both in their professional and in their personal lives. Simone Davis notes the psychological repercussions of the adjustment in the profession's gender balance: "When women began to generate advertisements, the men in their midst seem to have often grown nervous, wary of the threat leveled against [the] extremely gendered [female]-sucker-and-the-salesman model that helped organize their world" (81). Libby, as accounts manager, is advised by her firm's "new Creative guru" (24), the Australian Greg Grosz, that "[a] good ad grabs you by the balls but a great ad gives you a blow-job as well" (28), a sentiment in keeping with his surname. Little wonder if she says – of course, to herself – "God, these male egos" (28).

Libby's husband Nat, an unproduced playwright with a sizable male ego, is convinced that he is himself creative and his wife uncreative, merely a drudge grubbing for money. "Libby's horizons were horribly narrow these days" (22), he smugly reflects. "Like Harry, churning out copy for the local newspaper, she had sold her soul to Mammon. … [I]t wasn't their fault that they lacked creativity. But both were morally the worse for *ware*" (22, emphasis in original). The spavined pun neatly captures Nat's self-righteous condescension toward those "uncreative" souls befouling themselves in "trade." Nat views his own playwriting as exalted above such dross, which contaminates even high-minded scholarly work: "Less gifted colleagues used their days for academic research. Nat was a creator" (18). In Bourdieu's terms, Libby's work may bring in economic capital (which incidentally supports the family) but Nat's accumulates cultural capital. Nat lives, that is, in what Bourdieu calls an "upside-down economic world" (40) according to which financial success is failure and failure success. "Nat had always defined [success] inversely: if a book was a best-seller, it couldn't be worth reading; if a record was a hit, it couldn't be worth listening to; if a film made millions at the box office, it couldn't be worth watching. This aesthetic allowed him a happy coexistence with failure" (22). (As Bourdieu notes dryly, "The literary and artistic world is so ordered that those who enter it have an interest in disinterestedness" (40).)

Libby has been habituated to deprecate her personal career interests and to accept her husband's literary dabbling at his own heady valuation: "I'm not supposed to be the creative one" (73). She has internalized the notion that her work bears the stigma of base profit seeking; indeed, her marriage functions to offset her imputed inferiority. "He was her bit of culture, to show off to friends. Hey look, I'm not as shallow as a career in advertising would suggest, my husband is an intellectual, a writer, teacher and thinker – that's what his presence allowed her to say" (139). Nat's distaste for her calling, however, shades into a rude assault on her worth as a person: "She knew he thought adverts a waste of space – dead matter on arts pages which could more profitably be filled by an article on neglected British playwrights, or one particular neglected British playwright – but he shouldn't treat her as a waste of space, too" (84–5). She privately begins to challenge her husband's contempt for her job: "But she was creative. She had good ideas" (73). At last, after stumbling

upon her husband's extramarital affair, she has a "revelation," which
"came to her driving home through the Blackwall Tunnel in the new
Mercedes, and was as cataclysmic – and liberating – as his infidelity.
'Nat's uncreative,' she thought, then said it aloud, laughing, 'Nat's
uncreative,' then let it echo through the subterranean traffic-roar:
'Uncreative. Uncreative. Uncreative'" (257–8). It is a long-postponed,
comic moment of clairvoyance among the exhaust fumes: Nat,
whose desultory scribbling is narrowly self-indulgent, lacks any real
imaginative spark. The tendency of Morrison's novel is to reshuffle
Bourdieu's taxonomy: the "shallow" woman whose achievements
could strictly be classed as "mercenary" (and who drives a damningly opulent car) brings more true inventiveness to her work than
her self-important "disinterested" mate. One must credit Morrison
with impressive broad-mindedness in not reserving to his own métier
of literary writing a monopoly on creative distinction.

Much about Libby's career trajectory belies the "worse for *ware*"
stigma often associated with advertising in popular discourse, or in
best sellers like *The Hucksters* and *Aurora Dawn*. She gamely abandons her limiting job as salaried manager to set up her own agency,
where her entrepreneurial panache has more scope. She introduces
Nat's Uncle Jack, whose power mower business is sputtering, to
more efficient ways of marketing his product, including rebranding
through a timely change of name. Her campaign revives Jack's fortunes along with Jack himself, lonely and adrift since the loss of his
wife. Nat, by contrast, retreats further into narcissism, alcohol, and
his infatuation with Anthea, herself drifting from one disappointing
short-term job to another while struggling to get her own idiosyncratic writings published.

Where Libby's career provokes second thoughts about the imputed
venality of advertising, Anthea's trials as an aspiring writer unmask
the dark commercial underside of "high-minded" literary pursuits,
an insight that Bourdieu, again, would applaud. An old friend of
Nat's named Mike, a publisher, agrees to consider Anthea's collection of stories, entitled "Foxed." She is at length invited to lunch by
Mike's young colleague, Colin, whose sole interest (apart from luring Anthea into bed) turns out to be "puffing" books and authors. To
Anthea's chagrin, he proposes rebranding her collection by changing
the title to "Foxy," which he deems "more selling" (224). The publishing opportunity fizzles, but Anthea afterwards reflects ruefully,
"Thanks to Mike, she had avoided becoming a widget in a fiction

factory – a package, a product, a consumer commodity" (225). It dawns on her that, at least in the current English scene, there may be no such thing as unsullied cultural production for its own sake. Though she remains unpublished, she at least escapes turning into an edible author.

By setting Libby's solid accomplishments off against the literary dabblings of Nat and Anthea, *South of the River* suggests a hetero-dox idea: it is myopic to scorn promotional work as necessarily a distasteful prostituting of talent. This is not to say, however, that Morrison presents advertising in an unproblematic light. Some of the ads that Libby's agency produces stir tremors of distinct unease, like one for a beer unhappily named Raanch:

> The poster showed a black man's torso, rear-on, naked from butt to shoulder, with a woman's white hand curling round his waist, her fingernails painted silver, and the slogan: "For a cooler pull, try Raanch." Here's a stylish, multi-ethnic, post-macho lager, the subtext went, a better bet for attracting women than your lad-dish swill. The Raanch people loved the roughs and green-lighted the shoot, but Libby had argued with Tarquin [the ad's designer] about the positioning of the woman's hand on the man's torso: how obvious did it have to be that she was reaching upwards; that her head (half hidden from view) was level with his groin; that she was giving him a blow job? (287–8)

According to her quondam colleague Greg's criterion ("a great ad gives you a blow job"), the Raanch spread qualifies as great in the most palpable sense, but it makes even the tolerant Libby blench. By comparison, the macho lumberjack pitch used to sell Moose Beer in *The Edible Woman* – "Tang of the Wilderness" and so on – begins to look downright elegant.

A postmarital involvement more subtly focuses the troubled inter-play in Libby's life between the personal and the promotional. At her previous agency she has struck up a friendship with a young copy-writer, Damian, which later blossoms into an affair. Although the liaison flourishes for a time, it crashes noisily when it runs afoul of Damian's self-promoting manoeuvres. When he asks her to come to dinner to meet a Milanese businessman and his wife, a potential plum account, Libby begins to suspect that her value to her lover owes less to her personal charms than to the professional boost he stands to gain from them. Ironically, Libby finds herself serving as a poster girl in aid of promotion, a mode of careerist game playing uncomfortably akin to her own artifices as an ambitious "creative." "It was only after he dropped her, a judicious three doors up from [her] house, that she felt manipulated. How could she possibly have agreed to cook?" (348).

The crisis of the relationship occurs during the dinner party, when Damian learns from a phone call the news of Libby's mother's death but, to avoid fumbling a business coup, delays informing Libby until the Milanese have left. His cold-bloodedness prompts Libby, afterwards, to make a call to the Italian tycoon intimating Damian's behaviour and her own resentment, thereby spiking the deal. ("It was a gamble. But not much of one" (444).) The subterfuge seems warranted by the facts of the case; still, such moves and counter-moves transmit an unsavoury sense of advertising in general as a dog-eat-dog scramble. The narrative structure, featuring five inter-related but distinct centres of consciousness, imposes a further damaging perspective on the occupational straits Libby must navigate. Anthea, who, by comparison, has seemed drifting and naïve, by the end finds her true calling in helping to serve the needs of vulnerable civilians in a Third World war zone, while incurring serious hardship and risk. The contrast with her gallantry may not quite put Libby's world of advertising to shame, but it confers little glory.

Watching football on television late one night, a downhearted Jack Raven muses, "England would lose in the end. Defeat was the English condition" (178). While this may sound like the defeatist grumbling of a cranky, aging traditionalist, the surrounding action of *South of the River* reinforces the sense of a nation "going south." Anthea fears that prolonging her relationship with Nat will cause her to "dribble [her] life away in boring old England" (183). Only far from home, in a war torn country, does she achieve an exhilarating sense of personal mission: "She had a job to do" (455). As for Libby, even though her new agency is thriving, her urge to find horizons more ample than "boring old England" can offer impels her to broaden her business, and conceivably her life, by journeying to the United States. Unfortunately, to judge from the panorama offered by Joshua Ferris's *Then We Came to the End* such emigrant hopes risk being ill founded; defeat may reveal itself to be as much the American condition as the English.

In Ferris's aptly titled *Then We Came to the End*, advertising confronts mortality and loses. The quiet desperation of Ferris's agency people is summed up by the bizarre in-house ritual they perform with the firm's office chairs, one that involves filching a colleague's chair, then rushing frantically to replace it in dread that management may possess esoteric means of detection. It seems a purely farcical, aimless routine, but the farce has a portentous symbolic dimension. It mimics the frantic vying for status that prevails in the workplace, as well as the hectic competition for consumer goods that obtains in society at large – a competition the labours of the admen and women are meant to exacerbate. What Jean Baudrillard says about the tensions besetting modern urban spaces is exemplified by Ferris's Chicago and particularly by the chair thievery: "[T]he *language of cities* is competition itself. Motives, desires, encounters, stimuli, the endless judgements of others, continual eroticization, information, the appeals of advertising: all these things make up a kind of abstract destiny of collective participation, set against a real background of generalized competition" (65, emphasis in original).

The clash Baudrillard detects between collective participation and generalized competition is enacted in the daily routines of Ferris's agency people. For some, the tension proves too great to bear. After being pink-slipped Chris Yop disassembles his (or possibly a colleague's) chair and hurls the components, one by one, into Lake Michigan as a symbolic rejection of the rat race. Meanwhile Yop's office mates live in dread of the vengeful return of another released employee, the volatile Tom Mota, to spray everyone in sight with bullets. Yet this particular terror dissolves into slapstick; when Tom does run amok, the "bullets" he sprays turn out to be messy but harmless paintballs.

As Tom clamorously proclaims, the spirit pervading this workplace is disintegrative. While "shooting" his paint bullets he intones a mantra about the business which runs in part: "I content myself with the fact that the general system of our trade ... is a system of selfishness ... is not dictated by the high sentiments of human nature ... much less by the sentiments of love and heroism ... but is a system of distrust" (323). Although Tom is prone to acrid cynicism, and although his outbursts punctuate a scene of knockabout mayhem, his words need to be taken seriously. The smallest actions of the novel's characters, down to the obsessive chair theft, support his

jeremiad against the "system of distrust." Even Joe Pope, an out-
standingly level-headed employee, makes sure always to lock his
bicycle when he brings it to work (69).

One might expect Ferris's unorthodox use of the collective "we"
narrator to offset this social fragmentation by expressing the group's
solidarity, but its practical effect is the opposite: to accentuate the
dissonance between comradeship and competition. As Ferris avows,
his purpose is to trouble any benign promotional vision of corporate
amity; the novel "returns the 'we' to the individuals who embody it,
people with anger-management issues and bills to pay, instead of
letting the 'mystic we' live on unperturbed in the magic land promoted by billboards and boardrooms" ("A conversation with Joshua
Ferris" 5). When the economic downturn duly arrives, the "magic"
fades to dust. Ironically, what the collective voice for the most part
projects is not consensus but contention, at times heated. This has
little to do with the homespun ethos of individualism championed
by Tom's heroes Emerson and Whitman and nostalgically invoked
by Tom himself. (As Tom bitterly observes, "Those two fucks
wouldn't have lasted two minutes in this place" (86).)[1]

The choral voice is too splintered to engage with another, contrary national strain, the collective expression of common cause.
Foundational documents like the Declaration of Independence ("We
hold these truths to be self-evident") and the Preamble to the Con-
stitution ("We the people of the United States") speak gravely in the
first person plural, but in Ferris's novel the corporate voice is undercut by the characters' segregation within separate cubicles and their
similarly compartmentalized psychic spaces. All the employees live
in dread of being made to "walk Spanish down the hall" – by defini-
tion a solo rather than a collective act – if only as a consequence of
having a purloined chair tracked down. "I've been on *eggshells*
since the input yesterday," a distraught Marcia Dwyer confesses.
"Because *I'm* the one who took Tom Mota's chair" (107, emphasis
in original).

Even Lynn Mason, the redoubtable agency chief, the sole character to be accorded a singular point-of-view and the sole firm member
exempt from the dread of dismissal, is shadowed by fear, though of
a different and gender specific sort: her breast cancer diagnosis and
her scheduling for a mastectomy. Yet as even she acknowledges, her
professional life is itself founded on the inculcation of fear. When her

lawyer boyfriend Martin leaves a voice message wondering how a person with her intelligence can put off consulting a physician, she speaks a plaintive imaginary monologue into the telephone receiver:

"That's because ... intelligent people are not *always* guided by their intelligence. Sometimes, Martin, something called fear is a little more powerful." He would know that basic fact of human psychology, she thought, if he were in marketing, but as a practitioner of the law, he believed that the decision that was most rational, or at least most shrewd, would always triumph if it determined one's own self-survival. (212, emphasis in original)

The cunning use of advertising to implant irrational fear in a susceptible public is a familiar enough stratagem; in her professional tactics Lynn has simply been following standard industry practise. Yet it is a poignant irony that such a masterly orchestrator of fear cannot herself resist the irrationality she exploits routinely in others. Much of the brilliance of Ferris's novel stems from its adroitness in highlighting the subtle filaments linking promotional work and personal vulnerability.

But if fear is her vocational stock-in-trade, there are limits to the fear mongering Lynn will countenance. When Karen Woo, an office go-getter, is directed to redesign the packaging for a box of cookies to emphasize the product's nutritional value, she adds the notation "o g of Lastive Acid" (48). To her colleague Jim Jackers's query "What's lastive acid?" Karen replies evasively "Not something you want in your body" (48). In reality Jim has no lastive acid in his body nor has anyone else; Karen has invented the toxin out of thin air. It is an age-old promotional dodge, recalling the "pedic perspiration" scam performed by Orwell's New Albion agency, but it is one that Lynn firmly vetoes. The choral narrator comments admiringly: "It was this sort of thing that showed us how Lynn had developed over the years a moral principle that guided her in the practice of advertising, which she abided by with strict authority. We respected her for it and wanted to live up to those high standards" (50). While there is no reason to challenge this estimate – Lynn is clearly a "good" advertising boss by prevailing norms – the tone of the testimonial betrays the indeterminacy often lurking between the assured lines of Ferris's prose. What, after all, has Karen Woo done but take to its logical extreme the cultivation of groundless fear that Lynn herself sees as key to her agency's success? "I was trying to think out of the box," Karen righteously protests (49).

Karen may be thinking too far out of the box, but she is plainly responding to the perpetual need of the "creative" staff to be, in fact, creative. Like Morrison's, Ferris's novel insistently raises the question of "creativity" as an integral part of advertising. What is it, exactly, that is being created? How far does it coincide with accepted ideas of valuable imaginative production? When Jim Jaggers phones his shrewd Great-Uncle Max on his Iowa farm to get hints for a snappy slogan for a printer cartridge, Max proffers the headline "A Great Writer Needs a Great Ink Cartridge." Jim pays him a respectful compliment:

"You should have been a creative."
"A creative?" said Max.
Jim explained that in the advertising industry, art directors and copywriters were called *creatives*.
"That's the stupidest use of an English word I ever encountered," said Max. (188)

Soon after, with malice aforethought, Max returns Jim's call:

"You folks over there," said Max, "you say you call yourselves *creatives*, is that what you're telling me? And the work you do, you call that *the creative*, is that what you said?" Jim said that was correct. "And I suppose you think of yourselves as pretty creative over there, I bet."
"I suppose so," said Jim, wondering what Max was driving at.
"And the work you do, you probably think that's pretty creative work."
"What are you asking me, Uncle Max?"
"Well, if all that's true," said the old man, "that would make you creative creatives creating creative creative." (189)

Max's mocking redundancies threaten to undermine the industry's fondest pretensions; one begins to wonder whether even the invention of, say, the agency's flagship "Cold Sore Guy" ad properly qualifies as a gem of creative inspiration. What the echolalia evokes is, rather, a league of juvenile narcissists infatuated with their own cleverness.

Many of the day-to-day tasks performed by Jim and his colleagues seem less like masterworks of creativity than exercises in futility; the accumulated "useless shit" they haul away with them when they walk Spanish down the hall seems to sum up the worth of their labours, possibly even of their lives. Some, like Karen Woo, manifest few qualms, but others, like Carl Garbedian, are nagged by a haunting sense of triviality. Carl feels shamed by the painful contrast between his trifling as a "creative creative" and his wife Marilynn's literally lifesaving work as a surgeon. Marilynn, like Morrison's rehabilitated drifter, Anthea, has "a job to do" (238), one that places Carl's task in a cruelly demeaning perspective. And yet the "creative" elements that infuse the efforts of Carl and the others do appear to involve a substantial measure of inventiveness. The novel is the site of complex negotiations between the claims of diverse species of capital: the economic and the cultural.

At worst, advertising in *Then We Came to the End* can seem an affront to minimal standards of decency. This applies even to the well-meant billboard publicizing the disappearance of the young daughter of another employee, Janine Gorjanc, an ad thoughtlessly left up long after the girl's lifeless body has been retrieved. The billboard, which the grieving mother must pass on her daily commute, is bad enough in itself, but it becomes an insult added to a thoughtless injury: her colleagues' prurient eagerness to divine the reason for her haunting of a local McDonalds play area. (The behaviour is at length explained as the woman's sad, makeshift expedient for mourning her daughter's loss.) It is the dissident Tom Mota who launches a campaign to get the offending sign removed. Tom remonstrates with one of the firm's media buyers, Jane Trimble: "'He's got to take that goddamn billboard down,' he said to her after walking into her office without a knock or a greeting. Unfortunately Jane knew just what he was referring to: the vendor with whom she had placed the order" (98–9). Tom's compassionate efforts are thwarted by the inviolable logic of business: "The vendor might have taken a hit on the rental fee but to rent it at all was likely a great boon to him, and he probably never had a client complain about continued exposure after the lease expired. Free advertising – who could complain about that?" (99). To adepts of the trade the question may seem rhetorical, but not to Tom, who goes on complaining – "complained so much that Jane had to get on the phone with the vendor and complain. When she got off the phone with the vendor, Jane

called Lynn Mason to complain about Tom Mota – just one more
complaint that must have contributed to his eventual termination"
(100). The clash stages a pivotal confrontation of values, exposing
the grating discord between personal sensitivity and promotional
logic. Too active a concern for the feelings of one's coworkers spells
one's dismissal from their ranks.

Finally, in an epic small-hours sortie Tom drives to the remote
billboard, intrepidly scales its rickety ladder and obliterates the
image of the by now long-dead child, supplementing paint rollers
with his talismanic paintball gun: "[H]e walked back and forth
along the planks loading and shooting, covering over the dead girl's
image one bitter blot at a time, because his complaints to Jane
Trimble had gotten him nowhere – and because in conversation the
previous morning, Janine had said she couldn't bear to look at it one
day longer" (132). Tom's guerrilla assault on publicity, by trade
norms an egregious sin, is by more humane standards as close to a
heroic act as anything any of Ferris's people manage to accomplish.

Such literal adbusting exposes the meanness of the agency ethos
by impudently transgressing it. And yet, whatever the moral deficiencies of the business routine, there is enjoyment to be derived
from the daily desultory camaraderie, even from the dreaming up of
sales gimmicks. As Ferris says in "A conversation," "Ad agencies can
be a lot of fun. Creative departments are full of toys and games and
wacky surprises, and throwing a Nerf football down the hallway to
release tension isn't immediate cause for walking papers" (3). If the
"fun" here sounds juvenile, the novel itself gestures toward more
solid sources of shared *jouissance*. "[W]hile it lasted, work was a
well-spring, a real source of light, the nurture of a beloved community" (21). More than anyone else it is the dedicated Lynn who seeks
in her work the pathway to fulfillment. Urging her trusted assistant,
Joe Pope, to help her win some major new accounts, she tells him:
"This is it, Joe. This is my life" (319). Like Libby in *South of the
River* she is that still uncommon figure, a woman who has risen to a
prestigious position in the advertising hierarchy. As Joe quietly
assures her, "You've worked hard" (319).

It may be that Lynn has worked too hard; again like Libby she
cannot escape being a "driven woman." She asks Joe pathetically,
"But what am I missing? What have I missed?" (319). The question
resonates grimly now that she is prey to a life-threatening illness,
and her own response is weirdly configured by the professional

straitjacket that binds her. Ferris chooses to explore her subjectivity in greater depth than he accords to any of the other characters, and the result is a remarkable feat of empathy. But what is most distinctive about this psychological profile is the way in which it is governed by promotional pressures. To solace herself Lynn hits on the scheme of a pro bono campaign to promote a fictitious charity for breast cancer research, thus converting real private anguish to fantasized public service. In Bourdieu's terms, the process involves the translating of economic capital (commercial advertising) into symbolic capital, here of a private rather than artistic type. The same is true of the outlandish twist Lynn adds to the faux campaign, aimed at extracting humour from the gloom of acute illness. One employee, Genevieve Latko-Devine, raises a logical objection: "The point I'm trying to make ... is that there is really very little humor in a diagnosis of cancer. And what humor there is, is humorous only in the context of a whole lot of sadness" (184). Even the usually loyal Joe concurs: "'Make the cancer patient laugh,' he said, and his voice got quiet. 'Isn't this assignment a little screwy?'" (185). Carl Garbedian, himself no stranger to mental stress, attempts a snap psychoanalysis of Lynn's "screwiness": "He wanted to claim that Lynn had made up the assignment because Lynn's life was so much about marketing, the only way she could come to terms with her diagnosis was to see it presented to her in an ad. In a time of personal upheaval she fell back on the familiar language of advertising. She had to have it sold to her" (247). Owing to Carl's own record of instability, his coworkers hasten "to distance ourselves from that theory" (247), but their sceptical reaction is itself unconvincing. It smacks of denial, a refusal to confront what Carl has grasped: the hold the industry they serve exerts over Lynn's psyche and, for that matter, their own. The whole situation exposes the abject inadequacy of "marketing" to deal with ultimate issues of life and death.

Lynn's thinking cannot escape the consumerist maze that is the site of her life's work. A riveting episode is her hysterical breakdown in a department store fitting room where she tries to select a bra to wear to her surgery. The mountain of lingerie taunts her, mordantly reminding her of the limitless consumerist abundance upon which her career is predicated:

This is what makes the country great, isn't it? And it's what's made her life in advertising possible, the opportunity afforded by this glut to market one particular offering in a way that allows it to stand alone as the leader in the marketplace. She would know exactly what to do with any one of these brands, if they were fortunate enough to win that account. (210)

Here, in a scene that clinches Carl's "eccentric" theory ("In a time of personal upheaval she fell back on the familiar language of advertising"), Lynn strives to recast her sad task of bra selection as a marketing initiative, but all her selling expertise cannot blunt her dread of surgical mutilation. A line like "This is what makes the country great, isn't it?" strikes a note of bleak irony, casting doubt not just on Lynn's mental balance but on the sanity of the whole American consumerist project. Her life-options boil down, miserably, to a "choice" between Bra Brand A and Bra Brand B. "Picking the one bra in this haystack of bras that will define where they make the incision and that will, somehow, when all this is over, make her feel sexy again – even she admits there's not likely to be one bra here that can fill an order like that" (210).

The overall effect of this surrealistic episode is to transmit an image of the American marketplace as nightmare.[2] In a stifling cubicle (recalling her agency's meagre workspaces) jammed with a mountain of figure-flattering lingerie, the normally controlled and controlling manager yields to panic: "She's in the tiny dressing room with a thousand bras screaming as loud as she can. It sounds like AAAAAAAAARRRRRRRRRRRRRHHHHHHHHH!!!" (211). The howl conveys an emotional truth not contained in any of Lynn's advertising "messages."

Although it might be tempting to interpret Lynn's primal scream as the death rattle of late American capitalism, the novel does not encourage so tendentious a reading. The group sensibility knows that the show, however futile, must go on:

What was the point of it? No matter. Our job wasn't to ask what the point was. If that *had* been our job, nothing articulated to our prospective clients in our capabilities brochure and on our website would have escaped our rolled eyes. The point of another billboard outside O'Hare? Another mass mailer on your kitchen table? Good luck mustering an argument for more of that glut. If we had to call into question the point, we'd have fallen into an existential crisis that would have quickly led us to question the entire American enterprise. We had to keep telling ourselves to forget about the point and keep our noses down and focus on the fractured and isolated task at hand. What was funny about breast cancer? (233–4, emphasis in original)

Here again, as in Lynn's panic attack, the motif of *glut* – ultimately traceable back to the mountain of Gatsby's shirts – drives home the craziness of the "humorous" marketing project and by extension of "the entire American enterprise." The "fractured and isolated task at hand" – searching for laughter (reputedly "the best medicine") in breast cancer – is patently absurd. And yet, for the employees, there is no shunning, or even scrutinizing, the mindless imperative of promotional duty.

The iron clutch of the job on those who perform it calls to mind a legendary silent film sequence: the scene from Charlie Chaplin's *Modern Times* (1936), where Chaplin's assembly line worker cannot, when his shift ends, stop his hands from executing the spasmodic movements he has been industrially programmed to execute. Such automatism is at once comic and frightening. An example from the novel is the behaviour of Chris Yop, who returns robotically to the office even after "walking Spanish": "Can you believe I can't stop working in my head?" he asks. "I keep working and working and working – isn't that sick and twisted?" (106). Sick and twisted it may well be: "It was obviously just plain wrong that the man was still in the building a full day after being laid off. But to have concepts, too? Some nerve system crucial to an understanding of the agreement one enters into when engaging in the capitalist system had obviously gone haywire in him, along with the rest of his ailing networks" (192). What Ferris's novel (like Chaplin's film) suggests is that it may in fact be the system, not just some ailing networks, that has gone haywire. The same holds true for the "aberrant" actions of that other misfit, Tom Mota, who finally opts out of the system by joining the American military and serving in Afghanistan. At bottom, however, work in advertising may not be all that unlike military service; it is the collective consensus that "[n]obody talks about it, nobody says a word, but the real engine running the [agency] is the primal desire to kill. To be the best ad person in the building, to inspire jealousy, to defeat all the rest. The threat of layoffs just made it a more efficient machine" (109).

The Londoners of *South of the River* have at least avenues of escape, real or fancied, from the machines that imprison them; for two of them that avenue is the United States. The occupants of Ferris's sky-high Chicago cubicles lack such apparent alternatives. Carl Garbedian's landscaping business, a venture Mota has prompted him to undertake, is merely a return to a pallid suburban travesty of Emerson's Nature. Tom's own enlistment in the US army, eventuating in his death, is at best glumly patriotic: "He called this country the best republic that ever began to fade" (381). For most of Ferris's people, "real life" in the fading republic gets squeezed into the weekends, their refuge from anomie. Another type of release is humour, available at least to a few fortunate spirits. Lynn obviously possesses the gift of humour, though it cannot serve as the magic bullet for which she longs. Tom's "lunacy" is really a penchant for the comic grotesque he summons up under extreme duress. Or there is writing, an option that provides a welcome release for the "poetaster" Hank Neary, but is out of reach for most cubicle dwellers, the wannabe Hollywood screenwriter Don Blattner included.

According to Ferris, *Then We Came to the End* was meant to capture "what's universal about office life" ("A Conversation" 3); the choice of the specific type of work – advertising – was in some measure a fortuitous outgrowth of the author's own prior exposure to the industry. But while much of what the characters experience is no doubt generic in any workplace, the specific nature of the business they conduct is what gives the narrative its peculiar bent. A *mise en scène* presenting, say, a law office, in part the setting of Ferris's second novel (*The Unnamed*, 2010) or a dental surgeon's office as in his third (*To Rise Again at a Decent Hour*, 2014) would have quite different implications.[3] Still, because promotional work is central to the modern capitalist system, Ferris's treatment of the business is broadly representative, commenting on many elements that go to compose twenty-first-century American, or for that matter global, experience. The persistent ambivalence of treatment points to disquieting doubts about the future of the system itself. Speaking of the advertising agency in "A Conversation" Ferris says: "I thought such an awesome, malignant, necessary, pervasive, inscrutable place deserved a novel's attention" (6). One is immediately struck by Ferris's term "necessary"; not only is the place needed by those it employs but it is also indispensable to the great commercial apparatus it services. And yet the word "malignant" has equal force; it picks up and extends the symbolic resonance of Lynn Mason's life-threatening cancer. The Emersonian vision of individual promise crumbles as the workers, one after another, walk American down the hall. "We knew the power of the credit card companies and the collection agencies and the consequences of bankruptcy. These institutions were without appeal. They put your name into a system, and from that point forward vital parts of the American dream were foreclosed upon" (16). Ferris has composed a Farewell Symphony for the American dream, though he remains reluctant to blow out the last flickering candle.

Both *South of the River* and *Then We Came to the End* interrogate popular assumptions concerning creativity. On the one hand, the hierarchical thinking that situates "literary" writing in a creative empyrean and commercial work in an uncreative Hades is exposed as naive. On the other hand, the malignant offshoots of promotional work are made troublingly clear. In both books the most authentically "creative" people turn out to be the marginalized, those exiled to the perilous fringes of the capitalist universe: Morrison's Anthea in an NGO unit in a developing country, Ferris's Tom Mota among the beleaguered troops in Afghanistan. A rare exemplar of creativity closer to home is Ferris's house novelist, Hank Neary. Hank's first attempt at a novel takes the all too predictable form of a frontal assault on the system. In that version, he explains,

> I based a character on Lynn, and I made that character into a tyrant. I did it on principle, because anyone who was a boss in that book *had* to be a tyrant. Anyone who believed in the merits of capitalism, and soul-destroying corporations, and work work work – all that – naturally that person wasn't deserving of any sympathy. (377, emphasis in original)

Time and experience, however, mellow Hank's approach to the character from the stiffly doctrinaire to the more compassionately nuanced:

> But when I decided to retire that book, thank god, and write something different, I knew she was sick, so I went to see her. Just on a lark. Because what did I know about her? Nothing, really. I didn't know her – not in any meaningful way. And it turned out she was very open to talking with me, not only about her sickness, but also her personal life, a lot of other things. (377)

Hank's new novel (which, in metafictive fashion, replicates Ferris's or at least its lengthy central section) represents a generous step forward from angry, stilted preconception to more compassionate empathy. Yet while this shift signals the liberation of creative impulse on a personal level, neither it, nor Tom Mota's impulsive exit from the corporate centre, nor Anthea's move to selfless service in the Third World can ultimately impede the rumbling onrush of the relentless promotional juggernaut.

Enjoy the Best America Has to Offer:
Mad Men as National Brand

The specialization of images of the world is completed in the world of the
autonomous image, where the liar has lied to himself.

Guy Debord, Society of the Spectacle, Section 2

Amid the animated opening credits of the hit television series *Mad
Men*, in which a dapper executive plummets from a sky-high office
past emblems of consumerist glut – billboards, fashion models, alluring female body parts – a stirring directive slides by: "Enjoy the Best
America Has to Offer." It is an invitation that could apply to the
lavishly praised series itself; the show has had, according to Jesse
McLean, "a cultural impact unlike any television program in recent
history" (5). (The slogan derives from an ad for Old Taylor 86 bour-
bon dating back to 1963, an apt tie-in with the robust drinking
habits of the show's dramatis personae.) In its representation of
advertising as an industry and a way of life, *Mad Men* persistently
recalls the literary works already discussed. Yet the electronic
medium enforces its own message. Even more acutely than those
other texts, *Mad Men* is a site of tension between artistic impulses
and commercial imperatives, a tension stemming from its own conditions of production.

These have to do with the dual nature of commercial television, a
visual medium that serves as a vehicle for both entertainment and
persuasion. A TV series about advertising that depends on ads for its
own survival is obviously apt to involve complex negotiations. One
much publicized example was the delay in starting Season Five due
to a dispute between the show's originator, Matthew Weiner, and
the host cable network AMC /Lionsgate.[1] The network reportedly
demanded more product placement, added commercial breaks, and
the release of several cast members. Weiner's resistance testifies to

his commitment to the show's artistic integrity, as do his comments in published interviews and on bonus tracks included in DVDs. Nevertheless, Weiner has clearly been obliged to make substantial concessions to the exigencies of modern commercial programming. But even beyond those compromises, the medium itself imposes its own distinctive parameters on the responses of its users.

In its original AMC transmission format (as apart from subsequent iterations such as DVD sets) *Mad Men*, like other television series, has involved a recurrent alternation of dramatic sequences and commercial breaks. The viewer's experience has thus been in important ways distinct from that of readers of print texts like those discussed in previous chapters. Early editions of a novel like *Tono-Bungay* might contain advertising matter, but readers could take notice of this content or not, at their pleasure; their attention was not diverted from their perusal of the text itself. By contrast, a viewing of an original *Mad Men* episode would be interrupted every five to (at most) ten minutes by a commercial spot. Scenes of 1960s agency personnel creating advertisements would thus alternate with advertising in the ordinary sense, producing a highly self-conscious overlap between fictional and commercial narratives, most strikingly on the visual level. Boundaries could at times be confusingly crossed; some commercials for Lincoln automobiles featured the voice of John Slattery who plays a major character, Roger Sterling, in the series. Uncle Teddy Ponderevo's pet literary magazine, *The Sacred Grove*, with its pill-pushing cover, may have been aiming at something approaching such blurring of modes, but it certainly did not typify common publishing practise of the time.

Other sponsors of the show have introduced commercials (for which Weiner is not responsible) that similarly indulge in sly self-reference. A spot for Clorox cleanser displayed a white dress shirt with a telltale lipstick smear on the collar, appending a punning caption: "Keeping ad men out of hot water for generations." Apart from such promotional double entendres, the show has accumulated around itself a whole carnival of ancillary bric-a-brac: iTunes items, recipes for period cocktails, high-end clothing store tie-ins. As Daniel Mendelsohn reports, "The clothing retailer Banana Republic, in partnership with the show's creators, devised a nationwide window display campaign evoking the show's distinctive 1960s look, and now offers a style guide to help consumers look more like the show's characters." In the run-up to the Season Five debut this partnering reached its peak, Banana Republic staging "Mad Style Parties" "celebrating the launch of the limited edition Banana Republic Mad Men collection" (Banana Republic Canada e-mail, 27 February 2012). The show is thus deeply implicated in the promotional milieu it recreates. Inevitably, its treatment of that milieu betrays its compromised positioning.

Given that positioning, the seriousness of the show's intent to critique its nurturing industry is thrown open to doubt. Some have even questioned the industry's very relevance to the dramatic content. According to Barbara Lippert, "It's a show about timeless human frailty – that happens to use advertising as a backdrop." Such a verdict misses what the present chapter is meant to demonstrate: in *Mad Men* advertising operates as far more than a backdrop, and in fact the nature of the industry in that particular time and place – New York City in the 1960s – has everything to do with the specimens of "timeless" frailty on offer.

The opening scenes of the Season One pilot quickly establish that advertising is a zone of conflict. While agency personnel grope for ways of downplaying the health risks attendant on smoking, they themselves smoke and cough furiously. (While the epochal US Surgeon General's Report on Smoking would not be released until 1964, possible links between tobacco use and lung cancer were already suspected by 1960, the date of the action.) The chief copywriter and central character, Don Draper, insists that the key concern is not health but branding: "The issue here isn't why should people smoke. It's why should people smoke Lucky Strikes" (1.1., 14:44). The irony springs from the admen's complicity in a scandal that, as twenty-first-century viewers are well aware, will eventually convulse both the advertising and tobacco industries. Subsequent episodes frequently revert to the vexed matter of tobacco promotion. To personalize the problem, the tobacco company's chief representative, the overbearing Lee Garner Jr, is endowed with a disposition as noxious as the product he markets.

This ongoing strand of the drama feeds into a general concern with the social impact of advertising as a catalyst for capitalist enterprise. Historically, cigarette advertising stands as a landmark of modern mass marketing.[2] The issue of how and whether to promote this hazardous product comes to a head late in Season Four, when the agency calamitously loses the Lucky Strike account. But even this crisis does little to resolve the hard questions arising from the peddling of toxic merchandise. In a late episode of Season Five, Draper, attempting to land the massive Dow-Corning account, is asked provocatively by a Dow representative, "Tell me about napalm" (5.12., 34:17). Don launches into fulsome apologetics:

> Napalm was invented in 1942. The government put it in flame-throwers against the Nazis, impact bombs against the Japanese. It was all over Korea, I was there. And now it's in Vietnam. But the important thing is when our boys are fighting and they need it, when America needs it, Dow makes it and it works. (5.12., 34:22)

To promote a murderous product, Don (secretly an army deserter) glibly pushes the button of patriotism – "our boys" – while ignoring concerns of basic humanity. The irony is augmented early in the following season by a remark of Ken Cosgrove, another agency employee, about his father-in-law, a Dow executive: "If he wants people to stop hating him ... he should stop dropping napalm on children" (6.4., 7:39).

Yet while this aspect of the show may raise doubts about promotion as a practise, there are offsetting elements. Much about the treatment of advertising frames it as not a disreputable but rather a fascinating and indeed creative pursuit. The series, many have felt, casts an aura of retrospective glamour over the business as conducted half a century ago, largely owing to the meticulous recreation of period styles and manners. The visual prompts and the discursive import are in fact sometimes at odds. As Lippert puts it, "Does [*Mad Men*] romanticize the industry? Yes. ... *Mad Men* makes the industry seem exciting and sexy again. There's glamour in the trance-inducing visuals and smart narrative, and just enough facts in the story to sell us on Weiner's particular brand of Mad Ave. madness." It is hard to resist the excitement of episode-by-episode turns of plot, hard not to follow the fortunes even of unappealing characters, not to mention compelling ones like Draper and his protégé Peggy Olson. The opulence and panache of the characters' attire and milieu function as a metonymy for the imputed richness of their emotional lives, however turbulent these may appear.

For Mendelsohn, "*Mad Men* is much like a successful advertisement itself." The claim is by no means frivolous. Partly owing to the hectic sexual entanglements of characters like Draper, ably played by

Jon Hamm, *Mad Men* invites powerful viewer identification. Just as advertising eroticizes commodities in order to market them, so one could argue that *Mad Men* eroticizes the advertising industry in order to "sell" it.

This seductive allure depends heavily on facts of genre: above all the show's visual medium, which for obvious reasons is peculiarly appropriate to its promotional subject. As Sut Jhally has noted,

> Through the course of twentieth-century advertising there have been two significant parallel developments; the shift from explicit statements of value to implicit values and lifestyle images; and a decline in textual material with a correlative increase in "visualised images of well-being". Modern advertising is characterised by the growing domination of *imagistic* modes of communication. (22, emphasis in original)

What is striking is the symbiosis between *Mad Men*'s visual medium and the highly visualized commercial practises it reproduces. The series makes much of the resonance of optical images; mirrors proliferate, and admen and women are continually gazing at their reflections. A telling instance occurs in I 6, where a group of female employees participate in a trial session for Belle Jolie lipsticks, excitedly applying the cosmetics before a one-way mirror while agency males ogle them unseen from the other side, trading leaden wisecracks. A phrase repeatedly spoken by characters to one another, either in admiration or denigration or wonderment, is "Look at you!"

According to Jean Baudrilllard, "What the TV medium conveys ... is the idea (the ideology) of a world endlessly visualizable, endlessly segmentable and readable in images" (123) – in effect, a world that replaces critical insight with visual overkill. For Stuart Ewen, too, the medium tends to sideline reflective critique: "In its depiction of both the present and the past, television wrought a structure for past and present which would lead its audience to an uncomprehending adulation for the market economy and the *universals* that it projected" (*Captains* 210, emphasis in original). Ewen goes on to argue that "[w]ithin advertising, the social realm of resistance is reinterpreted, at times colonized, for corporate benefit" (218). Any episode of *Mad Men* could provide ample grounds for such strictures. The attractiveness of the people, fashions, and décor of the show's

world of 1960s advertising can operate to disarm critical judgment more powerfully than anything within the rhetorical ambit
of prose fiction.

And yet, in practise the visual dimension of *Mad Men* does not act
in the homogenizing, narcotic fashion theorized by Baudrillard and
Ewen. Frequently, images themselves propagate a subtextual or
ironic counterpoint to dramatic action. In the opening sequences of
Season Six, shots of Draper on a "business" junket lolling on a
Hawaiian beach are juxtaposed with clips of his neighbour, the eminent surgeon Dr Arnold Rosen, back in New York struggling to
resuscitate an afflicted man. (At the end of the episode, we see Rosen
leaving a New Year's Eve party and setting off into a blizzard – on
skis, no less – to perform emergency surgery.) The contrast with Don
wordlessly makes its point, and bears on our reception of the fact
that Draper is having an affair with Rosen's wife, Sylvia. In a later
episode (12), repeated shots of Don lying on his sofa in a foetal position enhance our sense of his psychological regression, amplifying
the impression made by other features of his behaviour, like his
compulsive drinking. Most memorably, in the closing minutes of the
Season Six finale, where Don has taken his unsuspecting children,
Bobby and Sally, to see the house where he grew up in Hershey,
Pennsylvania – a dilapidated brothel – the silent glance exchanged
between father and daughter vividly conveys the sudden, electric
understanding between them. (The idea of a breakthrough in perception is nicely enhanced by an aural accompaniment, Joni
Mitchell's song "Both Sides Now.") Such optical cues are too abun-
dant throughout the series to receive adequate notice here, but
their cumulative impact adds a complexity to the drama that belies
sweeping generalizations about the anodyne nature of the televisual medium.

While such visual suggestion can have at times a distancing effect,
the characters' daily predicaments invite empathy; the message
driven home is that brilliant copywriting calls for an inventive capacity bordering on genius. In addition, it often involves an uphill battle
to win over obtuse or truculent clients. In Season Six, when Don cuts
ties with the shifty Jaguar dealer Herb Rennet, his associate Pete
Campbell logically objects: "So he's demanding and unreasonable.
How does that make him any different from the other people who
walk through that door?" (6.3., 23:35). Such obstreperous types
play roughly the same adversarial roles as despotic sponsor figures

like Evan Llewellyn Evans in 1940s advertising fiction. The young "creative" Peggy Olson struggles to convince Raymond, from Heinz, of the merits of the pitch she has devised for baked beans: "You have to run with this. It's young and it's beautiful. And no one else is going to figure out how to say that about beans" (5.6., 5:50). If Peggy's "sales talk" for her own selling idea falls flat, it is Raymond's lack of receptiveness that bears the blame. Weiner observes: "I hope that people understand that the results of these advertising pitches are not related to the quality of the pitch; this is a great ad ... It's about the client" (6.1., Commentary 22:20). This "creative" side of the agency's work is contrasted with the more mundane accounts side; Weiner speaks of "the business versus the artistry" (2.1., Commentary 11:50).[3] In his comments Weiner stresses the expertise that advertising shares with more widely recognized forms of art. He even proposes a homology between such promotional endeavours and his own métier of television writing and producing: "Advertising, to me, at this period was probably the most glamorous job you could have in the United States, because it was a job that was creative, had a fairly substantial salary, had very loose working conditions, lack of respect for authority, was basically like working in television" ("Establishing *Mad Men*" 1.0., 0:10).

In *Mad Men*, as in several of the novels discussed earlier, advertising is set at odds with formal literary art. Roger Sterling, a senior partner, asserts: "I guarantee you that in the bottom drawer of every desk in this place is the first ten pages of a novel," an estimate Draper tersely amends: "Five" (1.5., 13:26). Ken Cosgrove has a story published in the *Atlantic*, a major gain of cultural capital that provokes malice and envy among his aspiring but less gifted colleagues. One of these, Paul Kinsey, defiantly rips Cosgrove's own copy of the magazine; as in *Then We Came to the End*, the agency is not notable for its fraternal climate. Another, Campbell, urges his wife, Trudy, to lobby an ex-boyfriend, now a literary agent, to place Pete's banal story about a bear hunter in a quality periodical. When her overtures misfire, Pete scolds her for not complying with her old flame's sexual advances. Draper's hyperbole, "Sterling Cooper has more failed artists and intellectuals than the Third Reich" (1.4., 16:43), has its grain of truth.

The friction between advertising and literary accomplishment reaches a crisis in Season Five. When Sterling becomes aware of Cosgrove's writing he erupts, rebuking the aspiring author with a

sarcastic solecism: "Who'd have thunk you were you by day and
Edgar Allan Poe by night?" (5.5., 36:30). Countering Peggy's protest
against his decision to stop writing his stories ("I read the one in
Galaxy about the girl who lays eggs. Wow!" (5.5., 43:55)), Ken follows Roger's lead: "I'm gonna leave the writing to the writers."
Weiner remarks, "It's really an issue for people in an agency to
indulge that part of their life and really be seen as taking their job
seriously" (5.5., Commentary 9:42). Simone Davis finds expressions
of this attitude in decades-old advertising archives, "where literary
ambitions and college educations are treated as embarrassing liabili-
ties that copywriters should suppress or at least disguise under all
circumstances" (58).

An analogous conflict troubles the career of Don's second wife,
Megan. Like Orwell's Gordon Comstock, Megan exhibits a formidable knack for producing advertising copy but has her heart set on
a more "artistic" pursuit (in her case, acting) in which her success is
far from assured. Reproached by her father, an academic, for selling
out – "I always thought you were very single-minded about your
dreams and that that would help you through life. But now I see you
skipped the struggle and went right to the end" (5.6., 43:26) – she is
prompted to quit the agency and devote herself full-time to the theatre. Weiner applauds: "[W]hat I love is that she is actually exhibiting an artistic conscience, and that is very disturbing in an advertising
agency. This is her novel that she has in the drawer, you know?"
(5.8., Commentary 17:45). Unfortunately, her "novel" is read by her
husband as a *de facto* repudiation of his own life's work. After they
see an antiestablishment Broadway play, *America Hurrah* by Jean-
Claude Van Itallie, his resentment boils over:

> DON: Let me tell you, people buy things because it makes them
> feel better.
> MEGAN: I'm sorry. People make fun of acting all the time, and
> you love it. And I didn't think it was such a strong stand against
> advertising as much as the emptiness of consumerism.
> DON: Well, no one's made a stronger stand against advertising
> than you. (5.10., 15:25)

Although Megan's acting career sputters at first, she announces
gamely, "I felt better failing in that audition than I did when I was
succeeding at Heinz" (5.8., 23:49). But eventually she is driven to

press Don to wangle her a place in a TV commercial ("Beauty and the Beast") advertising Butler Shoes; she feels driven to settle for the *pis aller* of promotion. Megan's difficulty in keeping her two possible career paths separate is not unique; as Davis notes, "The substance, form, and site of these two distinct genres – the literary and commercial – have interpenetrated at least since the rise of modern advertising" (13). Another adman who dreams of "finer" things is Paul Kinsey, who, though turned Hare Krishna votary, still cherishes the profane ambition of writing television plays. He shows the agency media head, Harry Crane, a manuscript – a *Star Trek* episode – confiding, "I think it's the most meaningful work I've ever done in my life" (5.10., 16:45). Sadly, Paul's "meaningful" script turns out to be feeble. Those toilers who look beyond advertising for creative fulfillment risk a harsh comeuppance.

But if, as Don Draper says, failed artists and intellectuals abound in the Madison Avenue Reichstag, their presence betokens at least a modicum of respect for art and intellect. As in Morrison's *South of the River*, condescending remarks about copywriting as a meanly mercenary pursuit are regularly undercut. Starting as a humble secretary, Peggy Olson manages, through grit and inventive flair, to achieve status as a copywriter in this male-centred industry. Yet even Peggy's friend Joyce and her boyfriend-to-be Abe Drexler are too bound by convention to grasp that Peggy might be considered a "real" writer (Joyce: "Peggy's a writer." Abe: "So am I. What do you write?" Peggy: "I'm a copywriter." Abe: "But what do you write?" Peggy: "That *is* writing." Joyce: "You're not working on something else?" (4.4., 36:43)). When the crass accounts man Herman "Duck" Phillips, phoning Peggy to engineer a midday assignation, urges her, "Come on, creative, be creative," his joke falls flat; Peggy is constantly being creative in ways Duck cannot fathom.

Yet even while it insists on the creative dimension of advertising, *Mad Men* persistently makes an issue of its suspect moral correlatives. Pete Campbell's pique at his wife for rebuffing her old flame's sexual advances implies his willingness to have her prostitute herself to further his own egotistical yen for artistic standing. References to prostitution, commonplace in print fictions involving advertising, run rampant in the television series. To cite a seminal instance, the male lead, Draper, is revealed to be the child of a young prostitute who died giving birth to him. When, in a flashback to Don's childhood, a hobo visiting the family farm refers to the farmer's wife as the boy's mother, Don (then known as Dick) sets him straight: "She ain't my momma ... Ain't you heard? I'm a whore child" (1.3., 36:56). The utterance sends vibrations through subsequent seasons, channelling our perceptions of the grown-up whore child. In the intervals between his more serious affairs, Don has several flings with sex workers. At an upscale Manhattan bordello to which an important prospective client has been escorted by agency staff, Don remarks to the hostess: "I grew up in a place like this." She snaps back: "There's no other place like this." Don returns, "You're right, it wasn't as nice. We called it a whorehouse" (5.5., 33:37). In Season Six, through flashbacks, we learn more about the damaging psychological consequences of Don's brothel upbringing. (He recalls a sex worker admonishing his adolescent self: "Little boy, find your own sins" (6.3., 5:09). In his later life on Madison Avenue, he assiduously follows that advice.)

But the figurative overtones of prostitution are more important than the literal fact. Weiner comments: "We've talked a lot about prostitution on this show and I'm obviously interested in it as a dramatic device" (4.1., Commentary 30:14). What makes the device dramatic is, above all, its damning relevance to the business affairs of the principals. Informed that the Sterling Cooper agency is once again to be sold, Roger Sterling, another sometime user of prostitutes, blurts: "Christ. From one john's bed to the next" (3.13., 7:13). When a British firm buys out Sterling Cooper, it seems only fitting that the supercilious office manager they import should be named John Hooker.

The prostitution motif culminates in Season Five, when the agency is desperate to land the Jaguar automobile account. Herb Rennet, boorish head of the Dealers' Association, lets it be known that he fancies Joan Harris, the agency's buxom administrator, a single mother with a trying home situation. Rennet makes spending a night with Joan a condition of the Jaguar deal. The incorrigible Campbell breaks the news to Joan: "[W]e're going to lose Jaguar unless an arrangement is made" (6.11.; 6:00).

JOAN: You're talking about prostitution.
PETE: I'm talking about business at a very high level. Do you consider Cleopatra a prostitute?
JOAN: Where do you get this stuff?

PETE: She was a queen. What would it take to make you a queen?
JOAN: I don't think you could afford it. (5.11., 7:07)

Despite her amply justified outrage, Joan eventually agrees to the "arrangement" for the sake of a partnership entailing a five percent stake in the firm. It is prostitution at a very high level indeed. Draper, who for all his libertinism has scruples, pleads with her: "I wanted to tell you that it's not worth it. And if we don't get Jaguar, so what? Who wants to be in business with people like that?" (5.11., 29:02). As Don does not know, but as the action ironically intimates, the arrangement has already been consummated. In a brilliant sequence of intercutting, shots of Joan arriving at her assignation with the porcine Rennet alternate with glimpses of Don "pitching" Jaguar; while he describes the car as a voluptuous woman, we see Joan disrobing. Machine and woman become figuratively fused in a disturbing tableau of commodification.[4]

An allied motif is the fluidity of sexual relationships among the characters, once again most vividly represented by the wayward amours of Draper. Although at the outset of the series "happily" married with a "model" family, during the years so far covered Don has a matching number of major extramarital affairs, leaving aside the casual flirtations. Like an earlier, operatic Don, he could use a Leporello to keep score. And, like Don Giovanni's "badness," Draper's is always ambiguous, at once shocking and titillating.

Don's penchant of wandering from bed to bed serves as a paradigm for the profession he practices, where commitment becomes a matter of *pro tem* convenience. When offered the prospect of securing a seven million dollar contract with American Airlines, the Sterling Cooper partners are readily persuaded to jilt the smaller Mohawk, which yields a trifling one million. (Agency etiquette forbids the concurrent servicing of rival firms, a species of monogamy less often observed in the admen's marital histories.) Don objects to this desertion of a long-time client, but he too eventually complies. ("He'll be fine," Sterling assures his colleagues after a discomfited Don stalks from the boardroom (2.2., 16:53)). In this business model, infidelity is inscribed in the very terms of engagement.

In his professional and his personal life alike, Don Draper approximates the prototype of the modern executive sketched by the Frankfurt School theorists, Max Horkheimer and Theodor Adorno:

The bourgeois whose existence is split into a business and a private life, whose private life is split into the surly partnership of marriage and the bitter comfort of being quite alone, at odds with himself and everybody else, is already virtually a Nazi, replete both with enthusiasm and abuse; or a modern city-dweller who can now only imagine friendship as a "social contact": that is, as being in social contact with others with whom he has no inward contact. (155)

While Don is no Nazi, the other attributes – the aloneness, the notion of marriage as a surly partnership, the dividedness of life and self – hit home. Yet for all Don's solitary egotism, he comes across as more than a Frankfurt School whipping boy. The ethos of boundless self-aggrandizement urged on him by the firm's senior officer, Bert Cooper, an admirer of Ayn Rand, is not to his taste. As J.M. Tyree observes, "[W]hile Don often appears to others as a self-reliant businessman-artist who wouldn't be out of place in … *The Fountainhead*, he's actually more like a living critique of Rand's ideas" (35).

A more apt model for Don might be that prevaricating hero Pinocchio, to whom repeated allusions are made. (Don's naïve secretary, Lois Sadler, reports to Peggy that Don has explained his failure to show up by saying that he was attending a showing of *Pinocchio* (2.1., 7:46). In Season Six, Sally Draper calls to her brother, Bobby: "Go up there and get Pinocchio and bring it down" (6.8., 8:43)). A striking feature of the show is its obsession with mendacity. Here again the leading exemplar is Draper, a master of self-misrepresentation whose very name is a lie. Born in poor circumstances as Dick Whitman, he has rebranded himself by appropriating the identity of the actual Don Draper, an officer killed by a freakish mishap during the Korean War. The faux Don has become that quintessential American hero, a man who has lifted himself up by another man's bootstraps. Because the other man is handily dead, Don can rise to entrepreneurial stardom through a brazen act of character theft. Several critics have noted the connotations of the alias (e.g. Mark Taylor: "Even his name implies hiding or shrouding"); this is a man who figuratively dons drapery. He is a false advertisement in a fedora.

To maintain his shaky status Draper must resort to concealment and subterfuge, constantly dreading exposure. And yet, as we learn, in his peculiar line of work the sort of imposture he has perpetrated need not be fatal. In Season One, episode 12 Campbell, who has accidentally unearthed Don's secret past, blackmails Don by threatening to reveal it to the almighty Cooper unless given a promotion. Don calls Pete's bluff by accompanying him to Cooper's office, where Pete declares that Don is not who he claims to be and is guilty of desertion from the US army and perhaps worse: "Mr Cooper, he's a fraud and a liar. A criminal, even" (39:04). Cooper responds with majestic *sang froid*: "Even if this were true, who cares? This country was built and run by men with worse stories than whatever you've imagined here. More profit in forgetting this." What counts in Bert's vision of business is not mundane factuality but rather the grand American myth of the trailblazing privateer. Long-dormant truths are irrelevant to the bottom line – "More *profit* in forgetting this." As Don himself declares flatly in a later episode, "[T]here is no such thing as American history, only a frontier" (2.4., 31:49). The malleability of history harmonizes with the fluidity of the agency's claims for the products it pushes.

Beyond his founding falsehood, Don makes a regular practice of lying to his associates and his family. Impromptu fabulation has long been a defining trait of the questing hero, as witness that champion fibber, Odysseus, but in Don's case the lying both colours and is in turn coloured by the vocation he pursues. On occasion the point is made by disdainful outsiders. When at a Village club Don informs the cryptobeatnik Roy that he is in advertising, Roy responds, "Perpetuating the lie. How do you sleep at night?", to which Don answers readily, "On a bed made of money" (1.6., 42:26).

But of course that is only one of many beds upon which the errant adman sleeps. If Don's professional role demands nimble dancing around the slippery rocks of factuality, his personal life likewise entails such capering. The keys to his true character – his mean origins and his change of identity – he conceals even from his first wife, Betty, until she stumbles on the literal key that unlocks the drawer containing the evidence. She then tells him, with natural outrage, "You lied to me every day. I can't trust you. I don't know who you are" (3.11., 33:48). On a day-to-day level Don devises intricate deceptions to shroud the details of his extramarital involvements. A business trip he takes to Baltimore in the company of the art director Salvatore Romano (whose closeting of his homosexuality is yet another ongoing lie) turns into a festival of prevarication. To abet his flirtation with a winsome blonde flight attendant, Shelly, he poses as an accountant named Bill who is probing the affairs of the notorious labour boss, Jimmy Hoffa. On his return home, he explains his tiredness by unctuously telling his wife, "I don't sleep well when I'm not here"; the stewardess's badge, which has awkwardly turned up in his luggage, he palms off as a thoughtful memento for his daughter (3.1., 45:15). Eventually even Sally begins to see through her father's web of falsehoods. Told by their mother that Don is leaving the family home, the children ask him why he is going. He temporizes, "I'm not going, I'm just living elsewhere," to which Sally rejoins hotly, "That's going! You say things and you don't mean them, and you can't just do that" (3.13., 33:44). She is developing a precocious resistance to promotional doubletalk.

Troubled by the memory of how his father, Archibald Whitman, was marked out by the visiting hobo as a dishonest man, Don assures his small son Bobby, "I will never lie to you" (1.8., 43:53). Nevertheless, he persists in foisting falsehoods upon his children, not to mention their elders. One is drawn irresistibly to connect Don's shifty improvisations with the promotional stage he treads. Mendacity, the series insistently suggests, is the advertising man's occupational disease. With Don, the syndrome reaches a crisis in Season Six when Sally stumbles on her father in bed with the neighbour, Sylvia Rosen. Afterwards Don, speaking through his daughter's locked bedroom door, as usual endeavours to explain away the embarrassment: "I know you think you saw something. I was comforting Mrs Rosen. She was very upset. It's very complicated" (6.11., 45:26). But by this point the teenaged Sally knows what she saw and knows that it is not very complicated.

Under the stress of Sally's disaffection, compounded by pressures at work, Don finally arrives at an emotional impasse that puts a brake on mendacity. The crisis arrives late in Season Six, when he makes a fanciful pitch to Hershey's Chocolate representatives. He begins, typically, on a fulsome note of patriotism, tying the product symbolically to all that is heart warming in his native land: "[Hershey's] relationship with America is so overwhelmingly positive that anyone in this room has their own story to tell" (6.13., 30:05). He then goes on to "tell a story" of a childhood episode in which his father rewards him for mowing the lawn by taking him to the drugstore and telling him he can have anything he wants. His choice, needless to say, is a Hershey bar. "And as I ripped it open, my father tousled my hair and forever his love and the chocolate were tied together. That's the story we're going to tell. Hershey's is the currency of affection. It's the childhood symbol of love" (6.13., 30:37). The "touching" narrative is, as viewers know, an outrageous travesty of the facts of Don's wretched boyhood; there was no lawn mowing, let alone hair tousling. The response of one Hershey representative – "Well, weren't you the lucky little boy" (31:04) – is so ludicrously misconceived that it sets off in Don a stunning reversal.

According to Davis, "The adman's alleged imperviousness to the seductions of his own rhetoric is connected to a cynical detachment from what he says, to an identity, in fact, that revolves around its disjunction from utterance" (43). This analysis precisely fits the Don Draper of earlier seasons, but for the distraught Draper of the Hershey scene, goaded by galling memories, the distance between identity and utterance collapses. As Weiner comments, "What I wanted was for you to hear that pitch and that phony childhood, and even feel a little emotional, even though it was so hollow. And he knew it was hollow – it was a lie and he didn't feel good about it" (*Vulture* interview). Don proceeds to tell his dumfounded audience a shockingly different story: "I grew up in Pennsylvania in a whorehouse. … Closest I got to feeling wanted was from a girl who made me go through her john's pockets while they screwed. If I collected more than a dollar, she'd buy me a Hershey bar. And I would eat it … Alone in my room … with great ceremony, feeling like a normal kid. It said 'sweet' on the package. It was the only sweet thing in my life" (6.13., 31:50). The sudden coarseness of Don's diction signals his relinquishment of the glossy evasions of advertising. He has, in effect, bared the seamy side, not only of his personal history but of his vocation as well. And his partners react in character to this apostasy; after a brilliant career of fertile and effective lying, this eruption of truth costs Don his place with the firm, causing him to "walk Spanish down the hall." The "moral" is plain: honesty and advertising are unsuitable bedfellows.

The entire scene recalls, perhaps by design, the culminating confrontation between Vic Norman and Evan Llewellyn Evans in the Hollywood version of *The Hucksters*, where Vic suddenly abandons bogus "sincerity" by pouring over the soap magnate's head a genuinely sincere tumbler of water. Here too, the sudden onset of truthfulness accompanies an abjuring of the distorted values of advertising business. It is the differences between the scenes, however, that are revealing. Where Norman melodramatically asserts his superiority to the whole occupational mode of sycophancy and greed, Draper publicly exposes his own fabricated life history as an abject lie. It is an act not of bravado but of penance, and what follows it is not a grandiose leave-taking of the industry but a humiliating expulsion from it. Yet by the same token it is a far more credible display of courage and conviction than anything in Wakeman's book, not to mention the film based on it. It is an act of exorbitant honesty rather than cheap bravado.[5]

One should add that Don and his fellow Madison Avenue Pinocchios have no monopoly on the production of falsehoods. Most of the show's characters, outside and inside the industry, lie with enough gusto to make prevarication seem a universal birthright. "It's incredible how fast some people come up with lies," Sally's friend Sandy (who has herself been lying about her admission to the Julliard School) remarks to Betty Draper (6.1/2. 19:47). As Elizabeth Moss, the show's Peggy Olson, comments: "Everybody's lying, everybody's covering something up, everybody has a secret; it adds such a tension to the show" (Commentary 1.5., 41:30).

The tension often emerges in domestic settings. Betty Draper, if a less enterprising liar than her husband, habitually adjusts truth to her convenience. When dismissed from her brief stint as a fashion model, she explains that she was offered a "whole string" of other possibilities but has tired of the work (1.9.), even though her initial hiring was (as Don knows) a mere ploy meant to lure him away to a rival agency. More seriously, her clandestine flirtation with the political consultant Henry Francis, whom she will marry after divorcing Don, is managed as furtively as any of Don's dalliances. But Betty's propensity to impose her own falsehoods on herself matches her readiness to hoodwink others. As Weiner observes, "Her ability to lie to herself ... to deny, that's something that's going on the entire [first] season" (1.11., Commentary 23:50). Indeed, the whole image of model American family life staged by Betty and Don is a sham, a flagrant misrepresentation. Even when the couple step out for a Valentine's Day dinner at a posh hotel, the occasion plays out as a "romantic" charade. Much later, when the now-estranged pair keep up appearances by taking Bobby and Sally trick-or-treating – the boy dressed as a hobo, the girl as a gypsy – their neighbour Carlton asks the two grown-ups, with cruel though unwitting irony, "And who are you supposed to be?" (3.11., 46:25).

The connections *Mad Men* establishes among its alliterative "four p's" – prostitution, promiscuity, prevarication, and promotion – work to offset whatever glamour may cling to the industry it scans. As Timothy Richardson argues, "Draper's position on the show functions both as the obvious point of identification for the viewer ... and as a difficult ethical example in the field of the series" (23). A running motif of *Mad Men* is the deforming clutch of advertising upon the lives of those enmeshed in it. As happens in works like *The Edible Woman* and *Then We Came to the End*, the action points to a troubling link between advertising's outreach and the stresses inflecting personal relationships. Weiner says of the media director Harry Crane, "Harry can only see things in terms of advertising" (5.10., Commentary 9:03), a penchant Harry and his coworkers share with Ferris's Lynn Mason.

"Seeing things in terms of advertising" frequently means playing a part. In the promotional theatre of *Mad Men*, presentation assumes a crucial importance. Many of the activities of the Sterling Cooper staff involve a large intermixture of *performance*. A trivial though repellent instance occurs at a garden party hosted by Roger Sterling, where Roger tastelessly regales the company with a minstrel show rendition of "My Old Kentucky Home," his face begrimed with shoe polish (3.3.). In the daily course of business, agency personnel must stage more sober presentations to sell clients on the merits of advertising ideas, "acts" that amount to self-presentations. On occasion these performances fall dismally flat. When Roger, who handles the key Lucky Strike account, is convalescing from a coronary, he is unwisely hustled before tobacco company representatives in a pitch meant to guarantee that he is still in control (1.11.). The aim here is to transform Roger into a "picture" of health. Joan applies her skills as a cosmetician to lend a spurious glow to the sick man's visage. In the event, the reassuring image disintegrates. Raising a glass in a toast to New York, Roger has a sudden recurrence. His wife, Mona, tremulously in attendance, rounds on the man who has been spurring Roger on: "I used to think you couldn't put a value on a human life, but I never asked Bert Cooper, did I?" (26:45). Such a performance shockingly exposes the consequences of privileging commercial expediency over emotional or even medical necessities.

At first glance, *Mad Men* appears to enact a clean separation between the characters' office lives and their home lives, a disconnect geographically expressed by the miles between Don Draper's Madison Avenue office and (in earlier seasons) his Ossining family residence.

After visiting her husband's workplace, Betty confides to her neigh-bour, Francine, "It's like walking into another country where I don't speak the language" (1.5., 30:21). Looked at more carefully, how-ever, the two "countries" prove to overlap. The supposed chasm between promotional Hades and personal Elysium disguises the rul-ing grip of marketing psychology over both spheres. Joan casually defines her relationship with her lover, Roger, in trade terms: "I mean we both know that I'll find a more permanent situation, and you'll find a new model. The '61s are coming out soon" (1.6., 15:35). And more literal types of overlap are built into the show's narrative line. Pete Campbell's father-in-law, Tom Vogel, an executive with the Vicks pharmaceutical firm, indulgently allows Pete to snag a contract for Clearasil ointment and later for a broader gamut of Vick's prod-ucts. He threatens to withhold his business, however, if Pete does not "produce" – that is, enable his wife Trudy to bear a (preferably male) child. Although the child (unluckily female) is eventually forthcom-ing, Vogel later cancels the Vicks account after he espies his son-in-law in a brothel he himself has been patronizing (6.5., *et seq.*).

Madison Avenue business, when brought home from the office, can transmit life-altering signals. When Salvatore Romano's wife Kitty complains of feeling neglected – "I don't need that much but I do need tending," she confides (3.4., 15:11) – Sal distracts her by acting out a television commercial he has been devising for a new soft drink, Patio. The commercial is a takeoff on a musical number from a recent film, in which Ann-Margret delivers the song "Bye Bye Birdie" with juvenile buoyancy, heightening the effect with coyly suggestive body moves. Sal mimics the starlet's performance with obvious relish, unconsciously revealing to the dismayed Kitty his closeted sexual orientation and the hidden cause for her neglect. It is one of the most arresting moments of the whole series and, in an ironic sense, its most memorable demonstration of "Truth in Advertising."

The impingement of office matters on home life can sometimes lead to more abrasive encounters. An especially revealing invasion of domestic space occurs when Don enlists the unsuspecting Betty in a promotional scheme for Heineken beer. As Davis observes, "Both mythically and statistically, a woman was and is the primary con-sumer, and so holds considerable economic power. ... As such, she must be read, examined, hailed, and mimicked in address so that she will relate to the pitch, and then respond with a purchase" (82). In the episode in question (2.8.), Don sets about "reading" his wife in just this fashion, to gauge her consumerist preferences. Wishing to give a Continental twist to a dinner party, Betty is attracted by a supermarket display of the Dutch beer – exactly what Don had predicted would be the response of the "typical" suburban housewife. When Betty learns that she has been the subject of a marketing experiment she angrily turns on Don. Weiner treats the Heineken experiment as a side-issue, arguing that the hidden cause of Betty's outburst is Don's sexual cheating: "For some reason she has had enough. This embarrassment is not about the conversation at the dinner party about Heineken; this is about Bobbie Barrett [the other woman], this is about people knowing" (2.8., 23:31). In fact, however, the episode suggests that the two sources of injury are intertwined. Don's willingness to use Betty as a sample buyer tells her that he regards her as a convenient "Housewife X" rather than as a uniquely precious individual. It follows logically that he himself will not scruple to "switch brands" as an avid sexual consumer. The next day, when Betty happens to see a television commercial featuring Bobby Barrett's comedian husband, Jimmy, her anger boils over, prompting her to phone Don and tell him not to come home. Betty's life is overdetermined by advertising; little wonder if she feels trapped in a space dominated by two allied and menacing forces: mass promotion and male infidelity.

At work, too, the personal can become messily ensnarled with the professional. In Season Four a focus group for the promotion of Ponds face cream is organized by the marketing psychology consultant, Dr Faye Miller, drawing on the experiences of young female secretaries (4.4.). The women soon launch into candid emotional confidences, and one of them, Allison, who has had a fleeting relationship with Don, bolts in tears from the room. The upheaval caused by the supposedly neutral session impels the girl to resign her position with the firm. Faye, meanwhile, remains cheerfully unaware that any problem has occurred. She is too wrapped up in applying her professional expertise to the niceties of consumer response to register niceties of personal feeling. Like Harry Crane and other coworkers, she "can only see things in terms of advertising."

The series itself clearly means to "see things" more comprehensively, but it cannot be called consistent in so doing. At times, *Mad Men* seems uncertain in its own take on the psychology of consumer response, its understanding of how ads persuade individual shoppers to purchase specific products. Don Draper's *ex cathedra* pronounce-ments are often at odds with one another. When, early in her career as copywriter, Peggy casually remarks, "Sex sells" (2.1., 30:15), Don reproves her:

> Just so you know, the people who talk that way think that mon-keys can do this. And they take all this monkey crap and just stick it in a briefcase, completely unaware that their success depends on something more than their shoeshine. You are the product. You feeling something. That's what sells. Not them, not sex.

What Don appears to be saying is that empathy with the consumer, rather than cynical manipulation, is the key to creative advertising. What he ignores is the possibility that empathy can *fuel* manipula-tion – can enable the stealthy activating of hardwired responses (sexual ones included) in the public.

In an earlier episode, Don produces a markedly different ratio-nale. Here, he plausibly gauges an ad's rhetorical clout in terms of its appeal to the public's dreams of commodity ownership: "Advertising is based on one thing: happiness. And you know what happiness is? Happiness is the smell of a new car. It's freedom from fear. It's a billboard on the side of the road that screams with reassurance that whatever you're doing ... it's okay. You are okay" (1.1., 31:58). Don's rhapsody plainly exposes the assumptions that guide his own life, and yet the message, a gospel of zealous but mindless material-ism, sorts oddly with the messianic tone. As Jhally asks, "[W]hat is advertising if not the new religion of modern life, the religion indeed of use value?" (200). Such a religion is an inherently unstable con-struct; it has negligible "use value" in resolving the awkward per-sonal dilemmas Don and his fellows must confront.

Draper casts himself in the mould of the classic American seeker of fortune, an updated version of the Emersonian spirit of individu-alism revisited by Ferris in *Then We Came to the End*. This para-digm of the aspiring self is well suited to Don's career trajectory; as Tyree says, "An American paradox is that the much-vaunted Emersonian characteristic of self-reliance dovetails rather nicely with the goals of big business to create a nation of isolated, vulner-able, and greedy selves who can be persuaded that buying products is a form of self-expression" (35). Like Jay Gatsby, Draper constantly reinvents himself, pushing onward while attempting (with imperfect success) to revoke the past. As he is fond of proclaiming, the secret of successful promotion is the idea of the new, seconded by the dynamic spirit of enterprise: a potent duo of canonical American bywords.

Mad Men's treatment of American dynamism, like its take on advertising, is chronically divided. The series' boldest incarnation of the "Emersonian" spirit is the fictionalized character of Conrad Hilton, an incarnate myth of the national imperial self. Draper, who through a chance meeting wins the job of promoting Hilton's New York properties, is for a time captivated not just by the golden business opportunity but by the entrepreneur's charisma; Hilton, like Draper, has undeniably "made something" of himself. Unfortunately, it soon emerges that the self Hilton has made is a Frankenstein's monster; his egomaniac outlook, coupled with the project of American world supremacy, is deeply unsettling. Presenting a pitch for a "Hilton Abroad" campaign, Don dutifully mouths the imperial theme: "The average American experiences a level of luxury that belongs only to kings in most of the world. We're not chauvinists. We just have expectations. Well, there's one word that promises the thrill of international travel with the comfort of home. Hilton. ... It's the same in every language" (3.9., 32:52). Don paints an alluring picture of trotting the globe without ever leaving the shadow of the American homeland. Yet even this pious cant fails to appease the hotelier; his expectations reach beyond the global to the cosmic: "You didn't give me what I wanted. I'm deeply disappointed. I expect the moon." He whisks Don and Betty away for a whirlwind jaunt to Rome, but he also imperiously summons Don to impromptu consultations at any hour of the day or (more often) night. When, at a moment of crisis for Sterling Cooper, Hilton summarily dismisses his underling, Don's faith in the American ideal of boundless aspiration is strained to the breaking point.

All the same, Don seldom swerves from his gospel of no-holds-barred self-advancement. His stance on professional issues regularly sidesteps ethical concerns. What at first blush appears to be the major exception, Don's antitobacco manifesto in the *New York Times* (Season Four), turns out to be a *coup de théâtre*, a stroke of opportunism calculated to provide a life raft for the agency when it has been torpedoed by Lucky Strike and the odious Lee Garner. The full-page letter, headed "Why I'm quitting tobacco," cleverly pairs tobacco addiction with the agency's own addiction to tobacco money. It runs in part:

> For over twenty-five years, we devoted ourselves to peddling a product for which good work is irrelevant, because people can't stop themselves from buying it. The product that never improves, causes illness and makes people unhappy. But there was money in it. A lot of money. In fact, our entire business depended on it. We knew it wasn't good for us, but we couldn't stop. (4.12., 29:44)

Draper's colleagues' dismay at this bold stroke is understandable but misguided. In fact, Don has no high-minded intention of "quitting tobacco"; he has acted not as an exalted crusader for health and safety but as a scheming huckster. The letter is a truthful lie.[6] In the following season a job seeker, Michael Ginsberg, voices his street-smart appreciation of Don's move: "I'll be honest. I've admired you since the letter. I thought it was the funniest thing I ever read" (5.3., 35:00). The humour, if present, is certainly dark.

Meanwhile, the more impressionable Peggy Olson has been jolted out of her professional complacency owing to her nascent relationship with the activist journalist, Abe Drexler. Although he is stumbling in his approaches and unperceptive about issues of sexual equality (he teases her smugly, "All right, Peggy, we'll have a civil rights march for women" (4.9., 10:50)), Abe's passion for social justice challenges her neutrality. Almost alone among the cast of characters, Abe questions the modern capitalist ethos that advertising subserves. To Peggy's demurral, "I'm not a political person. I don't have to defend myself" (4.9., 18:37), Abe replies with impeccable sixties assurance: "You're political whether you like it or not."

Although apt to carry his crusading zeal to a risible extreme – he presents the horrified Peggy with a manifesto equating her agency's dealings with war crimes prosecuted at Nuremberg – Abe is not a crank to be laughed off the stage. He exhorts Peggy, in terms recalling Jhally: "We have a religion in this country and it's business. You're not a priest, you're just another congregant. ... Why should you have to be a part of that corruption? It's a waste of your and a million other artists' gifts" (4.9., 18:18). Peggy rips up Abe's "Nuremberg" tract, but his words leave their mark. His ire targets an agency client notorious for its refusal to employ blacks in its southern operation: "Fillmore Auto Parts is worse than a corporation, what with the boycott and all. ... [A]nd obviously your company has an investment in looking the other way" (4.9., 9:25).

Peggy awkwardly justifies looking the other way: "Well, it's a complicated idea, but in advertising we don't really judge people. We try and help them out of their situations." Later, however, at a staff meeting, she begins to question her adherence to the guild code of profitable indifference: "Why are we doing business with someone who doesn't hire Negroes?" (4.9., 37:42). Weiner comments, "Peggy has been politicized by this guy" (4.9., Commentary 37:15). The politicizing, however, stops short of the road to Damascus. In subsequent seasons, though she lives with Abe, Peggy shows far more interest in furthering her professional status than in confronting the issues close to her friend's heart. It comes as no surprise when at length the relationship noisily collapses. As Abe tells her in an ambulance after she has accidentally but gravely wounded him with an improvised bayonet, "Your activities are offensive to my every waking moment. I'm sorry. But you'll always be the enemy" (6.9., 39:54). Peggy has, in effect, been the enemy from the start.

The questions raised by *Mad Men* extend beyond issues of individual character to the ideology undergirding the modern economy within which Peggy, Don, and the others operate. What room is left for ethical and political debate amid the whole money-driven machine in which Sterling Cooper is only one minor cog? Weiner's own sympathies are officially with Abe Drexler's jeremiads: "I love what he says about advertising, about what's happening in the world; it's all coming" (4.9., Commentary 14:32). Still, it is fair to ask how far *Mad Men,* overall, pursues the radical agenda Weiner professes to love.

Even if *Mad Men* often seems to be mounting a vivacious exposé of the industry that is its subject, revealing it as a manipulative machine for perverting decent social values, the glamour and excitement associated with day-to-day business act to buffer viewer unease. In encounters between copywriters like Don and Peggy and cranky clients, we are predisposed to sympathize with the "creatives." Willy-nilly, we admire the inventiveness that goes into their presentations and recoil from (or laugh at) the obstinacy or downright oafishness of the lingerie or baked beans or auto moguls they must struggle to propitiate. This channelling of sympathy tends in some measure to dampen down critical awareness of the dishonesty or even malignancy of the campaigns themselves. Weiner's series may habitually bite the promotional hand that feeds it, but for the most part the bite is not lethal.

The show's schizoid split finds its counterpart in the personality of its leading man. For all his testimonials to moving forward and his tributes to the worth of his work, Draper himself is dogged by crippling doubts. As he confides to Anna Draper, the widow of the authentic Don, "I have been watching my life. It's right here. I keep scratching at it, trying to get into it. I can't" (2.12., 18:01). In Season Three, episode 7, under the influence of drugs and alcohol, he hallucinates that his late father, Archie Whitman, is jeering that he is a "bum" and that his hands are disgracefully soft as a woman's: "What do you do?" the phantasmal Archie asks (42:39). "What do you make? You grow bullshit." The fantasized voice of the father is actually, of course, a projection of Don's normally silenced self-contempt, his fear that he is pursuing shoddy goals rather than performing honest, productive work like that of his father's generation.

That this prophecy of decline from ancestral virtue is pronounced by the shade of a threadbare and brutal drunkard has its ironic edge. Nevertheless, it contributes to a generalized premonition of national decline that now and then emerges in the series, clouding the surface glitter of the Madison Avenue milieu. In Season Three, episode 3 young Sally Draper is twice shown reading from Gibbon's *Decline and Fall of the Roman Empire* at the behest of her maternal grandfather, Gene Hofstadt. One extract describes how the Emperor Julian's austerity measures met with a hostile reception from the "soft" Roman populace. It seems an odd book for a child to be reciting to her grandfather, but the surreal tinge accentuates the symbolic overtones. After Gene's sudden death in Season Three, episode 4, the child is touchingly shown going to sleep cradling the Gibbon volume as a relic of the old man and perhaps as an augury of the fate awaiting the nation in which she will grow up. In Season Five, after Sally has come home from a visit to Manhattan that turns out to be a shattering initiation into urban decadence, she responds to her friend Glen Bishop's query, "How's the city?" with a single resonant word: "Dirty" (5.7., 46:30). When in Season Six Don takes Bobby to see the futuristic film *Planet of the Apes*, a clip of the film's closing tableau, showing the dismembered top of a shattered Statue of Liberty (5., 33:53), drives home the apocalyptic theme with unnerving bluntness.

The dissonance in *Mad Men* between period glamour and encroaching "dirt" or devastation is an insistently perplexing feature of the show. In a thoughtful essay, Jerome de Groot has proposed a rationale. He argues that the series invites nostalgia for a simpler, more hospitable time in American history only to subvert it by exposing that cozy image as a contrived memory:

> The show itself plays fast and loose with nostalgia, quite deliberately invoking it to explode it. On the one hand, it recalls paradisical postwar prosperity and confidence, the sudden expansion of the American economy, rampant unrepentant capitalism and, most importantly of all, a cultural milieu with much currency in the contemporary world – smoky jazz clubs, Sinatra, fine suits. On the other hand, the show gathers much of its historical otherness through its revelation of horrific ideologies in the past – racism, sexism, homophobia, class. The show is revisionist in its approach to the past, disrupting the historical imaginary by undermining the sheen of nostalgia. (279)

For de Groot, Don Draper's pitch for the Kodak Carousel slide projector using deceptively idyllic snapshots from his "perfect" family's past (3.13.) functions as a metonymy for the debunking strategy of the series as a whole: "Gradually ... the beautifully put together image is revealed to be rotten and fake, the key motif here being the picture-book household and family that Draper has slowly undermined and fractured. America was never beautiful and innocent, and any programme that tells you different is selling a lie, is selling a product using nostalgia" (280).

De Groot's thesis, framing the series as a determinedly deconstructive comment on the American illusions it projects, is an attractive one. The show's period allure hinges largely on peripheral matters of fashion and personal flair, while the lives of the principals betray alarming inward fissures. The figure tumbling from on high in the opening credits presages the arc frequently followed by these lives. The women relegated to suburban homes are stultified and bored; those working in offices are liable to be harassed and humiliated. The men's greater scope for action only leaves them fevered and aimless, both in their work and in their personal relationships. Those belonging to racial minorities are marginalized and patronized; those with the "wrong" sexual orientation, like Salvatore Romano, must at all costs keep it closeted.

De Groot provides an eloquent analysis of Draper's predicament:

He makes his own past, like America itself, denying what happened in order to live in the beautiful modern moment of possibility. Draper is an absence, yet he is the centre of a show which
articulates the continual state of becoming, of rejection of one's
roots, of modernity as a continual denial of pastness, of shiny
newness. Draper thinks he lives his life without history, and the
life he leads is mad as a consequence; similarly, he helps America
to deny and forget the reality for a dream of now, and everything
that was solid melts into air. (280)

An update is called for: by the end of Season Six (the Hershey's scene
and its aftermath) Don appears possibly on the verge of facing up to
the past he has so long denied. In general, though, de Groot's assess-
ment holds good. One needs to ask, however, just what it means to
call Draper an absence. The natural inference is that Don does not
possess an identifiable and sustaining "core" of self. (It is relevant
that, in the opening double episode of Season Six, when a photographer taking agency portraits tells him, "I want you to be yourself,"
Don looks at a loss (46:22).) Nonetheless, the trope of absence risks
obscuring the character's vivid episode-by-episode personal *presence*, upon which the vibrancy of the show heavily depends.[7] Draper
commands centre stage largely because his acutely conflicted nature
makes him so undeniably *there*; the more he attempts to repress the
past the more punishingly it returns to him in the form of flashbacks,
hallucinations, even photos. Don has, in fact, a superabundance of
selves contending with one another: the devoted husband and father
and the skulking philanderer; the man of mystery and the flagrant
self-publicizer; the fugitive from the past and its hapless prisoner;
the passionate advocate for his work and the jaded nihilist who que-
ries its worth.

Mad Men itself is similarly riven in its take on its subject industry.
It glamorizes the promotional project while expertly highlighting its
corruption. It would be fanciful to expect the show to resolve its
multiple contradictions in its remaining episodes; it is, for one thing,
too closely wedded to the vexed and vexing business it scrutinizes.
Yet for all that, by producing a complex and sometimes subtle
representation of that business, it gains an urgency that is more

engrossing than any simplistic, backward-gazing nostalgia. In *The Enchantment of Modern Life* Jane Bennett asks: "Can advertisements qualify as sites of an ethically useful kind of enchantment? Even if they can, should we not seek our enchantments elsewhere?" (113). *Mad Men* offers no clear-cut answer to Bennett's tantalizing questions; what it presents, instead, is a fascinating, open-ended contest between enchantment and its discontents.

The Price of Enchantment

The literary works I have considered in this study raise complex questions about the nature and influence of mass advertising; the answers – if any – they propose tend to be contradictory and elusive. As is natural, these fictions are not consecutive, closely reasoned anatomies of the issues arising from the dominance of promotional culture over modern life; for analysis of that sort one turns to studies like the British reports cited in my introductory chapter, *The Advertising Effect* and *Think of Me as Evil?*. The imagined careers of invented personages – an Edward Ponderevo, a Marian MacAlpin, a Don Draper – cannot offer conclusive pronouncements, only at best contingent but fertile impressions. Still, works of fiction have their own distinctive strategies for probing the allure of promotional enchantment, transmitting a more various and precise sense of the ambiguities of lived experience than any systematic survey. Careful acts of imagination can attempt to persuade Consumer A to purchase Brand B rather than Brand C, but applied to different ends they can convey fresh and valuable insights into branding and consumerism.

Some recent fiction, like the works by Morrison and Ferris treated in chapter 6, has focused on the psychological consequences of living in a promotionally saturated universe. A book that deals with such issues in a compellingly dialogic fashion is Jonathan Franzen's 2001 bestseller, *The Corrections*, which can serve as a fitting capstone for this discussion. Franzen's narrative traces the lives of two generations of the Lambert family, originally from the Midwestern city of St Jude (read "St Louis"). The generations correspond by and large to Zygmunt Bauman's "solid" and "liquid" phases of modern

society. The elder Lamberts, Alfred and Enid, lead more or less tradi-
tional lives in the aging, and significantly deteriorating, house they
have dwelled in throughout their marriage. They have travelled,
mainly as a result of Alfred's assignments with the Midland Pacific
railway company, but their routine and their outlook on the world
remain static. The three Lambert children, sons Gary and Chip and
daughter Denise, have chosen a contrasting mode of life. They have
all moved east to the Philadelphia/New York ambit; their fluctuat-
ing metropolitan lives exemplify Bauman's "liquid" phase.

In their approaches to living, however, the younger Lamberts
diverge not just from their parents but from one another as well.
Their differences can be roughly summarized in terms of the distinction between intrinsic and extrinsic values proposed in the report
Think of Me as Evil?. The eldest, Gary, a wealthy investment banker,
is enthusiastically committed to the "extrinsic" ethos of boundless
consumption. One of his ten favourite "points" about his wife,
Caroline, is her signature utterance (point number six on his list):
"Let's buy both" (184). The modern preeminence of "things" – the
Gatsby legacy – here reaches its zenith. Like his wife, Gary embodies
what Harms and Kellner call "a commodity self which sees buying
and consumption as a solution to problems and consumerism as a
way of life: the 'good life' in contemporary capitalism" (11). His
sister Denise's calling, that of a gourmet chef, because devoted to
consumption in the most literal sense might seem equally "extrinsic"; yet Denise brings to her work a passion for excellence that
qualifies as inward, indeed artistic. In addition, more than her broth-
ers she is preoccupied with the intrinsic value of family togetherness,
showing concern for the welfare of her aged (and in Alfred's case
ailing) parents.

While *The Corrections*, unlike *The Hucksters* or *Then We Came to
the End* or *Mad Men*, does not concern itself with advertising as a
means of livelihood, it consistently foregrounds the desired outcome
of advertising – consumption – as a dominant social paradigm.
Consequently, the narrative continually, and trenchantly, reflects upon
the universal grip of mass persuasion. It does so most penetratingly
apropos of the younger Lambert brother, Chip, in whose career consumption and promotion figure as channelling forces. Chip habitually
oscillates in a "liquid" fashion between intrinsic and extrinsic allegiances. His struggle to reconcile himself with the values of postmodern society culminates in a hilarious crisis in a mammoth futuristic

supermarket, the aptly named Nightmare of Consumption, a surrealist version of the sort of place where a mesmerized Marian MacAlpin does her shopping. Chip attempts to smuggle an unwieldy consumable – an absurdly expensive piece of salmon – out of the store in his trousers, where to his dismay he loses track of it. The enterprise's slogan, "Everything – for a Price!," succinctly sums up the culture it feeds.

The authors of *The Advertising Effect* observe that as consumers "we compete with each other for status and inevitably feel like failures." Chip, a reluctant competitor in the status-consumption sweepstakes, is tagged by the title of his opening narrative sequence as The Failure. He had "believed that it was possible to be successful in America without making lots of money" (32), but his misadventures severely test that fragile tenet of faith. "He'd always been a good student, and from an early age he'd proved unfit for any form of economic activity except buying things (this he could do), and so he'd chosen to pursue a life of the mind." Franzen's dry wit implies that if Chip is less than competent as an earner, he can nonetheless hold his own as a consumer, albeit one with highbrow tastes. Still, the flashback episode in which, as a child, he sits at the dinner table for hours refusing to eat the unpalatable food set before him already suggests the trials he will face even with consumption. The adult Chip recoils from a society in which "[a] lack of desire to spend money becomes a symptom of disease that requires expensive medication" (31) – the cure for the "disease" of under-consumption is more consumption. He draws the understandable conclusion that "the structure of the entire culture is flawed" (31).

Meeting his parents at LaGuardia Airport and finding them sporting shoulder bags from the cruise company they have engaged, Nordic Pleasurelines, Chip is "appalled by [their] willingness to make themselves vectors of corporate advertising" (16). Advertising, in fact, underlies the disaffected "failure's" quarrel with the Nightmare of Consumption that America has become. It is the crux of the frustrating argument Chip, a college instructor, has with his undergraduate class on contemporary cultural patterns, archly entitled Consuming Narratives. During the final meeting Chip exposes his students to a series of television spots by the W— Corporation, ostensibly a pro bono campaign for breast cancer diagnosis, though stealthily aimed at marketing computers. The campaign's stirring slogan is Help Us Fight for the Cure (40). The series features "a self-consciously 'revolutionary' plot twist that had generated publicity for the ad" (40); the young female office worker stricken with cancer dies, instead of recovering as she would in a standard, feel-good promotional vignette. The trick is to use paradigm-breaking novelty as an attention getting device. Chip hopes his class, primed by diligent semester-long deconstruction of dishonest advertising ploys, will see through those of the W—— Corporation. His expectations, in the event, are rudely defeated.

Chip's star student, Melissa Paquette, acts as tribune for the disloyal opposition. She argues that it was courageous of the W—— Corporation to opt for the offbeat, saddening denouement. Chip's sarcastic rejoinder – "So a wholly cynical strategy ... if there's a financial risk attached, becomes an act of artistic bravery?" (41) – unfortunately falls flat. For Melissa the politically correct end justifies the devious means: "It's celebrating women in the workplace. ... It's raising money for cancer research. It's encouraging us to do our self-examinations and get the help we need. It's helping women feel like we own this technology, like it's not just a guy thing" (43). She launches a belligerent but pertinent protest – "Why is it *inherently* evil to make money?" (43, emphasis in original) – and concludes with a disdainful shrug: "This whole class. ... It's just bullshit every week. It's one critic after another wringing their hands about the state of criticism" (44). At this late stage of the present study Melissa's rationale for shady advertising methods sounds a familiar note; such reasoning would have drawn a cheer from Uncle Teddy Ponderevo.

Cornered, Chip pulls professorial rank – "This is not about opinions" (42) – resorting to guilt by association to point out that the W—— Corporation is currently defending three antitrust suits. Had he had it to hand, he might usefully have quoted the authors' warning in *Think of Me as Evil?* that "even advertisements that appeal to intrinsic values may do more harm than good" because they risk "reinforcing the perception that intrinsic values can be meaningfully pursued through the [extrinsic] purchase of particular products" (33). Instead, the class wrangle leaves Chip feeling depleted, wondering whether his animus against corporate advertising is merely an offshoot of his social positioning: possibly "it was only straight white males like Chip who had a problem with this order" [the consumerist social order decried by critics like Zygmunt Bauman or Chip's pet philosopher, Jean Baudrillard] (45). The scene adroitly highlights the chronic difficulty in finding a genuinely impartial standpoint from which to critique trendy promotional stratagems.

Chip's crisis of self-doubt represents, however, a compulsive and short-sighted overcorrection What the class discussion accomplishes, in the wider purview of Franzen's novel, is to frame the whole issue of corporate promotion within a dialogic context, obliging the reader to weigh conflicting but not *prima facie* invalid propositions against each other. (The debate framework recalls the scene of Michael Wilde's antiadvertising "oration" in Wouk's *Aurora Dawn*, but Franzen's handling of the scenario is far less creakily didactic.) Melissa advances a coherent argument that the W—— commercial, whatever its ulterior motives, bolsters progress that has been achieved on the front of sex discrimination and contributes to medical research. She shows impressive spunk in standing up to an overbearing male instructor and in daring to dismiss his course as worthless. Nevertheless, the later course of the narrative implicitly demolishes her stance and vindicates Chip's. We at length discover that while the W—— firm burnishes its image by making charitable donations, the value of what it donates is negligible. "Critics ... complained that W—— was donating its slow and crash-prone Version 4.0 Desktops to the schools and its nearly useless 3.2 technology to the Community Computing Centers" (344). A reliable witness, Robin Passafaro, complains that "this horrible company is corrupting the city schools" (404–5). As for Melissa, despite her cockiness she too turns out to be crash-prone; she inveigles the unwary Chip into a sexual liaison that leads to his expulsion from academic employment.

Although the gap separating Chip, in his thirties, from his students is not vast, the standoff between him and the class can be called generational. The dispute about corporate advertising focuses a broader divergence in attitude toward a whole range of social structures that advertising itself underpins. Where Chip, along with the postmodern thinkers he reveres and expounds, perceives a world increasingly based on ugly materialism, manipulation of images, and corporate guile, his youthful audience perceives a world in which obsolete restrictions are unraveling and progress is occurring on a variety of exhilarating fronts. Ultimately, rather than professing an attitude of urbane neutrality, like Wouk's *Aurora Dawn*, Franzen's novel implicitly opts for Chip's position over Melissa's. It anticipates the critique of advertising's mass influence – its fostering of a treadmill world devoted to competition for material goods and status symbols – set forth a few years later by the more systematic British reports. But it accomplishes something no such document is apt to achieve: it transmits an immediate, experiential sense of the bewildering complexities, intellectual and emotional, of advertising as a massive, though often disregarded, social fact – the gaudy elephant in the room of modern society. That many-sided apprehension is the special province of literary imaginings, fictions designed to sell not cosmetics or electronics but awareness, to spur potential consumers to examine their own extrinsically programmed agendas, to replace "Let's buy both" with "Do I really need either?"

By an ironic caprice of fate, the reception of *The Corrections* confronted its author himself with a disconcerting experience of the contradictions embedded in modern publicity. The novel was chosen as a showpiece for the enormously influential book club presided over by Oprah Winfrey, that latter-day inheritor of the august American cultural maven, Christopher Morley. After initially acceding to this honour Franzen began to have qualms, which he rashly voiced during a book tour. The upshot was the withdrawal of his invitation to appear on Winfrey's show. In connection with his scheduled appearance, Franzen had agreed to pose for footage documenting his "homecoming" to his natal city of St Louis, an episode he recounts in his engaging December 2001 *New Yorker* piece "Meet Me in St Louis." There he describes how the filming gave him an uncomfortable sense of being (not unlike Chip Lambert) a failure as an avatar of commodity culture: "I'm a dumb but necessary object, a passive supplier of image, and I get the feeling that I'm failing even at this" (71). Franzen's chagrin at turning into a passive supplier of images, a billboard for his own literary talent, might have been predicted; such a project represents just the kind of promotional jamboree his fiction interrogates. For a contemporary novelist, any trumpeting of "the transition from a discursive book/print culture to a figurative media culture" (Harms and Kellner 5) is bound to set off uneasy vibrations. In his pained ambivalence toward the importunate Call of the Promotional, Franzen becomes a reluctant Exhibit A of the many literary encounters with advertising this study has traced.

Writers like Franzen can easily feel that their literary efforts are overwhelmed by the deluge of promotional matter constantly drowning out the work of cultural scrutiny they undertake. Our current period has been called the "Age of Persuasion";[1] a more precise label might be the Age of Manufactured Preference. In the face of the mighty commercial engines by which preference is produced, the literary imagination may seem to be at a loss. Not only is that imagination a modulated and often ironic voice amid the promotional din, it is also, as I have argued, itself chronically susceptible to the torque of commercial interests. Nevertheless, it remains uniquely available as an intellectual resource, placing in a resistant perspective the thundering onrush of the tidal wave of promotion.

Notes

1 As updated a decade earlier by Nathaniel Hawthorne, see "The Golden Touch" in *A Wonder-Book for Girls and Boys* (1852). Hawthorne added to the ancient Ovidian fable the significant detail of Midas's daughter ("Marygold") being inadvertently transformed into a lifeless golden statue by the fatal touch. Eliot, who was familiar with Hawthorne's work and may have known this story, plays the metamorphosis in rewind mode; Silas reaches out expecting to touch his lost gold and instead touches the living child's golden curls.

   In *A Sense of Things* Bill Brown discusses the attitude of Trina McTeague, in Frank Norris's *McTeague* (1899), to her windfall of gold pieces: "Trina isn't interested in gold as a medium of exchange; she is interested in gold as substance and form; like a collector, she wants to preserve her coins from the fate of exchange" (66). Although Brown does not note the parallel with *Silas Marner*, the resemblance seems compelling. My discussion in this Prologue is generally indebted to Brown's study of the evolving significance of "things" in American culture, though my approach to their literary treatment differs somewhat from his.

2 Miller's article includes a reproduction of the advertisement (352, Figure 6). Miller explicitly makes the connection with *The Great Gatsby* in a note (7, on 362).

1 Although *Mad Men* at time of writing still has one more season to run, with episodes to be distributed over two years, the series' treatment of

advertising is by this point well established. I therefore consider it eligible for analysis even in unfinished form.

2 Such violations of public space crop up with alarming frequency. An egregious example is noted in a *Guardian* piece by Owen Hatherley on plans for commercial use of the Rialto bridge: "The Rialto bridge in Venice, one of the most-photographed emblems of the Italian Renaissance, *is about to be sold as advertising space*, a symbolic desecration of a historic and famously beautiful cityscape that is, in theory, going to be renovated by the money the ads will raise" (emphasis in original). To adapt an infamous utterance stemming from the Vietnam War, it has in effect been found necessary to destroy the landmark in order to "save" it. However, it is worth noting that what most distinguishes this project from other instances of routine commercial depredation is that it has, at least, received outraged attention in the international press.

3 For a discussion of the episode, see John K. Young, "Woolf's Mrs. Dalloway," Marshall Digital Scholar 1-1-2000. Accessed 10 February 2013.

4 For an illuminating and troubling application of Barthes's methodology to the marketing of pharmaceutical products, see Linda and Michael Hutcheon, "Medical 'Mythologies': A Semiotic Approach to Pharmaceutical Advertising." *Queen's Quarterly* 94/4 (Winter 1987), 904–16.

5 The edition cited here is the seventh, dating from 1967.

CHAPTER TWO

1 See again Linda and Michael Hutcheon's article on the use of "scientific" appearances in advertisements in medical journals, referenced in chapter 1.

2 Herbert is adapting George's assertion that "radioactivity is a real disease of matter" (268).

3 It appears to have elements in common with what would today be called a Ponzi scheme.

4 The connection has been noted by Parrinder, who calls *Gatsby* "a novel on a similar theme." See Huntington 45.

5 In this doubleness Edward again anticipates Fitzgerald's Gatsby, another "saint" of materialism.

CHAPTER THREE

1 The name of the agency here varies slightly from that of the agency in the later "Story of the Ginger Cubes": "Grey-Matter" versus "Gray Matter,"

"Agency" versus "Service." Presumably Morley had the same (of course fictitious) agency in mind in both instances; the discrepancies are likely due to authorial absent-mindedness.

2 The only contact between Morley and Orwell known to me is an oblique one. As a regular member of the selection panel for the Book of the Month Club until he suffered a stroke in 1950, Morley would have been one of the judges responsible for choosing *Animal Farm* and (more hesitantly) *Nineteen Eighty-Four* as club selections during their years of publication.

3 The novel was apparently a work from which Orwell wanted to distance himself, since it was among those that in later years he left instructions to have suppressed. See Bowker 323–4. While in Germany in 1945 Orwell drafted a document headed "Notes for My Literary Executor" listing works he wished to have republished after his death and others he wished suppressed. Among the latter was *Keep the Aspidistra Flying*. On the other hand, Sonia Orwell claimed that when Orwell was near death and a uniform edition of his novels was being mooted, she and Fredric Warburg persuaded him to include *Aspidistra*, along with the other listed works.

4 See also O'Reilly and Tennant, xi.

5 According to Patrick Parrinder, "It is hard to say whether [the] absence of anything directly connected with the United States ... from Orwell's critical targets [in *Nineteen Eighty-Four*] is deliberate, or whether it results from an unconscious refusal to grasp the full implications of Britain's diminishing place in the world" (39). In fact, though, Orwell was by the early forties, if not before, well aware of the threat of American domination of British life.

6 Actually, the verse sounds less like Stephen's villanelle than like a stab at the manner of early T.S. Eliot.

7 Parrinder claims correctly that "Orwell's satirical exaggerations" of the deprivations besetting his Oceania "have a real basis" in the conditions of postwar London (38). But while consumer goods may have been scarce after the war, advertisements had not simply vanished from the London panorama.

CHAPTER FOUR

1 To *Marketing/Communications*. The final year of the magazine's publication was 1972.

2 Although some female copywriters rose to prominence in the industry, men were by far the numerical majority. The next chapter comments further on this gender imbalance. For a fuller discussion of women's roles

in the early phases of advertising, see Simone Weil Davis, *Living Up to the Ads*.

3 In an analogous distancing move, Wakeman has Vic Norman tell Kay Dorrance that "'the American intellectual ... always feels compelled to accept [any political act or idea] or reject it on the basis of Soviet interests. Always. Whether the issue is good, bad or indifferent'" (133). The early stirrings of Cold War ideology are already discernible here.

4 In the film version of *The Hucksters* Vic Norman delivers a judgment similar to Stanfield's. Alleging that radio has deteriorated during the war years, he complains that far too much time is being devoted to commercials, far too little to the entertainment they are supposed to support. Radio accordingly needs to "turn over a new leaf." His secretary Miss Hammer assures him that she never buys any product advertised on radio, Beautee soap included.

5 Nearly half a century earlier Henry James had made a strikingly similar point apropos of Trinity Church in lower Manhattan, progressively dwarfed by tall buildings: "What was the case but magnificent for pitiless ferocity? – that inexorable law of the growing invisibility of churches, their everywhere reduced or abolished *presence*, which is nine-tenths of their virtue, receiving thus, at such hands, its supreme consecration. This consecration was positively the greater that just then ... the vast money-making structure [an adjacent skyscraper] quite horribly, quite romantically justified itself, looming through the weather with an insolent cliff-like sublimity" (*The American Scene* 65, emphasis in original).

CHAPTER FIVE

1 See again, Simone Weil Davis, *Living Up to the Ads*, for discussion of female-authored memoirs and manuals emanating from the advertising industry of the 1920s and '30s.

2 A dramatic instance of such perceptual growth in *Surfacing* is the protagonist's reaction to her married friend David, who has just propositioned her: "The power flowed into my eyes. I could see into him, he was an imposter, a pastiche, layers of political handbills, pages from magazines, *affiches*, verbs and nouns glued on to him and shredding away, the original surface littered with fragments and tatters" (252).

3 The relation between the commercial and the perceptual emerges in a peculiar fashion in "Carved Animals," a poem dating from the same period as *The Edible Woman*. In the poem, first published (in the journal *Canadian Literature*) as part of a Hudson's Bay Company promotional

campaign and subsequently included in *The Circle Game*, Atwood focuses on the communal but noncommercial nature of aesthetic perception, involving apprehension through individual (but shared) touch. The company seated in a circle, passing from one to another a small native carving, come to a quasi-mystical understanding of its unique form: "and the hands, the fingers, the/hidden small bones/of the hands bend to hold the shape,/shape themselves, grow/cold with the stone's cold, grow/also animal, exchange/until the skin wonders/if stone is human" (*Circle Game* 75). The object "gives the gift of life" in a far more genuine sense than the banal nursing poster that Marian espies. With unintended irony, Atwood contributed for commercial use a poem that sets up a poignant counter-image to the conspicuous consumption of material commodities. See Michael L. Ross and Lorraine York, "Imperial Commerce and the Canadian Muse: The Hudson's Bay Company's Poetic Advertising Campaign of 1966–1972," *Canadian Literature* 220 (Spring 2014), 37–53.

4 See e.g. Keith (63–4) and Lauber (Moss 29).

5 An appropriately Canadian coinage. The reference is to *Adbusters* magazine, based in Vancouver, which began publication in 1989.

6 For a fuller discussion of this aspect of Atwood's career see Lorraine M. York, *Margaret Atwood and the Labour of Literary Celebrity* (University of Toronto Press, 2013), chapter 4.

CHAPTER SIX

1 The novel's take on Emerson, as on much else, seems ambivalent. The book's epigraph is a quotation from Emerson affirming his vaunted individualism: "Is it not the chief disgrace in the world, not to be a unit; – not to be reckoned one character; – not to yield that peculiar fruit which each man was created to bear, but to be reckoned in the gross, in the hundred, or the thousand, of the party, the section, to which we belong." The choral mode of the novel's narration may seem to expose the various characters to Emersonian criticism on the grounds of their group identity – their propensity to be "reckoned in the gross." However, since (as I argue) the general effect of the narration is by no means to blur the unique individualities of the characters, even despite the pressures on them to conform, the Emerson extract may itself be the object of retrospective irony.

2 Compare the monstrous supermarket dubbed "the Nightmare of Consumption" in Jonathan Franzen's *The Corrections*, discussed in the Epilogue.

3 References to advertising in *The Unnamed* are not numerous, but those that occur tend to be dismissive. The protagonist Tim's overweight daughter Becka is obliged as a teenager to abandon, like Atwood's Marian, "her good-faith efforts to fit in with the TV-commercial vision of life" (22). Later on, Tim himself reflects: "Commercials were poignant reminders of what a waste of time it was to watch TV" (90).

CHAPTER SEVEN

1 See James Poniewozik, "Mad Men Held Hostage: Drama over Advertising on an Advertising Drama," Time.com blog, 29 March 2011: "If current reports are true, the Madison Avenue drama is being held up at least in part over – yep – advertising. Reports Deadline.com AMC – which butted heads with Weiner two years ago by asking for more commercials during the hit show – wants to cut another two minutes for commercials, work in more product integration and ... cut a couple cast regulars to save cash."

2 A "special feature" included with the DVD set for Season Three: "Clearing the Air: The History of Cigarette Advertising," notes that cigarette advertising was at the forefront of the development of mass advertising. A promotion for Camel cigarettes was the first big nationwide advertising campaign.

3 Although Weiner is the series' head writer, all the scripts are the outcome of a collaborative effort. Weiner himself remarks on one of his commentary tracks: "As usual you see my name on the script, [but] it's the work of a lot of people" (4.7., 1:24). Nevertheless, since he has extensive input into all episodes and gives final approval to all the scripts, I have privileged Weiner's comments over those of other participants.

4 In an interview, Weiner comments: "I was kind of surprised that people were so scandalized by the Joan thing. I don't think she has exactly, as a character, been the model of propriety" (TV *Guide*). On occasion, Weiner can be surprisingly insensitive to the implications of his own script.

5 Weiner explains in interviews (e.g. *Vulture*) that it is not Don's "confession" alone that occasions his dismissal but his erratic behavior throughout the season. While this is plausible in the abstract, the palpable *dramatic effect* of the on-screen action is to couple inseparably truth telling and job loss.

6 During the episode in question a reference is made to Emerson Foote, an actual advertising man who also, after years of promoting tobacco products, began to publicize their hazards to health. Unlike Draper, however, Foote appears to have undergone an authentic change of heart. As Weiner

observes about Foote, "It is more of a moral stance than Don, at least appeared to be that way" (4.12., Commentary 31:45).

7 Compare Taylor: "[H]e is not really there; he is just a projection, or the outline of a man, like the one in the show's title sequence."

EPILOGUE

1 See O'Reilly and Tennant.

Works Cited

Adams, James. "Publish, and Your Book Will Probably Perish." *Globe and Mail* (7 February 2009).

Alexander, Jon, Tom Crompton, and Guy Shrubsole. *Think of Me as Evil?: Opening the Ethical Debate in Advertising*. NP: Public Interest Research Centre and WWF-UK, 2011.

Anderson, Linda R. *Bennett, Wells and Conrad: Narrative in Transition*. Basingstoke and London: Macmillan, 1988.

Atwood, Margaret. *The Circle Game*. Toronto: House of Anansi Press, 1978 [1966].

– *Conversations*. Edited by Earl G. Ingersoll. Willowdale, ON: Ontario Review Press/Firefly Books, 1990.

– *The Edible Woman*. Toronto: New Canadian Library, 1989 [1969].

– *In Other Worlds: SF and the Human Imagination*. Toronto: McClelland and Stewart/Signal, 2011.

– *Lady Oracle*. Toronto: McClelland and Stewart, 1976.

– Letters to Pamela Fry, 3 March and 14 March 1968. Thomas Fischer Rare Book Library, University of Toronto.

– "Margaret Atwood, Uncensored" (interview). *Globe and Mail* (29 April 2011). Web. 30 April 2011.

– *Payback*. Toronto: House of Anansi Press, 2008.

– *Selected Poems 1966–1984*. Toronto: Oxford University Press, 1990.

– *Surfacing*. Markham: PaperJacks, 1973 [1972].

– *The Tent*. London: Bloomsbury, 2006.

Barnouw, Erik. *The Sponsor*. New York: Oxford University Press, 1978.

Baudrillard, Jean. *The Consumer Society*. London, Thousand Oaks, New Delhi: Sage, 1998 ([970].

Bauman, Zygmunt. *Liquid Times: Living in an Age of Uncertainty*.
    Cambridge: Polity Press, 2011.

Bennett, Jane. *The Enchantment of Modern Life*. Princeton and Oxford:
    Princeton University Press, 2001.

Berland, Alwyn. *Culture and Conduct in the Novels of Henry James*.
    Cambridge: Cambridge University Press, 1981.

Berman, Ronald. *The Great Gatsby and Modern Times*. Urbana and
    Chicago: University of Illinois Press, 1994.

Bloom, Harold, ed. *H.G. Wells*. Philadelphia: Chelsea House, 2005.

Book, Albert C. and Norman D. Cary. *The Radio and Television
    Commercial*. Chicago: Crain Books, 1978.

Bourdieu, Pierre. *The Field of Cultural Production*. New York: Columbia
    University Press, 1993.

Bowker, Gordon. *Inside George Orwell*. New York: Palgrave Macmillan,
    2003.

Brown, Bill. *A Sense of Things*. Chicago and London: University of Chicago
    Press, 2003.

Cantor, Paul A. "*The Invisible Man* and the Invisible Hand: H.G. Wells's
    Critique of Capitalism." In *H.G. Wells*, edited by Harold Bloom.
    Philadelphia: Chelsea House, 2005, 99–113.

Cheyette, Bryan. "Introduction." In *Tono-Bungay*, by H.G. Wells, xiii–xli.
    Oxford and New York: Oxford University Press, 1997.

"Clearing the Air: The History of Cigarette Advertising." Supplementary
    feature, *Mad Men* Season 3.

The Contribution of Advertising to the UK Economy. The Work Founda-
    tion. Web. 25 November 2013.

Davis, Simone Weil. *Living Up to the Ads: Gender Fictions of the 1920s*.
    Durham and London: Duke University Press, 2000.

Debord, Guy. *Society of the Spectacle*. Detroit: Black & Red, 1977 [1967].

de Groot, Jerome. "'Perpetually Dividing and Suturing the Past and
    Present': Mad Men and the Illusions of History." *Rethinking History*
    15, no. 2: 269–85.

Eliot, George. *Silas Marner*. Harmondsworth: Penguin, 1967 [1861].

"Establishing Mad Men." Supplementary feature, *Mad Men* Season 1.

Ewen, Stuart. *Captains of Consciousness: Advertising and the Social Roots
    of the Consumer Culture*. New York etc.: McGraw-Hill, 1976.

– "Memoirs of a Commodity Fetishist." *Mass Communication and
    Society* 3, no. 4 (Fall 2000): 439–52.

Felski, Rita. *Doing Time: Feminist Theory and Postmodern Culture*. New
    York and London: New York University Press, 2000.

Ferris, Joshua. "A Conversation with Joshua Ferris."
– *Then We Came to the End*. New York: Back Bay Books, 2007.
– *The Unnamed*. New York: Little, Brown, 2010.
Fish, Stanley. "The Tobacco Horror Show." NYTimes.com. 14 November 2011.
Fitzgerald, F. Scott. *The Great Gatsby*. New York: Scribner's, 1953 [1925].
Foot, Michael. *H.G.: The History of Mr Wells*. Washington: Counterpoint, 1995.
Franzen, Jonathan. *The Corrections*. Toronto: HarperCollins, 2001.
– "Meet Me in St. Louis." *New Yorker* (24 and 31 December 2001): 70–5.
Frost, Robert. *Complete Poems*. New York: Henry Holt, 1949.
Fussell, Edwin Sill. *The French Side of Henry James*. New York and Oxford: Columbia University Press, 1990.
Gannon, Zoe and Neal Lawson. *The Advertising Effect: How Do We Get the Balance of Advertising Right*. London: Compass–Direction for the Democratic Left, nd. [2010].
Gilmour, Rachael and Bill Schwarz, eds. *End of Empire and the English Novel Since 1945*. Manchester and New York: Manchester University Press, 2011.
Grace, Sherrill E. and Lorraine Weir, eds. *Margaret Atwood: Language, Text, and System*. Vancouver: University of British Columbia Press, 1983.
Harms, John and Douglas Kellner. "Toward a Critical Theory of Advertising." *Illuminations: The Critical Theory Web Site*, nd [ca. 1990]. Web. 15 January 2012.
Hatherley, Owen. "Venice's Rialto Bridge Will Be Desecrated." TheGuardian.com. Web. 20 September 2012.
Hengen, Shannon. *Margaret Atwood's Power*. Toronto: Second Story Press, 1993.
Herbert, Lucille. "*Tono-Bungay*: Tradition and Experiment." *Modern Language Quarterly* 33, no. 2 (1972), 140–55.
Hettinger, Herman S. and Walter J. Neff. *Practical Radio Advertising*. New York: Prentice–Hall, 1938.
Hindley, Diana and Geoffrey Hindley. *Advertising in Victorian England 1837–1901*. London: Wayland, 1972.
Horkheimer, Max and Theodor W. Adorno. Dialectic of Enlightenment. New York: Herder and Herder, 1972 (1969).
The Hucksters. Dir. Jack Conway. MGM, 1947, film.
Huntington, John, ed. *Critical Essays on H.G. Wells*. Boston: G.K. Hall, 1991.

Hutcheon, Linda. "Afterword." In *The Edible Woman*, by Margaret Atwood, 313–17. Toronto: New Canadian Library, 1989.

– "From Poetic to Narrative Structures: The Novels of Margaret Atwood." In *Margaret Atwood: Language, Text, and System*, edited by Grace, Sherrill E. and Lorraine Weir, 17–31. Vancouver: University of British Columbia Press, 1983.

Hutcheon, Linda and Michael Hutcheon. "Medical 'Mythologies': A Semiotic Approach to Pharmaceutical Advertising." *Queen's Quarterly* 94, no. 4 (Winter 1987): 904–16.

Itzkoff, Dave. "Matthew Weiner Closes the Books on Season 4 of 'Mad Men.'" NYTimes.com. Web. 17 October 2010.

James, Henry. *The Ambassadors*. New York: Norton, 1964 [1903–09].

– *The American Scene*. New York: Penguin, 1994 [1907].

Jhally, Sut. *The Codes of Advertising*. New York: St Martin's, 1987.

Keith, W.J. *Introducing Margaret Atwood's The Edible Woman*. Toronto: ECW Press, 1989.

Kilbourne, Jean. *Can't Buy My Love: How Advertising Changes the Way We Think and Feel*. New York: Touchstone, 1999.

Konigsberg, Eric "'Mad Men' Creator Matt Weiner on His Hollywood Struggles, and How George Lois Is Like Tony Soprano, Not Don Draper." Web. RollingStone.com, (3 September 2010).

Kupinse, William. "Wasted Value: The Serial Logic of H.G. Wells's 'Tono-Bungay.'" *NOVEL: A Forum on Fiction* 33, no. 1 (Autumn 1999): 51–72.

Larkin, Philip. *Collected Poems*. London: Marvell/Faber, 1988.

Lauber, John. "Alice in Consumer-Land: The Self-Discovery of Marian MacAlpine" [sic]. In *The Canadian Novel Here and Now*, edited by John Moss, 19–31. Toronto: NC Press, 1978.

Lawrence, D.H. *Late Essays and Articles*. Cambridge: Cambridge University Press, 2004.

Lears, Jackson. *Fables of Abundance*. New York: Basic Books, 1994.

Lippert, Barbara. "Mad Men Unvarnished." *MediaWeek*. Web. 9 August 2010.

Lodge, David. *Language of Fiction*. London: Routledge, 1966.

MacLulich, T.D. "Atwood's Adult Fairy Tale: Levi-Strauss, Bettelheim, and *The Edible Woman*." In *Critical Essays on Margaret Atwood*, edited by Judith McCombs, 179–97. Boston: G.K. Hall, 1988.

Mad Men Season 1. Matthew Weiner et al. writers. Lions Gate 2007. DVD.

Mad Men Season 2. Matthew Weiner et al. writers. Lions Gate 2008. DVD.

Mad Men Season 3. Matthew Weiner et al. writers. Lions Gate 2009. DVD.

Mad Men Season 4. Matthew Weiner et al. writers. Lions Gate 2010. DVD.

Mad Men Season 5. Matthew Weiner et al. writers. Lions Gate 2011. DVD.

Mad Men Season 6. Matthew Weiner et al. writers. Lions Gate 2013. DVD

McLean, Jesse. *Kings of Madison Avenue: The Unofficial Guide to Mad Men.* Toronto: ECW, 2009.

McLuhan, Marshall. *The Mechanical Bride.* New York: Vanguard, 1951.

McCombs, Judith, ed. *Critical Essays on Margaret Atwood.* Boston: G.K. Hall, 1988.

Mendelsohn, Daniel. "The Mad Men Account." New York Review of Books. Web. 24 February 2011.

Meyers, Jeffrey, ed. *George Orwell: The Critical Heritage.* London and Boston: Routledge & Kegan Paul, 1975.

Meyers, William. *The Image Makers: Power and Persuasion on Madison Avenue.* New York: Times Books, 1984.

Miller, Lewis H., Jr. "Advertising in Poetry: A Reading of E.E. Cummings' 'Poem, or Beauty Hurts Mr Vinal.'" *Word and Image* 2, no. 4 (October–December 1986): 349–62.

Morley, Christopher. *The Haunted Bookshop.* NP: Grosset & Dunlap, nd [1919].

– *Parnassus on Wheels.* New York: 1931 [1917].

– *The Powder of Sympathy.* Garden City and New York: Doubleday Page, 1923.

– *Thunder on the Left.* Garden City and New York: Doubleday Page, 1925.

Morrison, Blake. *South of the River.* London: Chatto and Windus, 2007.

Moss, John. *The Canadian Novel Here and Now.* Toronto: NC Press, 1978.

Motion, Andrew. *Philip Larkin: A Writer's Life.* New York: Farrar, Strauss and Giroux, 1997.

Munro, Alice. *The Moons of Jupiter.* Harmondsworth: Penguin, 1982.

Nevett, T.R. *Advertising in Britain: A History.* London: Heinemann, 1982.

Oakley, Bernard and Joseph Browne. *Critical Essays on George Orwell.* Boston: G.K. Hall, 1986.

Oakley, Helen. *Three Hours for Lunch: The Life and Times of Christopher Morley.* New York: Watermill, 1976.

Onley, Gloria. "Power Politics in Bluebeard's Castle." In *Critical Essays on Margaret Atwood*, edited by Judith McCombs, 70–89. Boston: G.K. Hall, 1988.

O'Reilly, Terry and Mike Tennant. *The Age of Persuasion: How Marketing Ate Our Culture.* Toronto: Knopf Canada, 2009.

Orwell, George. *Animal Farm.* Harmondsworth: Penguin, 1951 [1945].

– *The Collected Essays, Journalism and Letters of George Orwell.* Volume 1: "An Age Like This, 1920–1940." Harmondsworth: Penguin, 1968.

– *The Collected Essays, Journalism and Letters of George Orwell.*
  Volume 2: "My Country Right or Left, 1940–1943." Harmondsworth:
  Penguin, 1968.
– *The Collected Essays, Journalism and Letters of George Orwell.*
  Volume 4: "In Front of Your Nose, 1945–1950." Harmondsworth:
  Penguin, 1970 [1968].
– *Coming Up for Air.* Harmondsworth: Penguin, 1962 [1939].
– *Keep the Aspidistra Flying.* Harmondsworth: Penguin, 1961 [1936].
– *Nineteen Eighty-Four.* Harmondsworth: Penguin, 1954 [1949].
Parrinder, Patrick, ed. *H.G. Wells: The Critical Heritage.* London and
  Boston: Routledge, 1972.
– "The Road to Airstrip One: Anglo-American Attitudes in the English
  Fiction of Mid-Century." In *End of Empire and the English Novel Since
  1945,* edited by Rachael Gilmour and Bill Schwarz, 38–51. Manchester
  and New York: Manchester University Press, 2011.
– "*Tono-Bungay* and *Mr. Polly*: The Individual and Social Change." In
  Critical Essays on H.G. Wells, edited by John Huntington, 36–52.
  Boston: G.K. Hall, 1991.
Patai, Daphne. *The Orwell Mystique: A Study in Male Ideology.* Amherst:
  University of Massachusetts Press, 1984.
Piercy, Marge. "Beyond Victimhood." In *Critical Essays on Margaret
  Atwood,* edited by Judith McCombs, 53–66. Boston: G.K. Hall, 1988.
Poniewozik, James. "Mad Men Held Hostage: Drama over Advertising on
  an Advertising Drama." Time.com blog. Web. 29 March 2011.
Pope, Daniel. *The Making of Modern Advertising.* New York: Basic Books,
  1983.
Richardson, Timothy. "The Looks of Men: Doubling and Nostalgia in
  Mad Men." *Popular Culture Review* (1 January 2010): 21–31.
Ritzer, George. "Introduction." In *The Consumer Society,* by Jean Baudrillard,
  1–24. London, Thousand Oaks, New Delhi: Sage, 1998 [1970].
Rodden, John. *The Politics of Literary Reputation: The Making and
  Claiming of "St George" Orwell.* New York and Oxford: Oxford
  University Press, 1989.
Rushdie, Salman. *Joseph Anton.* Toronto: Knopf Canada, 2012.
Salmon, Richard. *Henry James and the Culture of Publicity.* Cambridge:
  Cambridge University Press, 1997.
Sandage, C.H. and Vernon Fryburger. *Advertising Theory and Practice.*
  Seventh ed. Homewood, IL: Irwin, 1967.
Schumpeter, Joseph. *Capitalism, Socialism and Democracy.* New York:
  Harper and Row, 1942.

Seehofer, Gene F. and Jack W. Laemmar. *Successful Television and Radio Advertising*. New York: McGraw-Hill, 1959.

Smith, Dennis. *Zygmunt Bauman, Prophet of Postmodernity*. Cambridge: Polity Press, 1999.

Stein, Karen. *Margaret Atwood Revisited*. New York: Twayne, 1999.

Sullivan, Rosemary. *The Red Shoes: Margaret Atwood Starting Out*. Toronto: Harper Flamingo Canada, 1998.

Szántó, Andras, ed. *What Orwell Didn't Know: Propaganda and the New Face of American Politics*. New York: PublicAffairs, 2007.

Taylor, Mark. "The Past Isn't What It Used to Be: The Troubled Homes of Mad Men." *Jump Cut* (spring 2009). Web. 9 February 2011.

Twitchell, James B. *Adcult USA*. New York: Columbia University Press, 1996.

Tyree, J.M. "No Fun: Debunking the 1960s in Mad Men and A Serious Man" *Film Quarterly*, (summer 2010): 33–9.

US Bureau of Labor Statistics. www.bls.gov/OES. Web. 21 November 2013.

Veblen, Thorstein. *The Theory of the Leisure Class*. New York: Macmillan, 1899.

Wakeman, Frederic. *The Hucksters*. New York: Grosset and Dunlap, 1946.

Walker, Rob. *Buying In*. New York: Random House, 2008.

Wallach, Mark I and Jon Bracker. *Christopher Morley*. Boston: Twayne, 1976.

Wells, H.G. *The Correspondence of H.G. Wells*, Vol. 2, 1904–18. Edited by David C. Smith. London: Pickering & Chatto, 1998.

– *The History of Mr. Polly*. Cambridge, MA: Riverside, 1960 [1910].

– *Tono-Bungay*. Lincoln and London: University of Nebraska Press, 1978 [1909].

– *The War in the Air*. Lincoln and London: University of Nebraska Press, 2002 [1908].

Wernick, Andrew. *Promotional Culture*. London: Sage, 1991.

Wicke, Jennifer. *Advertising Fictions: Literature, Advertisement, and Social Reading*. New York: Columbia University Press, 1988.

Williams, Raymond. *Orwell*. London: Fontana, 1971.

– *Problems in Materialism and Culture*. London: Verso, 1980.

Williamson, Judith. *Decoding Advertisements*. London and Boston: Marion Boyars, 1978.

Witchel, Alex. "'Mad Men' Has Its Moment." NYTimes.com. Web. 22 June 2008.

Woodcock, George. "Margaret Atwood: Poet as Novelist." In *Critical Essays on Margaret* Atwood, edited by Judith McCombs, 90–104. Boston: G.K. Hall, 1988.

Wouk, Herman. *Aurora Dawn*. New York and Boston: Back Bay Books, 2004 [1947].

Young, John K. "Woolf's Mrs. Dalloway." *Marshall Digital Scholar* 1 January 2000. Web. 10 February 2013.

Index